Understanding Cultural Globalization

For Emma, Anna and my family

Understanding Cultural Globalization

PAUL HOPPER

polity

First published in 2007 by Polity Press
Reprinted in 2012

Polity Press
65 Bridge Street
Cambridge CB2 1UR, UK

Polity Press
350 Main Street
Malden, MA 02148, USA

ISBN-13: 978-07456-3557-6
ISBN-13: 978-07456-3558-3 (pb)

A catalogue record for this book is available from the British Library.

Typeset in 11.25/13 pt Dante
by Servis Filmsetting Ltd, Manchester
Printed and bound in the USA by
Edwards Brothers, Inc.

For further information on Polity, visit our website: www.politybooks.com

Contents

Acknowledgements

I would like to thank Andrea Drugan and her colleagues at Polity for their extremely helpful advice and assistance at every stage in the production of this book. I am especially grateful to my colleagues at the University of Brighton – Paddy Maguire, Stuart Laing, Peter Jackson and Aaron Winter – for their support. Luke Martell provided me with invaluable critical comments during the course of writing this book. As with my previous books, I dedicate this book to my family and in particular to my nieces Emma and Anna Hopper.

Introduction

Approaching Cultural Globalization

In late 2006 and early 2007, while I was completing the revisions for this book, there were a number of developments that took place in different parts of the world which arguably can be regarded as evidence of cultural globalization:

- Towards the end of 2006, the Iranian government was seeking to restrict online speeds and fast broadband packages in order to curtail Western cultural encroachment into the country and other influences considered 'un-Islamic'. *Resistance*
- One of the most disturbing of these developments was the way in which mobile phone video footage of the execution of Saddam Hussein circulated rapidly around the world only hours after the event via a combination of the Internet and transnational media organizations.
- In January 2007, a UK reality television show (*Big Brother*) attracted worldwide coverage and comment over the alleged racist abuse of an Indian contestant by some of her fellow (white English) 'housemates', provoking diplomatic uneasiness between the Indian and UK governments, and leading to fears in Britain that this would do lasting damage to the country's international reputation.
- At this time, the award-winning *The Last King of Scotland* was released, a film that from its subject matter to its production is perhaps an example of cultural globalization in action. The film is about the former Ugandan dictator Idi Amin, who was played by a leading American actor (Forest Whitaker), and it was shot in Uganda, internationally financed and distributed, had a British director, contained a cast and crew from numerous countries, and involved a fictional Scottish doctor.
- At Midem, the global music industry's annual conference in Cannes, held in January 2007, there was talk of the abandonment of digital rights management (DRM) – the technology that prevents the making of unlimited copies of digital files such as a song, film or video – for reasons ranging from it restricting download sales to it being easily

1

circumvented, a development which would make music even more globally accessible.
- More seriously, the publication of a report by the Intergovernmental Panel on Climate Change in February 2007 revealed the extent of global warming, and in turn generated international calls to rethink consumerist culture and to foster cosmopolitanism and environmentalism throughout the world.

These examples occurred during a particular two- or three-month period; however, they are not untypical of our age. There are numerous instances in the contemporary period of national governments endeavouring to curtail external and global cultural influences, of the music industry struggling to keep up with consumer behaviour, of films that are even more cosmopolitan in nature than the one cited above, of beheadings and other atrocities posted on Internet websites, and so on. But it is these types of developments, and the issues they raise, that are the concern of this work. In short, this book is an introduction to cultural globalization and associated debates. It addresses a range of issues and questions that are central to this subject, notably, what is globalization? What is culture? And, of course, what is the nature of the relationship between culture and globalization?

A differentiating and contextualizing approach to cultural globalization

During the course of the book, the emphasis will be upon the complex, plural and uneven nature of cultural globalization. It will be shown that there are multiple dimensions to globalization, reflected in its different histories, processes and forms of interconnectedness.[1] As will become clear, such complexity, plurality and multidimensionality are similarly evident when it comes to culture. Of great importance is that globalizing processes do not stand outside of culture or cultures, but are shaped by them, amongst other influences. By the same token, cultures will not be immune to the processes of globalization and are, in fact, at least in part, constituted by them. Moreover, while globalization both informs and disrupts culture, culture is arguably the most direct way in which we experience globalization. In exploring the nature of this interrelationship, the focus will be upon how the multiple forms of global interconnectedness are encountered and played out by different groups and societies. In turn, this will make it easier to determine the points and locations where the relationship between culture and globalization is reflexive, dialectical, or assumes some other form. Consequently, the necessity of employing a differentiating and contextualizing approach to cultural globalization will be stressed here. More specifically, it will be claimed that the cultural dynamics of globalization emerge from the interaction of numerous processes, flows, networks and interconnections, which are interpreted, experienced and contributed to by different actors and agencies in a range of cultural, political and social environments or localities. Such contexts may be regional, national, local, religious, institutional, historical, and so forth, while the extent and nature of our engagement with these forms of globalization are similarly important. As a result of this interplay between these different forces and groups within these different settings, we perhaps should not be surprised that heterogeneity and complexity are the prevailing tendencies of our globalizing era.

Moreover, individuals, groups and societies will have their own cultures and histories, which will inevitably shape the nature of their interaction with the different aspects of globalization and further serve to generate diverse responses. Indeed, in the case of individuals the nature of this interaction will be additionally dependent upon, among other things, our respective social and educational backgrounds, occupations and personal dispositions, as well as our knowledge and perceptions of globalization.[2] For example, the bombardment of images and ideas from Western media may be the most significant way that many Muslims interpret and experience globalization. For nationalists, flows of refugees threatening their national culture may be what they come to associate globalization with, and they then react accordingly. Globalization should therefore not be viewed in the abstract; we experience its processes in tangible ways.

Thus, it will be argued that rather than simply relying upon general theories and accounts, understanding cultural globalization requires us to focus upon the intersection of the global and the local within different contexts. In fact, as will be shown, globalizing developments serve to complicate matters even further and in doing so merely reinforce the need for such differentiation. For instance, as a result of the increased flows of people, images, sounds and symbols under contemporary globalization our place-based contexts or localities are constantly changing, while global information and communications technologies (ICTs), and in particular unequal access to them, ensure differential involvement in global and transnational networks. Likewise, some people will be utilizing jet airlines and traversing the globe and experiencing different places much more than others. In short, we inhabit complex social and cultural spaces, and operate from multiple and shifting contexts. And in order to encapsulate this diversity, it is appropriate to view cultural globalization in the plural as *cultural globalizations*.

In substantiating this conceptualization of cultural globalization, numerous examples will be provided in each of the chapters, though the book will not undertake detailed case studies as this has been undertaken elsewhere – see, for example, Eade, 1997; Hay and Marsh, 2001; Hopper, 2006; Monaci et al., 2003; Xavier Inda and Rosaldo, 2002 – and, to repeat, the primary concern of this work is to deal with the main debates surrounding this subject.

The importance of the criteria that we employ in defining globalization

There are further themes and contentions that lie at the heart of this work. Important among them is that the source of a lot of the disputes over globalization lie with the different perceptions of it and the criteria employed in conceptualizing and defining it. As a consequence, it can often appear that writers on the subject are writing about different things. In large part, this stems from the fact that academic disciplines have different approaches to the study of globalization. Within sociology, for example, globalization is often associated with modernity, whereas economists tend to discuss it in relation to capitalism and the global economy, and within international relations, globalization is invariably linked to global governance. Moreover, broadly speaking, a division persists between the social sciences, like sociology, economics and international relations, and the humanities (e.g., cultural studies, history and anthropology) towards this subject.[3] For instance, from a cultural studies perspective, Janet Wolff (1991) believes the social sciences present an inadequate and undifferentiating account of culture and the processes of globalization. Conversely, some of the social science models of globalization barely seem to register within cultural studies. For example, discussions of hybridity in our globalizing era rarely acknowledge the existence of sceptical accounts of globalization, such as those presented by Paul Hirst and Grahame Thompson (1996), who are discussed in the next section. However, Hirst and Thompson have themselves been criticized for privileging the economic at the expense of the cultural dimension of globalization (e.g., Tomlinson, 1999a).

Contested globalization and the need for an interdisciplinary approach

All of the above highlights two additional themes of this work, namely the contested nature of globalization – reflected in ongoing debates over its existence, history, nature and future trajectory or trajectories – and the need to pursue an interdisciplinary approach when investigating it. In the case of the latter, quite simply, no single discipline can adequately encompass and account for its different dimensions, manifestations and influences. Most importantly, given that the processes of cultural globalization do not operate in isolation but are inextricably intertwined with globalization's other dimensions, an interdisciplinary approach is also employed here. For example, our accounts of cultural globalization will be incomplete if they do not acknowledge the potential for dominant players (such as media TNCs, international institutions and certain national governments) to shape its processes and underlying forces like capitalism and rationalism to drive it, and that this in turn necessitates incorporating political, economic and sociological analyses into our investigations. In this regard, capitalism is undoubtedly a powerful influence informing many aspects of globalization, including its cultural dimension, though their relationship is not necessarily a straightforward one.

To begin with, there is now a tendency to identify different types of capitalism, with some – notably the Anglo-Saxon market-driven model – considered to be exerting a greater influence upon globalization than others (see chapter 5). Indeed, this particular model is even cited as one of the reasons why the Spanish siesta is in decline, with critics claiming that Spain's relatively relaxed Mediterranean culture is becoming more work-oriented and individualistic because of the pressures to compete within a globalized capitalist marketplace. But further complicating matters, Scott Lash and John Urry (1987, 1994) maintain that capitalism has actually departed from its organized national/societal form to become both disorganized and global, characterized by highly mobile and complex economies (of signs and people). As for a possible dominant player shaping cultural globalization, the USA is often accused of performing this role. More specifically, in the recent period the administration of George W. Bush has been widely criticized for employing American power in order to spread its conception of freedom and democracy throughout the world. However, the amount of chaos and violence in Iraq following the recent war, as well as the international criticism generated by this episode, strongly suggest the employment of force cannot guarantee global cultural influence. All of which means, as we will see in chapter 4, that it is debatable whether capitalism, American power, or some other influence, is producing a unitary global culture. Indeed, it will become clear during the course of this work that the view that cultural globalization is being controlled by a particular force or power is problematic, because cultural globalization should more accurately be viewed as a multi-centred phenomenon contributed to by a range of sources, powers and influences. Nevertheless, it remains the case that in approaching globalization through an examination of its cultural tendencies and manifestations, we should not lose sight of the wider picture and its other dimensions.

Analysing cultural globalization

Despite the considerable debate that globalization has stimulated, and the myriad of definitions and descriptions that have been postulated by writers seeking to encapsulate and explain it, three broad approaches to this subject, or waves of analysis, have emerged. These approaches will now be outlined and expanded upon during the course of this book, especially with regard to their respective positions on globalization and culture.

First-wave approaches to globalization

First-wave theorists or *globalists* consider that contemporary developments and global processes constitute a new condition or phase within human history (see Greider, 1997; Guéhenno, 1995; Julius, 1990; Ohmae, 1990; Wriston, 1992).[4] They write of the emergence of an integrated global economy with the emphasis upon open markets and the breaking down of national borders. Production is viewed as a global process evident in the growing volume of international trade, the greater mobility of capital, information and people, increased levels of foreign direct investment (FDI), and the heightened importance of multinational corporations (MNCs) and transnational corporations (TNCs). As well as having potentially profound cultural implications, such as arguably contributing to new global cultural formations like 'world music', these developments are considered to pose particular challenges to the nation-state, notably restricting the autonomy of national governments to pursue independent political and economic management, with some *globalists*, such as the Japanese business writer Kenichi Ohmae (1990), anticipating its demise.

This challenge to the nation-state is also apparent in the cultural realm, with some states struggling to control global cultural and information flows, and this even applies to authoritarian regimes. As we will see, even the powerful Chinese party-state cannot monitor and block all satellite television and Internet usage within its domain. Global information and communications technologies are therefore ensuring Chinese citizens have greater contact with the rest of the international community and, it follows, increased access to a range of perspectives on news and global affairs. Indeed, not only does Beijing no longer have a monopoly over information, it appears unable even to deal with the scale of pirating and distribution of foreign films and television programmes within China. In a globalizing era, it is not only external cultural influences that can present problems for national governments; such difficulties can also arise from domestic cultural products. For example, towards the end of 2006 the US military appealed to the producers of the popular and globally distributed American television series '24' to tone down federal agent Jack Bauer's torture scenes because of the damage it was doing to America's reputation abroad (Buncombe, 2007).

Second-wave approaches to globalization

Among second-wave theorists, more often labelled *sceptics*, there exists a range of perspectives that are highly critical of the globalist position. For example, many on the Left consider globalization to be simply a further expansion of international capitalism, and deny it constitutes a new epoch (Burbach et al., 1997; Sklair, 2002), while writers operating from the realist tradition stress that the international order continues to be dominated by certain powerful economic and military states, most notably the USA (Gilpin, 1987). Other critics, like Paul Hirst and Grahame Thompson (1996, 2000), have highlighted the 'myths' that have become associated with globalization. Based upon their research they maintain that the world economy is far from being genuinely 'global'. Trade, investment and financial flows are concentrated in a triad of Europe, Japan and North America and look likely to remain so; they therefore contend it is more appropriate to talk of 'triadization' rather than globalization. Hirst and Thompson also argue that genuinely transnational companies are relatively rare, and indeed most companies are nationally based in part because it is costly to relocate. They acknowledge certain developments in the flows of trade, people, finance and capital investment across societies in the contemporary period, but point to historical precedents such as the period 1870–1914 when they claim the world economy was even more internationalized than it is in our own time. Hirst and Thompson therefore conclude that contemporary trends can best be described as a process of economic internationalization, rather than fully developed globalization.

If the sceptics are correct, then this would raise doubts about the extent of contemporary cultural change. Put simply, if the global infrastructure does not yet exist, whether in the form of global capital, companies or trade, then there is not much that is sustaining global cultural formations, while to take the example of 'world music' cited above in relation to first-wave approaches to globalization, some critics deny it constitutes a genuine cultural form with its own distinct style or sound, viewing it simply as a marketing strategy that encompasses and promotes a vast and diverse range of music. Likewise, returning to the example of China, despite all of the discussion about global and transnational cultural flows, the Chinese Communist Party (CCP) continues to exert tight control over the media. For example, China has over 25,000 newspapers and magazines, but the authorities determine whether they report on sensitive political issues, and provide guidance on how to do so. The state also censors television news coverage, determining the stories that must not be reported, and even though there are many terrestrial television channels in China, they are all run by the state or provincial government. Indeed, such is the extent of state control that television presenters have been instructed by the State Administration of Radio, Film and TV to stop imitating Western ways in their appearance and manner, including refraining from using English words (Watts, 2004). Furthermore, Beijing has been known to jam the shortwave radio broadcasts of foreign news providers and routinely blocks access to Internet websites, notably those of Falun Gong, as well as human rights groups and some foreign news organizations. Beijing would also not appear to be without power and influence when it comes to dealing with some of the driving forces behind the Internet as its handling of the Internet search engine Google demonstrated. In 2006, after the Chinese authorities blocked its service in their country, the owners of Google agreed to Beijing's demand that what it considers to be politically sensitive information, such as the Tiananmen Square massacre of 1989, cannot be retrieved via searches from Google's China Web service engine. In effect, Google had to agree to self-censorship if it wanted to continue operating in China.

Third-wave approaches to globalization

There is similarly a range of opinion among third-wave theorists towards globalization. It includes writers such as Anthony Giddens (1990) and James Rosenau (1997) who have been identified as *transformationalists* (see Held et al., 1999). Writers from this tradition, stress the unprecedented nature of current economic, political and cultural flows and levels of global interconnectedness as a result of the combined forces of modernity (ibid., 10). Globalization is therefore not just motored by capitalism, but by industrialization, the nation-state, technological and scientific developments, critical thinking, and so on. From this position, globalization is seen as a powerful, complex and essentially indeterminate and open-ended transformative force or process responsible for massive change within societies and world order (ibid., 7). This particular approach therefore raises the issue of the relationship between globalization and modernity, which is a recurring theme within the globalization literature. From a cultural perspective, if modernity and globalization are indeed interrelated, should globalization be understood as primarily a Western project, given the European origins of modernity? In short, is globalization westernization? For Giddens, globalization is 'one of the fundamental consequences of modernity', but he challenges the association of globalization with westernization, arguing that the former 'introduces new forms of world interdependence' (1990: 175). In contrast, world systems theory makes such connections, equating globalization with the spread of Western institutions and capitalism (Amin, 1996, 1997; Wallerstein, 1974, 1980). From a different perspective, Roland Robertson (1992) believes globalization predates modernity though modernization is able to help accelerate globalization, with, crucially, Europe lying at the heart of these processes, whereas Martin Albrow (1996) considers the global age has actually ousted the modern age: that globality has supplanted modernity. John Tomlinson, however, believes the notion of global modernity 'remains a highly compelling way of understanding our present complex connectivity (1999a: 70). These different positions will be addressed in more detail during the course of this work. However, greater emphasis will be attached here to non-Western developments (notably that capitalism is no longer a Western phenomenon), the notion of multiple modernities, the ways in which globalizing processes may have predated and contributed to 'modernity' as well as the constructed nature of 'the West' and 'Europe', in order to avoid presenting a Eurocentric approach and gain a more accurate understanding of cultural globalization.

However, as mentioned above, there is more to the third-wave analysis of globalization than just the transformationalist position. For example, Colin Hay and David Marsh make the case for avoiding conceptualizing globalization as a causal process having specific effects, and instead emphasize fluidity, multiple processes, contingency, resistance and contestation, arguing that globalization is that which needs to be explained (2001: 6). More broadly, within third-wave thinking a greater role is assigned to human agents in both negotiating and contributing to globalizing processes (see Holton, 2005). This in turn adds to the significance of our perceptions of globalization and the dominant ideas and rhetoric surrounding it. In this regard, Angus Cameron and Ronen Palan (2004), in their analysis of the discourse of globalization, stress the influence that conventional narratives are able to exert upon individuals, governments and businesses. In other words, there is an ideational dimension to globalization that can indeed lead to it having particular effects, and in doing so it becomes a self-fulfilling prophecy.

Given the emphasis in this book upon complexity, multidimensionality, unevenness and human agency in relation to globalization, the approach taken here is in accord with third-wave analysis. But the starting point of this work is more straightforward, with globalization viewed simply as multiple forms of global interconnectedness, both taking into account its potentially long history (because arguably such behaviour can be detected in earlier epochs; see chapter 1), and allowing for possible changes to its nature and form in our own time. In this regard, it will be stressed that the contemporary phase of globalization is marked by an intensification of multiple forms of global interconnectedness. This conceptualization of contemporary globalization is common to many writers on this subject, though it has been expressed in different ways. In particular, there has been considerable emphasis upon globalization marking a new stage or epoch in the organization of time and space. David Harvey (1989), for example, views this change to be a form of 'time–space compression', whereby space is eroded or shrunk due to modern developments (such as jet air travel), new information and communications technologies, and changing economic and social processes. As a consequence, the pace of life is greatly increased. Moreover, Anthony Giddens (1990) articulates the notion of 'time–space distantiation' to describe the 'disembedding' of relationships and personal contacts from particular localities or contexts, meaning that social relations are 'stretched' across distances and extending our phenomenal worlds from the local to the global. However, as we will see in chapter 3, the persistence of a global digital divide does raise questions about the extent to which technology is transforming human relationships, as well as our conceptions of time and space. But to return to the wider contention of this work, if the contemporary phase of globalization constitutes an unprecedented intensification of multiple forms of global interconnectedness, then it is likely to be transforming our social and cultural experiences. For this reason, when considering the debates that have come to be associated with cultural globalization, the concern will be to determine the nature and extent of these cultural transformations.

The structure of the book

In examining cultural globalization, each chapter deals with a particular debate surrounding this subject, as well as identifying key writers on these areas:

- Chapter 1 examines the history of cultural globalization, addressing the issue of when it began and whether it should be regarded as a long-term historical process. A number of different phases of globalization are delineated during the course of the chapter, and this forms part of the case for considering this subject in plural rather than singular terms, as globalizations rather than globalization. The chapter also shows that the contemporary phase of globalization, though constituting a distinct epoch with regard to the extensity, intensity and velocity of cultural flows, has nevertheless built upon earlier developments and processes. Lastly, the chapter will show how our conceptualizations of globalization inform debates about its history and origins.

- Chapter 2 examines the nature of culture in order to gain a more informed insight into cultural globalization, exploring such issues as how culture travels through the world and impacts upon our sense of place. As part of the investigation into the interrelationship between culture and space, a number of related themes will be examined, notably cultural flows, deterritorialization and transnationalism, as well as the works of key writers, such as Arjun Appadurai and James Clifford.

- Chapter 3 assesses the contribution of the media and contemporary information and communications technologies (ICTs) to cultural globalization, focusing upon recent technological advances such as information processing, digitization, the Internet and bandwidth. Questions covered include: what aspects of mass communication are truly global in territorial extent and impact? Is media globalization a myth? And how plausible is Manuel Castells's notion of the network society?

- Chapter 4 examines the issue of whether the processes of cultural globalization are leading to the emergence of a global culture, and, if so, the form that it is taking. This will entail exploring claims that it is a culture driven by capitalism, modernity, America or a combination of these and other forces, as well as examining the work of Roland Robertson, a leading writer in this area. In line with the general theme of this work, it will be argued that it is more appropriate to conceive of global culture in the plural as global cultures.

- Chapter 5 contests the claim that globalization is undermining national cultures. In doing so it looks at both the challenges facing nation-states and national cultures in a globalizing era, but also the claims of writers, such as Anthony Smith (1995), who stress their continuing relevance and vitality. The chapter considers the implications for national cultures of increasing cultural hybridization under contemporary globalization, taking into account the view that the hybridity case has been overstated (e.g., Friedman, 1990, 1999).

- Chapter 6 seeks to determine whether aspects of globalization have contributed to forms of cultural conflict. It will examine the primary social, economic and cultural processes associated with globalization, such as post-industrialism and detraditionalization, as well as those writers who have explicitly made the linkage between globalization and cultural conflict, such as Benjamin Barber and Samuel Huntington. But as may be anticipated given the emphasis here upon cultural complexity and plurality, it is argued that globalization does not readily provide an explanation for rising cultural and civilizational conflict.

- In contrast, chapter 7 explores the potential for aspects of globalization to generate cosmopolitan attitudes and lifestyles, assessing the possible effects upon individuals and societies with greater access to other cultures and traditions through travel, migration and global communications technologies. Of course, the varied cultural manifestations of globalization further reinforce the cultural globalization thesis defended here.

- The Conclusion synthesizes the key themes of this work, outlines recent developments within globalization studies notably in relation to network analysis, and makes the case for a more 'anthropological' or human-centred approach to cultural globalization.

Recommended reading

Globalization has generated a vast literature, but there are a number of works that have done much to shape the study of this subject. These include the following: Anthony Giddens, *The Consequences of Modernity* (1990); David Held et al., *Global Transformations* (1999); Paul Hirst and Grahame Thompson, *Globalisation in Question* (1996); Roland Robertson, *Globalisation* (1992); and Jan Aart Scholte, *Globalisation: A Critical Introduction* (2000). Texts that relate to particular cultural globalization debates are listed at the end of each chapter.

1

The Histories of Cultural Globalization

This first chapter examines some of the key debates surrounding the history of cultural globalization. It begins by delineating a number of historical phases of cultural globalization, before considering the problem of determining when it begins and the appropriateness of viewing it as a long-term historical process. It was emphasized in the Introduction that the cultural dimension of globalization is intertwined with globalization's political, economic, military and other dimensions. Likewise, in order to understand the history of cultural globalization we must undertake a wider examination of the history of globalization. But as will become clear during the course of this discussion, in determining the path of globalization much rests upon our conception of what it is and entails. Put simply, the criteria that we employ as part of our definition of globalization go a long way in deciding questions about origins, the form it has taken, and how it has spread. It will also be argued that an appreciation of the history of cultural globalization demonstrates that the contemporary condition, while constituting a distinct epoch, has built upon a number of earlier developments and processes. Furthermore, to be able to understand the historical forms of cultural globalization we must examine the confluence of the history of globalizing cultural flows with the history of particular settings or locations.

The different phases of cultural globalization

In tracing the origins and development of cultural globalization, it is useful to conceive of it as passing through a number of different phases. Broadly speaking, these may be categorized as the premodern (the period prior to 1500), modern (1500–1945) and contemporary (1945 onwards) phases of globalization.[1] It would be impossible to describe all forms of globalizing activity during these different periods, rather the aim is simply to identify the key forces and processes contributing to globalization within each epoch, such as technological innovations, political and economic developments, social transformations and institutional changes. Above all, given the analytical focus of this book, the emphasis will be upon a consideration of the cultural dimension of these developments. What, then, were the defining features of these different phases of globalization?

Premodern globalization (from the early civilizations to 1500)[2]

If we conceive of culture in a very basic sense as involving people, ideas, goods and artefacts, then cultural globalization could be said to have a very long history because such entities have been circulating the globe for several millennia. And there is a growing body of work and opinion emanating from world historians, hybridity theorists, world systems theorists and civilizational theorists, detecting forms of globalization, both cultural and non-cultural, in the premodern age (e.g., Frank and Gills, 1996; Nederveen Pieterse, 2004; Sanderson, 1995). Some of this research will now be indicated as part of an examination of the primary processes or transformations that are often cited as either manifestations of or contributing to globalization in the premodern period. These include the following:

1 early human migration
2 the emergence of world religions
3 the early imperial systems
4 the development of transregional trade networks.

The common feature of these human activities is that they ensured cross-cultural encounters whereby ideas, beliefs and technological developments were exchanged and absorbed, and hence must be considered as part of our investigation into the history of cultural globalization.[3]

1 Early human migration
Early patterns of human migration are considered by some writers to provide evidence of globalization in the premodern period. For example, Robert Clark (1997) detects a 'global imperative' – the innate need for humanity to spread itself throughout the world – dating back to pre-agricultural *Homo erectus*. Thus human groupings have moved across the globe in order to ensure their own survival and to counter entropy, seeking to supply their energy and other needs as their societies became increasingly large and complex and hence more difficult to sustain. In demonstrating this human drive to globalization, Clark identifies seven episodes of globalization that span our history: from the original migration of *Homo erectus* and

Homo sapiens out of East Africa through to the digitization of information in our own computer age. For Clark, therefore, far from being a recent phenomenon, globalization is rooted in human life: we are a global species. As he puts it, 'the essence of the human condition is a fundamental connectedness with parts of the universe across time and space' (ibid., 2).

Whether it was for the motives that Clark cites, it is certainly possible to identify examples of human expansion and movement during the premodern era, three of which will be cited here. The first concerns the shifting incidence of disease that was a feature of the age, occasionally assuming the form of epidemics and even pandemics. While the occurrence of infectious diseases in particular communities and countries was invariably the result of a combination of factors, their spread across regions provides some indication of the extent of population movements prior to 1500. For example, William H. McNeill notes that within the vast Mongol Empire large numbers of people travelled 'very long distances across cultural and epidemiological frontiers', which he maintains greatly contributed to the emergence and spread of bubonic plague (1979: 142–3). The second example of human movement during the premodern era concerns the prevalence of nomadism. During this time, nomadic empires, such as the Germanic peoples and later the Mongols, as well as pastoral nomadism and agrarian expansion, were facilitated by the lack of established territorial borders. Moreover, nomads were able to influence and shape sedentary societies, culturally, politically and economically. In this regard, Anatoly Khazanov (1984) has charted the ways in which nomads impacted upon such societies within the Afro-Eurasian region. He also identifies the different modes of nomadic adaptation to new regions and places, including the formation of nomadic states, though these tended to be short-lived. However, it should be borne in mind that nomadic empires and migratory waves could often be powerfully disruptive episodes, generating conflict that served to break up existing long-distance trade flows and interconnections (Cowen, 2001; Held et al., 1999). In the third example, a number of diaspora communities existed in different parts of the world in the premodern period. For instance, the Jewish diaspora emerged largely as a result of the actions of a series of regional military powers, notably the Assyrian, Babylonian and the Roman empires, which forced many Jews to flee their homeland from the eighth century BCE onwards. Furthermore, diaspora communities emerged for reasons other than those of regional politics and religious persecution. For example, Chinese commercial diaspora communities were prominent in parts of Southeast Asia in the fifteenth century, serving to facilitate trade and the creation of social networks (van de Ven, 2002).

However, equating early human migration with globalization is problematic. To make such a linkage, we would need to know more about the nature of the human integration this migration was generating, such as the intensity and extensity of the interconnections. In this regard, it is estimated that it took about 150,000 years for *Homo sapiens*, emerging first, as it is generally believed, from Africa, to disperse across the rest of the planet, and that is excluding Antarctica (Fagan, 1990). It was a process that happened so sporadically and unevenly, and over such a long period of time that it negates any notion of meaningful global interconnectedness. Moreover, even later population movements within Africa cannot be viewed in this way. For example, the migration of the Bantu-speaking peoples from Central Africa around Lake Chad between 500 BCE and 1000 CE throughout much of the rest of the continent was a gradual process involving relatively small groups who generally did not return and retained little contact with their places of origin (Maylam, 1986). In a similar vein, should nomadism be regarded as constituting, or at least as an indication of, globalization? In other words, is the spread of humans into new geographical territories evidence of global interconnectedness and interdependency? Of course, the conceptualization of globalization articulated here is likely to be challenged, a theme that is returned to in the next section of this chapter.

2 The emergence of world religions

The spread of world faiths is often considered to be another indication of globalization in the premodern era, serving to generate transregional allegiances and identities. Religions such as Christianity, Islam, Buddhism, Judaism, Zoroastrianism and Hinduism emerged during this period and in some cases came to gain adherents in areas far from their origins, carried in part to other regions by traders and travellers. Their spread was also aided by the development of writing, which enabled core texts, and hence the central tenets of these religions, to be widely disseminated (Held et al., 1999: 333). The globalizing tendencies of Christianity and Islam were further reinforced by and indeed founded upon the universalist claims that lay at the heart of these faiths. Moreover, in the case of Islam, while sectarian disputes (Sunnis and Shiites), dynastic divisions (the Umayyads and the Abbasids) and the establishment of rival caliphates in Córdoba and Cairo in the tenth century undermined Islamic political unity, the notion of the *ummah*, the universal Muslim community, and the Arabic language helped to override territorial boundaries and ensure a high degree of cultural unity. Nevertheless, it is debatable whether any of these faiths can be viewed as truly world religions, and hence as expressions of globalization.

This is because in the premodern era, with the exception of Islam and Christianity, most of these faiths remained centred upon a particular region. And even Islam, which stretched from South Asia to North Africa, could not be found in all continents prior to 1500. As for Christianity, by the fifteenth century it was an ailing force in Asia and only became a global phenomenon in the modern era, something achieved in part by attaching itself to the different waves of European imperial expansion. With regard to Buddhism, Confucianism and Hinduism, they remained Asian religions, and even today, while they have adherents globally, their spiritual centre remains in Asia (ibid., 332). Lastly, it should be noted that the spread of these faiths took many centuries to achieve; again Islam is the exception here with Arab conquests spreading the faith from Spain to India within a century of the Prophet Muhammad's death in 632 CE. But in general, while these religions contributed to global interconnectedness, they did so only very slowly. There was, however, an additional way in which religions expanded into new regions during the premodern period, and this was the result of their association with empires, as will now be discussed.

3 The early imperial systems

Imperial ruling elites came to see particular faiths as a way of buttressing their own position. Confucianism in China, Zoroastrianism in Persia, and Christianity within the Roman Empire were officially adopted as the religious doctrines of these empires (Cowen, 2001; Held et al., 1999). And as the empires expanded, so did the religions. Indeed, the early imperial systems, such as the ancient Sumerian (Mesopotamia), Egyptian, Greek and Roman empires through to the later Chinese and Islamic empires, have come to be viewed as globalizing forces. These empires were frequently forged from a combination of military conquests, strong political authority and commercial networks. What they had in common was their incorporation of different cultural groups within a single geographical territory or unit. This also meant that the peoples of these empires were often unconstrained by internal borders and boundaries and hence fairly free to move within them. Such conditions facilitated both trade and cultural interaction. These multicultural empires therefore provided the overarching authority that enabled cultural diffusion and the spread of ideas, and at the same time challenged local identities.

But on the whole premodern empires were relatively small in size at least in comparison with the globally spread British Empire of the nineteenth century, so in this respect they were at most limited manifestations of globalization. Nevertheless, some imperial systems like the Roman and Han Chinese empires became in time genuine regional powers (Held et al., 1999: 334). Indeed, in the case of the Roman Empire, such was the nature of its authority, economy and territorial extent that it is possible to detect the existence of a transregional culture, which was forged as a result of the tendency to incorporate conquered local elites into the imperial system (Millar et al., 1967). However, this culture was largely confined to those in the imperial elite or ruling class, who were bound together by their collective project, common cultural customs and shared socio-economic position, as well as by the high rates of literacy that existed among them, all of which contributed to their 'growing ideological integration' (Mann, 1986: 268). In addition, Roland Robertson and David Inglis (2006) detect a global consciousness among social elites not just within the Roman Empire, but more generally within the Graeco-Roman era dating back to Alexander the Great in the late fourth century BCE, reflected in the concern of ancient Greek scholars with cosmopolitanism and in their attempts to write histories of the world. Similarly, many Roman citizens considered their city to be the capital city of the world, which they believed was demonstrated by the fact that peoples, foods, goods and even entertainments (from gladiators to exotic animals) from throughout the world could be found in Rome (ibid.). In the case of the powerful Han Chinese Empire, the imperial dynasties oversaw the considerable diffusion of Chinese script and literature within their vast dominion (Buckley Ebrey, 1996; Held et al., 1999).

However, as Held et al. (1999) have noted, broadly speaking, such forms of cultural dissemination could not be matched by other premodern empires. Moreover, because many of these empires were essentially military entities sustained by authoritarian structures they often inhibited cultural diffusion, and it follows that some were not renowned for their cultural achievements. For example, some of the nomadic warrior empires of the Eurasian steppes left behind no lasting cultural legacy and often a trail of devastation (Osterhammel and Petersson, 2005). In the case of the Mongols (1206–1405), while they did serve to generate cross-cultural encounters by facilitating travel throughout the empire, as was mentioned above, this also aided the spread of bubonic plague throughout Eurasia (ibid., 37–8). As a consequence, travel and trade and hence cross-cultural encounters were significantly reduced in the late fourteenth century (Bentley, 1993). Of course, this does not mean that these other premodern empires did not have any cultural impact. The Assyrians, for instance, were known for their sophisticated art and architecture, and a tradition of deporting difficult populations encouraged cultural and ethnic mixing within the empire, but their influence was confined to the Near East and it waned with the collapse of Assyrian power in the seventh century BCE.

Overall, it is difficult to determine the extent to which premodern imperial systems contributed to cultural globalization because the empires varied in size, military power, political structures, and in their longevity. All of which ensured that the imperial centres of power differed in their ability to communicate with and shape their respective territories. Furthermore, whenever empires fragmented this could significantly disrupt trade routes and migration patterns, and hence reduce the amount of cultural interaction. This was evident with the break-up of the Chinese and Roman empires, which disrupted these flows and interconnections both within and between these empires.

4 The development of transregional trade networks
Another important globalizing force of the premodern period was the long-distance trade and trade networks, many of which were centred upon huge cities, such as those in China and India. In particular, trade networks such as the Silk Route are often viewed as evidence of early forms of globalization. The Silk Route was a term that came to describe an elaborate network of land and sea routes linking the Roman Empire and the Chinese Han Empire roughly between 200 BCE and 400 CE, one of the consequences of which was the spread of Roman coinage to Arabia, India and China (Dalby, 2000). But even prior to that time, it is possible to detect intercontinental trade as far back as the first civilizations of antiquity, a period which also witnessed a great expansion of maritime activity (see Sabloff and Lamberg-Karlovsky, 1975). For instance, the early empires of Mesopotamia (*c*.3500 to 1600 BCE) depended upon trade and the import of raw materials to sustain their societies and rapidly expanding populations, encouraging 'cultural cross-fertilization' between Sumerians, Indo-Europeans (Hittites), Hurrians and Semites (Barraclough, 1984: 54). Philip Curtin (1984) has undertaken an analysis of the long history of trade diasporas, which were networks of commercial communities), investigating their cultural impact and legacies. In this regard, he shows how the beginnings of Chinese settlement and influence in Southeast Asia can be traced back to Chinese trade diasporas that began operating in the area in the first centuries of the Common Era (CE).

Andre Gunder Frank and Barry K. Gills (1996) argue that patterns of long-distance trade, market exchange and capital accumulation indicate the contemporary capitalist world system is at least 5,000 years old.[4] Leaving aside the issue of the relationship between the world system and globalization, the relevance of their thesis for this discussion is that it suggests international economic interconnections go back much further than the early modern era, the period when capitalism is generally considered to have emerged. This notion of a pre-1500 form of economic internationalization can also be found in the work of Janet Abu-Lughod (1989), who identifies the emergence of a world system in the thirteenth century, consisting of eight overlapping circuits of trade that incorporated China, India, the Middle East and parts of Europe and Africa. This complex and sophisticated system of exchange, which included arrangements for pooling capital and monetization, predated the rise of the West by several centuries. Moreover, much of Europe was only on the periphery of this system in the mid-thirteenth century, while China, for example, was engaged in extensive trading relations with regions as far away as East Africa. Abu-Lughod also highlights the extent of the linkages between Africa and Eurasia during this period. The thirteenth-century world system was therefore a multi-centred system.

It would seem, then, that in relation to trade, Asia, the Middle East and parts of Africa were as much involved as Europe in contributing to the premodern phase of globalization. However, whether this activity marks the beginning of trade globalization or even evidence of an integrated world economy in any meaningful sense is a moot point. As Abu-Lughod herself concedes, the trading networks she identifies were not truly global in scope and the whole system was 'extremely uneven' (ibid., 353). For example, the contact between China and Europe at this stage was still relatively limited. Furthermore, there were aspects of the thirteenth-century world system that for a range of reasons were later to recede, and were to do so even by the middle of the fourteenth century. In this regard, Abu-Lughod notes the 'calamitous impact' of the Black Death at this time, which decimated populations and cities, upsetting the terms of exchange and breaking up trade routes in the process (ibid., 19).[5] Moreover, looking at the premodern period as a whole, we need to acknowledge the existence of different types of exchange and to consider how they may have informed cultural encounters. For example, in some regions trade was at times in the form of tribute trade rather than market exchange. This was the case in China from about 60 BCE when the Han dynasty imposed this system upon the northwestern barbarians (Curtin, 1984). To what extent did tribute trade inhibit trading relations and networks and hence curtail the spread of trade? Alternatively, was tribute trade able to regularize and deepen trading relationships?

Irrespective of these particular debates, what can be said about the premodern period is that while we can detect many of the roots of globalization, the majority of cultural flows and interconnections were at this stage trans-Eurasian only (Held et al., 1999: 433). Moreover, cultural flows, such as they were, were likely to be both sporadic and slow, making it difficult to sustain forms of cultural interaction over any distance. This was a consequence of limited communications and transport infrastructures, as well as the conditions of everyday life for those other than elites, which combined to hamper long-distance travel and trade. But crucially what undermines any notion of global cultural flows during the premodern era is that the Americas and Oceania were separated from Africa and Eurasia, which in turn contributed to a lack of knowledge of other regions of the world – the peoples of Europe were unaware of the existence of the Americas, and vice versa, for example (ibid., 416). While there was a development towards the end of the premodern period that was in time to have international significance, namely the invention in the 1450s of movable metal type by Johann Gutenberg (c.1398–1468), which resulted in nearly all European countries having printing presses by the 1480s, this particular revolution in communications only really began to have an impact in the early modern period, and was initially centred upon Western Europe (Deibert, 1997).

The modern phase of globalization (1500–1945)

There is some dispute about when the modern phase of globalization begins and ends, with some writers breaking it down into early modern and modern or late modern periods but diverging over their particular timescales (see Held et al., 1999; Holton, 2005; Hopkins, 2002). However, as with the premodern phase, the aim here is merely to identify the key elements contributing to modern globalization, especially its cultural dimension:

1 European imperialism
2 an emerging international economy
3 international migration and developments outside of the West
4 the spread of modernity
5 the rise of the nation-state
6 industrialization

1 European imperialism

A notable feature of the modern period was the emergence of forms of economic, political and military expansionism, notably in the shape of European imperialism. Indeed, some writers consider the defining feature of the modern age to be the 'rise of the West' (McNeill, 1963). European expansionism was given impetus in 1492 with Columbus's voyage to America, which paved the way for Europe's encounter with the New World, a momentous episode that led to flows of goods and people criss-crossing the Atlantic, albeit at a relatively low level. Such transatlantic flows were later contributed to by the African slave trade, which reached its height during the seventeenth and eighteenth centuries, and resulted in parts of the African continent being incorporated into these trading patterns. These flows were not just economic, and even included the spread of diseases. The latter was an unintended consequence of transatlantic migration, one which particularly affected the indigenous peoples of the Americas as their immune systems struggled to resist the diseases that the Europeans had brought with them (McNeill, 1979). A further motivation for some Europeans to go to the New World was religious, and specifically the desire to gain converts to Christianity. Indeed, one cultural manifestation of this need to spread the Christian message was the Christian names that many places in Latin America received. For example, Columbus used the names of saints in renaming many of the territories that he seized.

As well as the Americas and the Caribbean, Europe began to forge connections with other regions prior to 1850, notably Oceania, India, the Middle East and Africa. In the case of India, for example, the East India Company did much to open up the country to British colonial trade and cultural imperialism, resorting to military methods when necessary. Yet there remained large parts of the world that remained at this stage immune from European encroachment, including large parts of Africa and China. With regard to Africa, at the beginning of the nineteenth century, Europeans had established settlements along coastal areas, but they had failed to penetrate significantly into the interior owing to factors such as the extent of African resistance, with Europeans not establishing their overwhelming military superiority until later in the century (MacKenzie, 1983). And on the theme of warfare, while there were military encounters in different parts of the world, such as the clash between British and French forces in India in the mid-eighteenth century, it is implausible to talk of military globalization in this early modern period, as the global power blocs, weapons technologies and international institutions did not exist. Indeed, even the military skirmish between Britain and France in India was fought as part of the Seven Years' War (1756–63), and was therefore a European rather than global engagement.

In general, prior to the nineteenth century, economic and cultural flows were hindered by the lack of mechanized oceanic shipping, railways, international communication systems, and established and powerful nation-states with their strong industrialized capitalist economies, all of which were to develop later in the modern era. This ensured that such global cultural flows and interconnections as there were continued to be thin and uneven, with most centred upon the transatlantic region. Nevertheless, there were signs during the early modern period of what was to come, with the development of mechanized printing, canal and road building, and the establishment of postal systems within Europe (Held et al., 1999: 434). Europe's empires continued to expand in the second half of the nineteenth century, notably across the rest of Africa and into new areas within Asia, such as China, becoming truly international in the process. Indeed, the European empires, and in particular the vast and powerful British Empire, achieved their greatest territorial extent around the turn of the century. America had also expanded rapidly into new areas such as Alaska (Brogan, 2001). In fact, the period between 1870 and 1914 is notable for the increased extensity and intensity of international flows of trade, people, finance and capital investment, with episodes like the so-called 'Scramble for Africa' – in which the European colonial powers seized new territories in Africa for themselves creating new states in the process – encouraging this trend.

2 An emerging international economy

These late nineteenth-century developments were part of a significant internationalization of economic relations, reflected in the incorporation of Africa and large parts of Asia into the international economy and the Gold Standard becoming its currency. Indeed, such was the dramatic rise in the level of world trade and investment that Hirst and Thompson consider the international economy was more open and integrated from 1870 to 1914 than the current regime (1996: 2). Moreover, the popularity of free trade ideas earlier in the nineteenth century, especially with British governments, arguably paved the way for the emergence of this type of economy. However, we should not overestimate what was taking place during this period. For instance, forms of economic protectionism returned prior to the outbreak of the First World War. Furthermore, at the turn of the century there were limits to the amount of international activity that even Britain, the most global of all the major powers, could engage in. Most British overseas investment was still concentrated in established markets such as the USA and Latin America, and relatively little had been diverted to the newly acquired territories in Africa (Fieldhouse, 1961). In fact, it was only from the 1940s onwards that Britain and France, the major European colonial powers in Africa, started to invest substantially in their African possessions, and began what has been termed a 'second colonial occupation' of Africa, seeking to ensure the colonies made a more significant contribution to the colonial economy.

3 International migration and developments outside of the West
The period 1870–1914 was also a notable moment in the history of international migration. For instance, many Europeans took advantage of the 'Scramble for Africa' and began to uproot and settle in the new colonies, a pattern that continued well into the twentieth century. But migration was not just the preserve of Europeans. This period also witnessed the emergence of Asian global diaspora communities, motivated largely by the desire for employment and moving to Africa, North America, the Caribbean, to cite just a few places. For example, significant numbers of people from the Indian subcontinent went to South Africa in the late nineteenth century, many of them initially as indentured labour, to work on the European sugar plantations, but choosing to remain there after their contracts had expired, and encouraging their families to come to join them.

Asian migration is a reminder that we should not ignore the non-Western developments contributing to the modern phase of globalization. In this regard, Islam was a significant universalizing force during this period, with the Ottoman Empire, the largest Islamic state, incorporating at its height vast swathes of territory, stretching from Persia to the Austrian border, while in the early modern period, two other important Muslim dynasties, the Mughals and the Safavids, established control over India and Persia respectively, creating their own empires in the process. More generally, this was an important time in the history of the *ummah*, with the expansion of Muslim trade and cultural influence in Africa, Indonesia and the Indian Ocean, the legacies of which continue to the present day (Bennison, 2002).

4 The spread of modernity
European imperialism was not just a globalizing economic force, but had important cultural and political dimensions, notably contributing to the spread of modernity throughout the world. Western modes of thought such as science and secularism, and ideologies like socialism, Marxism, liberalism and democracy, spread across the globe during the modern age due to a combination of their universal claims, European power, and the certainty of Europeans in their own intellectual traditions. Arguably, this meant that compared to earlier eras the impact of global cultural flows tended to be more profound and lasting in the late modern period. For example, the cultural and political legacy of British imperialism in India is evident in its parliamentary system, the prevalence of the English language, and the popularity of cricket. And the cultural legacies of European colonialism can still be detected in other countries and continents, such as Hong

Kong, Australia, Latin America and Africa. In the case of the latter, it can be seen in the persistence of anglophone and francophone states, as well as the extent of the geographical spread of Christianity on the African continent.

But we should not overestimate the impact of colonialism and, it follows, the extent of the colonial legacy in Africa and elsewhere. In this regard, many African states in the post-colonial period have dispensed with European parliamentary systems, reasserted their Africanness, and generally sought to loosen ties with their former colonial rulers. Moreover, the African encounter with European colonialism was a relatively brief one; in some cases European colonial rule lasted no more than 40 or 50 years. As a consequence some Africans rarely if ever saw their colonial rulers, and many persisted with their traditional ways of life and customs. All of which, of course, does not detract from the fact that the Western metropolitan powers were the dominant players during the modern period.

As well as possessing the military, technological and economic capability to take over new territories, many European countries had imperial projects to export and a general sense that they were on a civilizing mission. For instance, France pursued a policy of assimilation, seeking to turn its colonial subjects into Frenchmen. Amongst other colonial powers, the notion of the so-called 'white man's burden' was a widely held sentiment with European elites seeking to inculcate the colonized with their own culture and cultural values. In doing so, they inevitably influenced the path of development of non-Western societies. For example, a combination of Western military and economic power and cultural influence contributed greatly to the fall of imperial China. Successive military defeats by European armies during the nineteenth century engendered debate within China about the need to imitate the military methods, science and system of government of the foreigner. This led to internal calls for reform and modernization that culminated in Sun Yat-sen (1866–1925) and his supporters establishing the country's first republic in 1911. In short, European imperialism ensured that cultural flows were predominantly from the Western to the non-Western world during the modern period. Hence any cultural mixing that took place was frequently a one-sided process with the colonized in the main incorporating the culture of the colonizer. This was evident, for example, in the Anglicization policy that the British implemented in India in the 1830s, which was geared to providing India's middle classes with an English education so that they could become agents of cultural dissemination.

Nevertheless, the colonized retained the capacity to resist the imposition of these alien cultures, and this was true in Asia as much as it was in Africa and elsewhere. In the case of India, a powerful motivation behind the Indian Revolt of 1857 was the perceived attack upon the indigenous cultures by the British authorities. A similar concern to protect traditional cultures from foreign influence can also be detected in the Boxer Rebellion in China at the end of the nineteenth century, with foreign embassies and Christian mission stations often the focal point of their attacks. Furthermore, the extent to which Western cultures were indigenized by colonial subjects, rather than simply absorbed, should not be underestimated. This tendency was evident in the Ethiopian movement, an Africanist form of Christianity that was also an early expression of African resistance to European colonialism, while some non-Western states retained the capacity to forge their own path to modernization during this age of European imperialism, with Japan being an obvious example of this tendency (Held et al., 1999).

Nor should we simply assume that these cultural encounters were always dominated by the Europeans and that they themselves did not learn and incorporate many things from this experience. In this regard, Europe's engagement with the New World is considered by many commentators to have had a profound impact upon European culture and society. For example, the discovery of the Americas challenged the authority of Christianity and the classical civilizations, as neither had any knowledge of the New World. It encouraged the view that if these sources had been mistaken about the geography of the world, it would be better to derive knowledge from actual experience and first-hand observation, rather than rely upon traditional authority. Arguably, therefore, Europe's encounter with the New World contributed to the development of a more critical or modern attitude.[6] Moreover, this episode marked the beginning of a shift towards more historical and comparative methods of learning within Europe. This was especially evident amongst many of the French *philosophes*, with figures like Voltaire employing Confucian China as part of his critique of the *ancien régime* (Clarke, 1997). Similarly, in the nineteenth century, as a result of Europe's encounter with Middle Eastern and Asian cultures, what became known as 'orientalism' had a considerable influence upon European thought, art, architecture, design, music, film and theatre, as well as tastes and sensibilities more generally (see Clarke, 1997; Macfie, 2000; MacKenzie, 1995). Even in the twentieth century, its influence could be seen in Hollywood films, as well as the counter-culture of the 1960s. These forms of intercultural mixing challenge the conception of globalization as a Western project, and there is now growing recognition of both the Western and non-Western origins of globalization (see for example

Hopkins, 2002). In part, this shift stems from a critical examination of the idea of 'the West', and recognition of its constructed nature, and that it was formed from a synthesis of many sources and influences, Islamic, Ethiopian, Egyptian, Indian, and so forth (see Nederveen Pieterse, 1994).

5 The rise of the nation-state

One of the most notable features of the modern age was the emergence of the nation-state, an institution that many commentators consider to have contributed greatly to globalization. But the nation-state experienced a complex relationship with globalization during this period. On the one hand, the formation of powerful nation-states in Western Europe, paved the way for the imperial expansion of the late nineteenth and early twentieth centuries, and hence contributed to the modern phase of globalization. More generally, however, the arrival of the nation-state upon the international scene was also accompanied by a greater emphasis upon maintaining national borders, a development that inhibited freedom of movement and cultural diffusion. While demarcated territories were evident in the premodern period, the consolidation of national cultures frequently entailed excluding those who were perceived as not belonging and the dismissal of other cultures as inferior. Thus the modern era witnessed the construction of ideologies of exclusion. Alongside exclusivist and romantic forms of nationalism other ideologies emerged opposing all forms of cultural mixing and miscegenation, such as racism and social Darwinism, which in turn paved the way for fascism and Nazism. The establishment and preservation of borders and boundaries was therefore a particular feature of the late modern era, serving to restrict cultural mixing as well as marginalize for the time being the cosmopolitanism that had existed at least amongst some eighteenth-century European intellectuals.

6 Industrialization

Another significant development facilitating modern globalization was industrialization. While Britain experienced its industrial revolution in the eighteenth century, the rest of Western Europe and the USA industrialized in the following century. Industrialization generated demand within these countries for raw materials to supply their industries, as well as new markets for the goods produced by their industries. Industrialization was therefore a spur to imperial expansion because the acquisition of colonies was seen as a way of meeting these competing demands (Hobsbawm, 1987). Furthermore, there were other developments associated with industrialization and modernization generally, and science in particular, such as mechanized shipping, railways and telegraphy, that greatly contributed to global interconnectedness. These technological developments facilitated trade, made it easier for people to traverse the globe, and increased the velocity of communications. In particular, the successful laying of telegraph cable across the Atlantic in 1868 is often viewed as a landmark event in modern communications. And the British in particular built a fairly elaborate telecommunications infrastructure, employing cable technology, submarine telegraph systems and hundreds of thousands of kilometres of cable, as a means of securing and maintaining their empire (Headrick, 1988). Finally, as we move into the twentieth century, further technological advances, such as telephony, radio, television and the combustion engine, greatly contributed to globalization in the period leading up to 1945.

Thus there were a number of contradictory developments at work in relation to globalization during the modern era, but overall its primary forces, such as industrialization, capitalism, imperialism and science, generated powerful globalizing tendencies, albeit often in an uneven manner.

The contemporary phase of globalization (1945–present)[7]

Some of the major developments and processes providing the momentum behind contemporary globalization will now be indicated, although both they and their implications for cultural globalization are not addressed in any detail here, as they are covered in the remainder of this book. But to begin with, it should be noted that even within the contemporary period, there have been factors working against globalization. First, while the Cold War was a system of global conflict, evident for example in the ways in which it contributed to the development of international security structures and a global arms market, and hence an expression of globalization, it inevitably served to inevitably restrict international trade, as well as the freedom of movement of people, information and ideas during the post-war period. Second, the continued vitality and relevance of the nation-state in our own time – though globalists would deny this is the case – serve to inhibit the development of the institutions of global governance. National governments could also be said to be acting as a fetter upon globalization in their attempts to restrict migration and asylum. This point equally applies to their attempts to control global capital and financial flows in their pursuit of national economic management. Third, global economic inequalities ensure that globalization remains an incomplete process. This is because one of the ways in which such inequalities are manifested is in the unequal access to communication and information technologies. It means that certain regions and continents, notably many African countries, as well as poor parts of Latin America and the Middle East, remain on the edges of these important global changes, and inevitably as a result do not participate fully in some forms of global interconnectedness. Fourth, and following on from the previous point, because of the form that globalization is taking – or at least is perceived to be taking – it has provoked an anti-globalization backlash and considerable popular resentment and protest. Taken together, it is likely these counter-globalizing tendencies have contributed to the unevenness and complexity of contemporary globalization.

Nevertheless, the contemporary period is in general marked not only by the greater intensity and extensity of cultural flows, in the form of the movement of peoples, ideas, goods, symbols and images, but also by the greater velocity with which they travel from place to place, and is in turn serving to deepen forms of global cultural interconnectedness. This pattern is the result of a number of developments, notably the significant and ongoing improvements in transport and transport infrastructures. In particular, jet airlines, the construction of road and rail networks across the globe, containerized shipping, and the dramatic rise in ownership of cars and other vehicles have all facilitated forms of global interconnectedness. For example, improvements in aviation have contributed to the development of tourism and shifting patterns of global migration, while major advances in communications and information technologies, notably in the areas of telephony, computing and digitization, ensure that international communication is both cheaper and instantaneous. Similarly, individual cultures and cultural forms now have a global reach, through a combination of satellites, fibre-optic cabling, the greater access worldwide to television and radio, and the spread of the Internet. Contributing to these developments has been the emergence of powerful international media corporations. And perhaps underpinning many or all of these developments has been the continuing expansion of international capitalism, evident in the spread of the global market and the incorporation of new countries into it like China, the emergence of MNCs and TNCs, as well as in the heightened role and influence of business generally in the contemporary period. The cumulative effect of the advances described here is that cultural interaction and consumption, in comparison with earlier eras, which, as Held et al. (1999) note, tended to be between the elites of different societies, under contemporary globalization are experienced in the main at the popular level. In addition, some globalizing tendencies are assuming new or heightened importance in our time compared to earlier eras, notably the condition of the global environment and the prospect of a different type of world politics with the formation and continuing evolution of international institutions.

In sum, while it has built upon and extended earlier tendencies and patterns, especially of the modern period, there are aspects of the contemporary phase of globalization that make it distinct from other periods, something which, as we will see later in this work, generates its own cultural debates and issues.

Interpreting the history of cultural globalization

Some of the key aspects of the history of cultural globalization having been outlined, a case could perhaps be made that the different phases delineated here do not adequately encapsulate its complexity. For instance, the early phase of globalization could be broken down further into pre-settler societies and settler societies. Likewise, as was mentioned earlier, it may be more appropriate to view the modern age as being constituted by early modern and late modern periods, say, c.1500–1850 and c.1850–1945, respectively (for example see Held et al., 1999). From a specifically cultural and social perspective, the modern phase of globalization may be regarded as having come to an end with the First World War, so momentous and disruptive was this episode. The contemporary phase should arguably be divided into pre- and post-1990 periods, as the popular dissemination of the Internet during the 1990s has ensured a surge in global interconnectedness. Irrespective of the accuracy of the historical periodization presented here, the more substantive point being made is that we should not become too preoccupied with delineating and thinking about historical phases in relation to cultural globalization. In this vein, the different phases identified here are not neat and enclosed entities, and it will be possible to find globalizing processes transcending them and existing in different epochs. It is also highly unlikely that any of these processes will be found in all regions throughout the world during any particular historical epoch.

Globalization is therefore not a uniform phenomenon. Rather, it is multi-centred and uneven, and we run the risk of producing simply a linear history of globalization if we do not acknowledge this reality. Indeed, Fredrick Cooper (2001) detects a teleological bias in current histories of globalization, whereby the present is simply read back into the past. Recognition of this unevenness includes taking into account that globalizing flows, cultural or otherwise, have provoked varying degrees of resistance in some societies and regions, thus influencing the trajectory of globalization and reinforcing the need to examine particular contexts in relation to this subject. Further complicating matters is the fact that some globalizing forces can work to cancel out or counter other universalizing tendencies. For example, the expansionism of European powers in the nineteenth century was in some regions achieved by pushing back another globalizing force, namely Islam.

As was stated earlier, a difficulty that arises when studying the history of cultural globalization concerns the issue of when it began. The premodern phase discussed earlier potentially covers many millennia prior to 1500, and for this reason we need to consider when it is plausible to talk about the emergence of globalization. Tackling this matter, in turn, raises questions about what we mean by globalization, and the criteria we employ in order to determine its existence. For example, should we conceive of it as: the movements of people; long-distance trading activities; the amount of inter-cultural contact; the development of an international society; or, in relation to the formation of a global consciousness? Or, should it be viewed as a combination of these and other yardsticks? Moreover, a frequently raised question within globalization studies concerns whether a cultural form has to be found all over the world to be evidence of globalization. Or, is it simply sufficient that it should transcend a number of regions? Furthermore, in what quantities must artefacts or traces of artefacts be found in different parts of the world to be recognized as constituting cultural globalization? In short, can globalization be traced back to the earliest civilizations or is it a product of more recent times?

Jan Nederveen Pieterse: the long history of globalization

Jan Nederveen Pieterse (2004) believes globalization should be viewed as a long-term historical process. He conceives of globalization as human integration and hybridization, arguing that it is possible to detect forms of cultural mixing across continents and regions dating back many centuries. Indeed, for Nederveen Pieterse, civilizations are not discrete entities, rather they are forged from the intermeshing of a range of influences over long periods of time, and as we saw in the previous section a case can be made for the West's own mixed cultural heritage. Moreover, in Latin America, a folk Catholicism was generated from the intermingling of Spanish, Portuguese and Catholic influences with indigenous cultures as a result of Europe's encounter with the New World. Hybridity, as Néstor García Canclini observes, 'has a long trajectory in Latin American cultures' (1995: 241). Similarly, the religious beliefs and social customs that constitute Hinduism emerged from the mixing of Indo-European culture, a process that began from 1500 BCE onwards when Aryan invaders encountered and intermingled with indigenous pre-Aryan and Dravidian societies. In support of his conception of globalization as a deep historical process, Nederveen Pieterse points to developments such as the ancient population movements across and between continents, long-distance cross-cultural trade, the spread of world religions, and the diffusion of technologies including agricultural and military technologies. And arguably there are other expressions of the long history of human interaction, such as the spread of languages, literatures, music, cuisines, foodstuffs, plants, cartography, maritime regulation, military technologies and planning, medical knowledge, ideas about statecraft and state formation, and the dissemination of scientific discoveries and technological innovations. It also follows, Nederveen Pieterse argues, that if we accept the naturalness of hybridity then contemporary globalization has to be read in a certain way, namely that it accelerates the human condition, which is one of cultural mixing. As he puts it: 'contemporary accelerated globalisation means the hybridisation of hybrid cultures' (2004: 82).

However, Nederveen Pieterse's thesis has attracted criticism. In particular, his conception of our cultures and identities as hybrid, and hence inherently unstable, is far from universally accepted. For example, as we will see in chapter 5, some writers on nationalism and national cultures, such as Anthony Smith, identify the *ethnie* (ethnic core) of nations and for this reason emphasize continuity in relation to this particular cultural identity. Similarly, Nederveen Pieterse's conception of history as one of constant human integration is not without challenge, especially as there are arguably some historical periods when civilizations did not interact to the extent that he contends. Felipe Fernández-Armesto argues in his book *Millennium* (1996) that at the start of the second millennium the Chinese, Islamic and Japanese civilizations were fairly discrete worlds developing in relative isolation. In this vein, it is often claimed that China became more insular after 1500 (Holton, 2005). The Chinese government banned maritime trade and emigration to Southeast Asia for a period in the sixteenth century because of the growth of piracy and smuggling (van de Ven, 2002). More significantly, China's imperial rulers, especially the Qing Dynasty (1644–1912), sought to avoid becoming involved with 'foreign barbarians', notably from the West.

But for Nederveen Pieterse, to repeat, these civilizations are themselves a product of human integration: cultures overlap, collide, and are shaped by these encounters, a process that has been going on since time immemorial. This is evident, he maintains, in the spread of the world religions and the degree of diversity that exists within them, which is a consequence of interacting with and adapting to local cultures and often the presence and influence of other faiths within particular regions (2004: 25). Nevertheless, it is appropriate to enquire whether – as Nederveen Pieterse insists that it is – human integration is tantamount to globalization? If we are to answer this question, we clearly need to know more about the nature or form of this human integration. For example, does it involve or include sources from all over the world? Or, have these civilizations emerged from, in the main, forms of regional mixing and interaction? Unfortunately, Nederveen Pieterse does not provide us with any detailed analysis or case studies to be able to investigate these questions. Rather, he leaves us with the general claim that integration is what human beings *do*.

Anthony Giddens: the modernity of globalization

The position sketched out by Nederveen Pieterse contrasts with that of economists and sociologists, who generally trace the origins of globalization to capitalism (1500 onwards) and modernity (1800 onwards), respectively. Indeed, Nederveen Pieterse is critical of the renowned sociologist Anthony Giddens for conceiving of globalization as one of the 'consequences of modernity'. For Nederveen Pieterse such views are Eurocentric because they conceive of globalization as westernization, 'which is geographically narrow and historically shallow' (ibid., 4), neglecting the fact that globalization predates the rise of the West. However, this disagreement, as well as reflecting the particular spheres of interest of individual academic disciplines, is rooted in differing conceptions of globalization. For Nederveen Pieterse, globalization is about human integration; for Giddens, it is about time–space distantiation. It is therefore inevitable that these writers have different understandings of the history of globalization. Again we can see that much rests upon the criteria we employ in defining globalization.

While the work of writers such as Jan Nederveen Pieterse and Robert Clark help to counter the conception of globalization as a uniquely contemporary phenomenon by reminding us of its historical antecedents, we need to be cautious about how far back in time we go when considering this subject. As we have seen, such factors as limited transport and communications and territorially separate continents inhibited cultural flows and other forms of global interconnectedness in the premodern period. We should also bear in mind that there can be discontinuities when it comes to globalizing tendencies and processes. For example, there may have been times over the centuries when particular trade or migration patterns contracted or simply disappeared. Hence we should not discount the significance of the relationship between globalization and modernity. In relation to this issue, Giddens maintains that modernity 'is inherently globalising' (1990: 177). He contends that two of its defining institutions – namely, the nation-state and capitalism – significantly extend globalization into new geographical areas. Indeed, developments within the modern period increase the intensity, extensity and velocity of global cultural flows to such an extent that there are substantive qualitative and quantitative differences from the premodern era, while developments within the contemporary period, such as advances in information and communications technologies, merely exacerbate this tendency. All of this raises the question of the appropriateness of applying the term 'globalization' to the premodern era, and in so doing returns us to the issue of how we define globalization. Lastly, Giddens emphasizes that the nation-state and 'systematic capitalist production' have their origins not only in a particular period of history, but also in Europe. As Giddens puts it, they 'have few parallels in prior periods or in other cultural settings' (1990: 174), and he would undoubtedly argue that this historical fact counters the charge of Eurocentrism made by Nederveen Pieterse.

Conclusion: the histories of cultural globalization

However, perhaps the most appropriate and productive way of conceptualizing globalization is simply to look for patterns and clusters as well as degrees of global interconnectedness, whether this is in the form of migration, intercultural contact, trade, the movement of ideas or some of the other criteria raised here. We should therefore conceive of globalization as stronger or weaker, deeper or shallower, thicker or thinner forms of global interconnectedness, or whatever adjectives we deem applicable (see Held et al., 1999; Rosendorf, 2000). By adopting this approach, we will be better able to map the historical development of globalization and recognize that it did not emerge from nowhere, but also to identify the qualitative and quantitative changes that have taken place in our own era. In other words, we cease conceiving of globalization as an absolute condition with a specific starting point at a particular moment in history. Thus some of the developments discussed earlier as part of the premodern era, such as the early imperial systems and world religions, would be instances of thin globalization, for example. Furthermore, if we follow this approach, it is likely that we will have a more informed understanding of contemporary globalization, delineating areas and aspects of 'strong globalization' but also those where patterns of weaker globalization persist.[8]

In summary, given the vast range of material covered here it has been impossible to undertake a comprehensive analysis of the history of cultural globalization. Instead, the aim has been to delineate broad historical trends. What we have learnt is that cultural globalization is not distinct from the other dimensions of globalization, and is in fact intertwined with many forms of human activity, and consequently studying it necessitates undertaking an interdisciplinary approach. We have also seen that globalization has evolved over a number of millennia from multiple origins or sources, though this history has been uneven and contingent in nature, depending upon the contexts in which its processes are being both contributed to and experienced. Furthermore, at various stages there have been forces working against globalization. Overall, therefore, it is appropriate to conceive of globalization as a plural rather than unitary phenomenon. Indeed, when thinking about the history of this subject, it is more accurate to think of a number of histories as opposed to the history of globalization: as globalizations rather than globalization. Given that cultural globalization is bound up with globalization's other dimensions, this emphasis upon plurality is equally applicable to it. Hence the title of this chapter: the histories of cultural globalization. Finally, while globalization, historically speaking, has been a long time coming, the distinctiveness of its contemporary phase has been emphasized here. This stems from the coming together of a particular set of processes, technological, economic, social and political, environmental and cultural, that takes us to a new and unprecedented level of global interconnectedness, as will be further demonstrated in subsequent chapters.

Recommended reading

Classic works on world history include William McNeill's *The Rise of the West: A History of the Human Community* (1963) and Janet Abu-Lughod's *Before European Hegemony* (1989). An important work on global history is *Conceptualizing Global History* (1993), edited by Bruce Mazlish and Ralph Buultjens. Jürgen Osterhammel and Niels Petersson's *Globalisation: A Short History* (2005) is a succinct, thoughtful introduction to the subject, which goes back seven or eight centuries in tracing the emergence of globalization, but focuses mainly upon the early-modern and modern periods. The edited collection by A.G. Hopkins, *Globalisation in World History* (2002), is a serious attempt on the part of historians to engage in the globalization debate. While *Global Transformations* by David Held and his co-writers (1999) is a thorough and impressive attempt to map the history of globalization in its different forms. For works stressing the long history of globalization, see Robert Clark, *The Global Imperative* (1997) and Jan Nederveen Pieterse, *Globalization and Culture* (2004); for works emphasizing the modernity of globalization, see Anthony Giddens, *The Consequences of Modernity* and Jan Aart Sholte, *Globalization: A Critical Introduction* (2000). Finally, the volume edited by Barry K.Gills and William R. Thompson entitled *Globalisation and Global History* (2006) presents a series of detailed scholarly investigations into this subject.

2

Travelling Cultures

To understand cultural globalization, we need to be clear, or at least as clear as we possibly can be, about what we mean by culture. For this reason, this chapter will explore the concept of culture and associated debates, with the notion of culture as process espoused. It is not my intention to set out a fully developed thesis on the nature of culture, merely to suggest appropriate ways of thinking about and approaching it under contemporary conditions. I will then turn to examine the relationship between culture and globalization, looking at how culture moves through the world, focusing in particular upon the idea of cultural flows and cultural deterritorialization. The final part of the chapter will concentrate upon an issue that is receiving increasing critical attention in relation to this subject area, namely transnationalism, examining what it tells us about the ways in which the relationship between the cultural and the spatial has progressed in the contemporary period.

Interpreting culture

If we assume that culture is more than just the creative arts and learning, we are immediately confronted with the problem of trying to pin down and define a concept that is notoriously slippery and contested. For this reason, it is tempting to conceptualize culture in a very basic sense as 'a way of life' (e.g., Williams, 1976). But such a broad-brush approach struggles to encapsulate the individual experiences of people inhabiting particular cultures. Within any cultural group, there will be different ideas and attitudes reflecting people's individual positions, lifestyles and outlooks, as a result of factors such as age, class and gender (Eriksen, 1997). At certain times, there will be some groups as well as some forces able to exert a dominant influence upon a particular culture, either from within the culture or from outside of it. Further, the idea of culture as a 'way of life' underplays the different types of culture – national, regional, popular, local, elite, business, Western, as well as subcultures – to cite but a few. There are also different dimensions to culture and cultures, notably institutional, political, social, economic and historical. Indeed, the protean and complex nature of culture has led some writers to work with other analytical categories when theorizing about the concept. In this regard, Pierre Bourdieu (1977, 1990a, 1993) has articulated his conception of 'habitus', a realm or system in which groups and individuals learn and develop over time cultural attitudes and dispositions, which are not uniformly pursued but are instead exercised uniquely in relation to particular contexts or fields. However, this 'system of acquired dispositions' (1990b: 13), as Bourdieu describes it, does not take sufficient account of the ways in which cultures are permeated by the flows and processes of globalization. In fact, many would argue that the very notion of system is problematic under contemporary conditions of circulation and mobility.

The lack of conceptual consensus over 'culture' is especially evident within academia. Not only do disciplines such as anthropology, sociology and cultural studies have their own approaches to the subject, but even within these disciplines there is a diversity of opinion towards culture. Thus, while a recurring theme within sociology is that we acquire culture through a range of socialization institutions and practices, Marxists and functionalists have different perspectives on the political ends that this serves, which lack of space dictates cannot be discussed here. In the case of anthropology, Adam Kuper (1999) employs the phrase 'culture wars' to indicate the extent and nature of the debates surrounding culture within his discipline. Moreover, early anthropological approaches to culture are criticized for exoticizing the 'other' and contributing to the domination of non-Western cultures, and even some anthropologists would rather dispense with the concept of culture, viewing it as a discredit to their profession (Shweder, 2000: 162). In response to these criticisms, anthropologists have been sensitive to the issue of cultural pluralism, a view that dates back to the noted anthropologist Franz Boas (1858–1942), who emphasized the necessity of respect for cultural difference and of recognizing that each culture pertains to a specific, historically contingent way of life. But as with Pierre Bourdieu's conception of habitus, it is pertinent to ask whether the cultural discreteness that this implies is applicable under conditions of globalization? As we will see during the course of this work, cultures are not immune to globalizing processes; rather they both inform and are informed by these external forces. In sum, to state the obvious, the lack of consensus over what culture actually is and how we should study it makes determining its relationship to globalization rather difficult.

Finally, some academic disciplines arguably have certain limitations when it comes to dealing with culture. For example, in the case of sociology, the emphasis within functionalism upon viewing culture as the learned norms and values of a society is, in an era of globalization, perhaps too attached to an outdated conception of the nation-state. Indeed, Ulrich Beck (2000) believes sociology has generally paid insufficient attention to the global. Of course, functionalism is only one branch of thought within sociology, and Bryan S. Turner (2006) contests the notion that sociology is fixated upon nation-states and national societies, arguing that generations of sociologists – dating back to Emile Durkheim and Talcott Parsons – have incorporated global processes into their approaches. In the case of anthropology, it has traditionally investigated 'the local', in all its various manifestations, thereby potentially ignoring global and transnational influences upon culture and the possibility of universal values and practices (Wilson, 1997), although contemporary anthropologists such as Ulf Hannerz (1992a, 1996, 2003) now actively engage with the external, and in his case it has led him to delineate cultural diversity, complexity, creolization and innovation or creativity as ongoing tendencies. More broadly, if, as hybridity theorists claim, globalizing processes are generating greater heterogeneity within cultures then this presents all disciplines with obvious analytical challenges. For example, it is often maintained that a culture requires an 'other' in order to define itself, but this becomes more problematic under conditions of hybridity.[1] Such conditions can even unsettle the concepts that we employ, something that is evident in the way in which the notion of 'the West', and implicitly the 'non-Western' world, is being undermined by contemporary patterns of global migration, with the exchange of peoples ensuring that the two regions become less culturally distinctive.

Culture as process

Having outlined some of the difficulties in analysing 'culture', the approach that will be employed here will now be set out. As with globalization, the stress will be upon its multifaceted nature or form. Hence, rather than being overly preoccupied with establishing a precise definition of culture, which for reasons that have been indicated is never likely to gain universal acceptance, it will be considered here in relation to a number of themes – namely process, travel, networks or webs of meaning, and plurality – and, in so doing, draw upon the insights of a number of disciplines, notably cultural and social anthropology, sociology and cultural studies. The reasons for considering culture in this way will now be set out.

To begin with, it should be noted that culture has always been a dynamic and protean concept in the sense that its meaning has changed over time and it assumes different forms (see Williams, 1976). In our own time, it is increasingly viewed as a process rather than an entity, a verb rather than a noun, especially within anthropology and cultural studies (Eriksen, 1997; Street, 1993; Wilson, 1997). As the anthropologist Roy Wagner (1986) has argued, cultures are continually changing and being re-created as part of an ongoing process. In particular, cultures are informed by numerous internal pressures and influences, ensuring that they are neither static nor stable. They are also shaped by external forces and hence are not homogenous, discrete and bounded entities; rather, they overlap and draw from other traditions. For example, patterns of global migration, and more specifically immigration into the UK since the 1950s, have led to Britain becoming a more visibly multicultural society, which in turn has influenced its national culture (chapter 5). At the same time, there have been internal pressures working upon this culture. Developments within British society, such as the decline in deference, the changing position of women, improved levels of education and devolution reforms, have all in varying ways impacted upon British national culture. Cultures are therefore continuously evolving, and as will be shown during the course of this work, contemporary globalizing processes almost certainly increase this tendency, and in doing so, arguably widen awareness of the essential malleability or changeability of culture.

James Clifford (1992, 1997) is the writer most associated with making the connection between culture and travel or movement. Clifford contends that culture can no longer simply be understood in relation to location or place, but should be seen as something that is mobile and travelling. Travellers, tourists and migrants are physically moving around the world, taking their cultures with them and interacting with other cultures and peoples, reproducing, negotiating and defining themselves as well as helping to ensure that cultures transmogrify into new cultural forms. Of course, not everyone is travelling. But even if we choose to stay at home, we still encounter travellers, these strangers from distant lands. Indeed, for Clifford, places should be viewed as sites of both residence and travel encounters. Moreover, the conception of culture as travel applies not only to people, but also to the flows of images, ideas, sounds, symbols and objects that circulate the globe, criss-crossing national borders in the process. For the individual, therefore, travel becomes a curious engagement with the familiar and unfamiliar, and in effect it leads to the blurring of home and abroad (Rojek and Urry, 1997). Cultures are therefore not motionless; they move, adapt and change. For this reason, the idea of 'cultures in motion' has been advanced as a useful way of thinking about this subject (e.g., see Lury, 1997).

All the above has implications for identity and identity-formation, because, if cultures are continuously evolving and moving, how is it possible to have stable identities? But we must not overstate the extent and the pace of the change taking place at any one moment. This is because if cultures were simply fluid and ever changing, then it would make it very difficult for people either to identify with or inhabit them. Therefore, there must be moments of stability: periods of time when networks or clusters of people come to identify with – depending on the particular type of culture – such things as a set of ideas, values, symbols as well as associated artefacts, texts and objects, and are able to internalize these elements of the culture. In other words, even in a world of motion, cultures are still being reproduced within a myriad of social contexts, providing us with interpretative frameworks, value-systems and sources of identity. Acknowledging the existence of these, to use Clifford Geertz's term 'webs of meaning' (1973), is also a recognition of the reality that the majority of people reside in their countries of birth and hence are subjected to its socialization processes, and many will even continue to work and/or live in the same localities for significant periods of their life, invariably developing attachments to them and their respective cultures.[2] Conceptualizing culture in this way is also better able to account for the diversity or plurality that exists within cultures because the numerous clusters and webs that go to make up a culture will often be a particularist rather than a universal experience, reflecting regional, local and other forms of distinctiveness. For example, there are a plethora of groups that constitute and inform British culture, ranging from groups connected to the monarchy and the establishment to immigrant communities, each with their own take upon what British culture is and able to shape it in different ways to a varying extent. Cultures are therefore multi-centred and multi-layered. They also evolve over time, a point that is evident in the case of Islam, within which a number of different religious cultural traditions have emerged over the centuries. For all cultures, such internal differentiation is exacerbated by entanglements with other cultures. Nevertheless, there must be processes of cultural formation and internalization, otherwise the implication is that we are all leading cultureless lives, making it in turn difficult to explain the persistence of cultural conflicts. Nor is it the case that cultural construction belongs to an earlier and less mobile era, as new cultures continue to emerge, such as rap and hip-hop, to take just the example of popular music, and do so in part because of this very mobility.

Thus, viewing cultures as constituted by different networks or webs of meaning, rather than as distinctive, bounded and coherent entities, implicitly acknowledges the diverse relationships that people have with particular cultures. Quite simply, within any culture there will be variations in degrees of commitment to it as well as different perceptions of what it *is* or means. Further, clusters and networks are inherently dynamic and continuously evolving – they form, develop, occasionally fragment, but also re-form – and as such give us an insight into and describe the amorphous and changing nature of cultures. Nor does such an approach deny the possibility that the constitutive elements of culture, such as customs, practices, institutions and traditions, can be constructed or invented, and hence that power relations are often involved in the shaping of cultures. In addition, employing the idea of webs and networks in relation to culture expresses the way in which culture stretches across distances, and in doing so overlaps and merges into other cultural networks, ensuring that cultures are endlessly mixing, with different permeations and new cultural forms emerging as part of an ongoing process. This helps to explain the commonalities that exist between different cultures and, further, accounts for the complexity and differentiation that exists within them. Indeed, recognition of such mixing goes some way to address Lila Abu-Lughod's (1991) concern that the concept of culture denies the existence of 'halfies' or the hybrid. Cultures are therefore cross-cultural, which implicitly implies movement and change rather than stasis and stability. Wolfgang Welsch (1999) describes this tendency as transculturality, meaning that cultures increasingly exist across cultures. Yet cultural distinctiveness persists partly because of the particular histories of different cultures, but also because of the myriad of outcomes that will arise from the mutual interpenetration of cultures as a result of individuals and groups entering these encounters with their own cultural predispositions and outlooks. Lastly, conceptualizing culture as stretching across distances and other cultures should in theory encourage us to take note of how cultures change when they travel, and specifically how they are appropriated, adapted and even resisted in different places.[3] And by adopting this approach we will be paying closer attention to the existence of variations within cultures.

When thinking about culture we also need to take into account that people can and do inhabit multiple cultures, which in turn will come to shape their sense of identity. At any moment, therefore, it is likely that numerous cultural influences will be informing our behaviour, even though we will not always be consciously aware that we are being shaped in this way. This latter point touches upon another aspect of culture, namely that there is an intangible quality to it, and we often only become aware of our cultures when we encounter otherness or difference. Yet it is

[handwritten margin note: Such as church controlling Bible, who does what, when + where – as Government]

also the case that we are not passive and unknowing when it comes to culture, that is, simply products of our respective socialization processes and surroundings; rather, we retain the capacity to critique our own cultures, distance ourselves from certain cultures, become more committed to some cultures than others, and experience and try out new cultures or at least aspects of them. Thus, as human beings we will carry around our cultures with us, but we will also pass through different cultural flows and networks during the course of our daily lives, absorbing new influences, though again not always consciously so. We are therefore not just bearers of culture, but also gatherers of culture. In this regard, Tim Ingold has observed that 'it might be more realistic . . . to say that people *live culturally* rather than they *live in cultures*' (1994: 330, his italics), though again we should not forget that we are considering culture within the context of the rise in forms of cultural fundamentalism.

In sum, it is appropriate to conceive of cultures as internally diverse or plural and engaged in an ongoing process of development, while recognizing that they are able to provide meaning for members by solidifying around common themes, ideas and identities as well as shared values and practices. Having outlined ways of thinking about culture, the remainder of this chapter will turn to consider how cultures are being informed by and in turn informing the multiple processes of contemporary globalization.

Interpreting cultural flows

There is something of a consensus among cultural globalization writers that contemporary processes and technologies are resulting in the greater mobility and fluidity of culture. This means therefore that we are likely to be gathering cultural influences to a much greater extent than in the past, with media, information and people flows in particular ensuring that we do not have to move far in order to undergo a range of cultural experiences. The consequence for us as individuals is that we become involved in a more reflexive and idiosyncratic relationship with these cultures (see chapter 7). Put simply, we enter a more negotiated and critical relationship with culture. Such reflexivity is indicative of a modern attitude, and as such it is one of the reasons that Anthony Giddens (1990) considers globalization to be a modern phenomenon. But attention will now turn to Arjun Appadurai, a writer who in making the linkage between globalization and modernity places great emphasis upon the movement of culture.

Arjun Appadurai: flows, 'scapes' and the new global cultural economy

In works such as *Modernity at Large: Cultural Dimensions of Globalization* (1996), Arjun Appadurai employs metaphors of mobility to describe the heterogeneous nature of culture and how it moves through the world in the contemporary period. More specifically, he identifies five dimensions of global cultural flows in the form of *ethnoscapes, technoscapes, finanscapes, ideoscapes* and *mediascapes*, which provide spaces or opportunities for the construction of new 'imagined worlds'. These landscapes are 'deeply perspectival constructs, inflected very much by the historical, linguistic and political situatedness of different sorts of actors', ranging from nation-states to neighbourhoods (Appadurai, 1990: 296). *Ethnoscapes* concern the demographics of the world, consisting of both the movement of people (travel, migration, tourism, displacement, exile) and stable communities, especially the former, given that people are more mobile than ever before. Moreover, as a result of electronic media and modern travel our imagined communities are no longer confined to the nation-state and are increasingly able to cut across national boundaries. *Technoscapes* describe the distribution of global technologies, much of it uneven, which facilitate the spread of global flows and ensure instantaneous communication, and in turn generate increasingly complex relationships between money, politics and employment (1990: 297–8). As may be anticipated, *finanscapes* are the ever more rapid flow of capital, currency and investment, which Appadurai considers has become detached or disembedded from territories. For Appadurai, the relationship between these three 'scapes' is both unpredictable and disjunctive 'since each of these landscapes is subject to its own constraints and incentives', but arguably more importantly 'each acts as a constraint and a parameter for movements in the other' (1990: 298). Moreover, *ideoscapes* refer to the flow of ideas, ideologies, counter-ideologies and images, such as freedom and democracy, which are always modified by context, and *mediascapes* to the mass media constructions formed from mechanical and electronic mass hardware. Both of these scapes are ideational. In the case of the latter, for instance, viewers use these mass media constructions or images to construct cultural narratives of the 'other'.

For Appadurai, taken together these interrelated global cultural flows form the basic framework of the complex, overlapping and disjunctive order that is the new global cultural economy. What he means by this is that these flows of people, objects, images and discourses follow increasingly non-isomorphic paths, 'have different speeds, axes, points of origin and termination, and varied relationships to institutional structures in different regions, nations, or societies' (2001: 6). And for Appadurai 'these disjunctures themselves precipitate various kinds of problems and frictions in different local situations' (ibid.). For example, when a region is saturated by media flows presenting images of alternative lifestyles this can stimulate imaginations and in turn generate internal tensions and pressures for change. In short, it is through their 'disjunctures' that the five scapes inform and influence culture, and establish the conditions under which global flows occur.

Is it possible to map cultural flows?

If we accept uncritically for the time being that flows are a useful way of conceiving of culture in relation to globalization, we are still faced with the complex task of mapping these flows, whether in the form of people, commodities, images or ideas, as well as the myriad of interconnections and, in turn, reactions that this generates.[4] Indeed, can the sheer quantity of cultural movements be measured and evaluated in any meaningful way? How do we quantify both the vast number and different types of cultural intrusions into any given country or region? The number of billboard and television advertisements selling products from other countries, the amount of foreign music being played on radio stations, and the extent to which foreign languages are being spoken in a country are all instances of cultures being permeated by other cultural influences. In short, it requires the identification of an array of objects, signs, sounds and images as well as peoples moving across regions and intercontinental space. Despite these challenges, David Held et al. (1999) believe that with the emergence of telecommunications, which entail disembodied signs instantaneously circulating the globe and usurping the artefactual nature of cultural transmission, it is possible to discern and trace cultural flows. As they put it: 'We can map the globalisation of culture in terms of the geographical extensity of these movements and the intensity or volume of such movements relative to the national and local. Cultural globalisation can also be charted in terms of the speed – the velocity or rapidity – at which images or ideas can be communicated from one place to another' (Held et al., 1999: 329).

While such cultural mapping may be possible, focusing upon cultural flows does not tell us how they are being interpreted and experienced by recipients, nor the motives of those who are generating them. We have to address, for example, why it is that some cultural flows engender forms of resistance, whereas others do not. In short, monitoring the volume, speed and location of such movements will reveal little about the nature of the cultural interaction.[5] There is also the attendant difficulty of trying to determine what is happening when cultural flows lead to different cultures encountering each other. From the perspective of an external observer, it will often be difficult to interpret accurately the nature of the interaction process, and to determine the meaning that the respective parties attach to the intercultural exchange. Moreover, in reality different groups and individuals will interpret and experience other cultures in a myriad of ways. Furthermore, since cultural flows can have a superficial and transitory quality, as well as being uneven, in some instances their impact upon recipients will be negligible. We will therefore require regular contact with, or exposure to, such cultural flows if they are to have a lasting impression and influence upon us. In short, the nature and intensity of cultural flows, alongside their extensity and velocity, are important determinants of their impact.

Similarly, we need to take into account whether there are some powers or influences dominating and defining global cultural flows and processes. Do cultural flows emanate in the main from a particular source or sources, and travel mainly in certain directions (see chapter 4)? Most significantly, cultural flows are not travelling within a power vacuum, rather they are operating within a world where structural inequalities persist, and we need to scrutinize how this influences their nature and form. Doreen Massey (1994, 2005) in particular has stressed the need to recognize the power-geometry that is present in despatialized social relations. As a result of differences in power, social groups and individuals operate or are situated in very distinct ways in relation to global flows and interconnections. Some initiate and/or are a part of cultural flows, while others are mainly on the receiving end of them. For Massey, this even applies to places, with Chad an example of the latter, and London providing evidence of the former.[6] All this leads Aihwa Ong (1999) to argue that, to understand cultural globalization and move beyond presenting generalized accounts, our analyses need to combine political economy with, as she terms it, 'situated ethnography'. Moreover, Marxist writers emphasize that what is circulating the globe in the form of objects, goods, images and people is doing so as a result of capitalism, which in their view remains the driving force behind cultural flows.

Many writers maintain that cultural flows also move from the local to the global, and for this reason globalization cannot be viewed as a one-way process, that is, as a movement from the global to the local (chapter 4). In this vein, Anthony Giddens has written of the 'local–global dialectic', arguing that 'local lifestyle habits have become globally consequential' (1994: 5). He continues, 'my decision to buy a certain item of clothing has implications not only for the international division of labour but for the earth's ecosystems' (ibid.). Yet it is even more complicated than this, as global fashions and tastes can also influence our decisions about the clothes and other products we purchase. Moreover, such decisions do not remain confined to the cultural realm. Economic, political, social and environmental influences will also inform our behaviour, and have both global and local dimensions. To take just one of these influences, the environmental: if we decide to buy local produce, for obvious reasons our decision will be based upon and have local/global considerations and consequences. It would seem then that the local and the global function in a reciprocal manner, though as will be indicated in the Conclusion, it is likely that what is taking place under conditions of contemporary globalization is even more complex than a global–local dualism.

The emphasis upon cultural flows and fluidity in general in relation to globalization presents certain challenges for a number of academic disciplines, notably sociology and anthropology. In the case of the former, John Urry (2000) has sought to respond to these developments by pursuing a 'sociology of mobilities', believing that existing sociological approaches and concepts are struggling to encapsulate the changes taking place in our more globalized era.[7] In the case of the latter, anthropologists, as was touched upon earlier, have had to revise the notion that cultures are homogenous, discrete and bounded entities, as this becomes difficult to sustain when these cultures are increasingly permeated by external flows and forces (see Eriksen, 1995; Wilson, 1997). In particular, it has highlighted the shortcomings of the traditional 'fieldwork approach' within anthropology – though, as we saw with James Clifford's emphasis upon travel in relation to culture, there have always been exceptions to this approach within the discipline – and has led anthropologists to pay greater attention to how cultures and places are constituted by a wider set of social and cultural phenomena. Such an approach has also enabled anthropologists to identify the limits of globalization, the localities where globalizing flows and processes have not yet properly or deeply permeated, and in turn contributed to an emphasis upon the transnational (see below). Finally, and continuing a theme of this work, we should note that the approaches to this subject area are very much a product of disciplinary constraints and traditions, with cultural studies stressing mobility and fluidity in relation to globalization and areas such as political science and legal studies focusing upon institutions and frameworks, examining how culture is structured by corporate and state power (Holton, 2005). But ultimately, while metaphors such as flows and scapes provide us with a vocabulary and an imagery to describe the way culture moves, these are not analytical categories, and there is always the danger that in employing them our investigations and discussions of cultural globalization remain general and abstract.

Cultural deterritorialization

What is cultural deterritorialization?

In a very broad sense, cultural deterritorialization marks a transformation in the relationship between culture and territory, necessitating that we re-examine how we conceive of culture. Contemporary globalizing tendencies are considered to be disrupting the linkage between culture and territory, ensuring that our cultural experiences, identities and practices are becoming separated from the places we inhabit. This can be seen in the manner in which cultures and cultural communities can develop in new and multiple locations or places. Indeed, cultural deterritorialization is especially associated with migrant and diaspora communities, many of whom will employ a range of strategies to preserve and adapt their cultures to new conditions, including utilizing some of the developments that are contributing to globalization, such as advances in transportation and communications technology. In this regard, global communications technologies allow dispersed and migrant communities to maintain regular contact with each other, their families, and with their homelands. At the same time, the modern media inform them of events taking place in their homelands and of news of their compatriots elsewhere in the world. Moreover, jet air travel means that those who have resettled can make return trips to their respective countries of origin, in many cases within a few hours. For example, some of the more affluent Korean migrants working in the USA are able to return to their home country on a regular basis, and effectively lead dual lives by becoming involved in two cultures (Douglass, 1994). Thus, with cultural communities emerging in different parts of the world, and often in different places within a single country, culture becomes multi-local and thereby deterritorialized. For Nikos Papastergiadis, cultural deterritorialization describes 'the ways in which people now feel they belong to various communities despite the fact that they do not share a common territory with all the other members' (2000: 115). Electronic communities or global networks are the most extreme manifestation of this development, displaying forms of cultural commonality despite the absence of any territorial base.

It is therefore not necessarily the case, especially under conditions of globalization, that deterritorialization serves to weaken cultural attachments on the part of those on the move. In fact, quite the reverse: the nature of the diaspora or migrant existence will often mean that a particular community will try all the harder to hold on to their original territorial-based culture, and hence will not simply or uncritically absorb the culture of their host nation. As Appadurai (1996) has noted, the issue of cultural reproduction for Hindus living abroad has become closely associated with the development of Hindu fundamentalism within India. Indeed, an attachment to their particular homelands on the part of the 'deterritorialized' can apply even when those homelands do not yet exist. Sikhs living in Canada, the UK and the USA have been at the forefront of the campaign for Khalistan, an independent Sikh homeland in India. Furthermore, there is the prospect that such activities and sentiments will generate among some migrants a desire to return to their territorial homes, real or imagined.

There are other instances of cultural deterritorialization in the contemporary phase of globalization. For example, the increased flows of trade, capital, people, media images and cultural symbols can serve not only to disrupt, but actually alter locations. In practice, this often means that the places we inhabit are being subjected to constant bombardment by images, ideas and sounds from around the world, whether via our television screens or radios, or by billboards advertising products from distant parts of the globe. Similarly, the shops and malls into which we walk will have foodstuffs, clothes and consumer items from countless places that we are unlikely ever to visit. The architectural styles of many of the new buildings that we enter will draw from influences as well as materials from around the world. Thus, global cultural forms and goods imbue the cultural spaces or territories in which we live, shaping them in the process. It is not only cultural formations and goods that are able to exert this influence: patterns of global migration mean that there are new peoples in our midst with different cultures and traditions who will want to practise these cultures and shape their own living space within their new societies. Moreover, as migrants interact with locals there will be the possibility of mutual intercultural borrowings and the development of new cultural formations. Hence, cultural deterritorialization does not only affect those who are migrating, but it will also have an impact upon the culture or cultures of host countries. In sum, an important consequence of such movement is that cultures and cultural forms can inhabit or exist within other cultures, albeit often being indigenized in the process. In fact, today's cultures can be so full of such 'foreign' elements that it is difficult if not impossible to detect authentic culture, if such a thing exists or indeed has ever existed. For example, within German culture and society can be found Pokémon, Elvis, reggae, Kung Fu films, hip-hop, rap, salsa dancing and Buddhist schools, which are cultural forms and influences that all originated in other countries and cultures. Such cultural complexity can in turn serve to disrupt our sense of place, making it more difficult for all of us to retain a notion of what is our cultural home.

Thus, under conditions of increased mobility, culture becomes increasingly detached from territory. For some writers, the dislocation of culture and cultural embeddedness is the cultural condition of globalization (e.g., Thompson, 1995; Tomlinson, 1999a). Arguably, it can even lead to cultures or cultural forms evolving largely free from association with a particular place. This would seem to be evident in the case of Bhangra music. While Bhangra is originally a form of folk music from northern India, it has been evolving in the UK and most importantly it has been drawing upon a large spectrum of musical influences, such as rap and urban punk jungle, many of which are not indigenous to Britain. The new cultural forms that emerge from such hybrid encounters are therefore frequently not tied to or associated with any specific territory, though we should not overlook the fact that this tendency may have a longer history, with jazz, for example, arguably displaying some of these characteristics as it evolved during the twentieth century.

Cultural deterritorialization: critical perspectives

The contribution of contemporary globalizing processes to cultural deterritorialization should not be overstated as arguably its existence dates back to early diaspora communities. The Jewish people, for instance, have maintained their religious culture despite the loss of what they consider to be their cultural homeland and being dispersed among Gentiles for most of their history. We also need to take into account that rather than aspects of globalization enabling cultures to survive deterritorialization, it is the strength of the cultures themselves that ensures this development. For example, during the period of 'the Troubles' in Northern Ireland, some of the most ardent supporters of the goal of a united Ireland could be found in the USA among Irish-Americans. In this instance, it is not just the nature of the diaspora's existence ensuring such interest in their 'homeland', and a transnational media and communications technology facilitating awareness of what was going on in it; the actual strength and vitality of the culture also contributed to this behaviour.

Furthermore, we should not overestimate the extent to which culture has been deterritorialized in the contemporary period. People are still prepared to resort to violence for the exclusive right to 'their' cultural homeland or territory and to exclude, and in some instances slaughter, communities that they consider do not belong, with the ethnic cleansing committed in the Balkans during the 1990s an obvious manifestation of this tendency. Territory and a sense of place therefore remain important and perhaps even constitute a deep human need, affording us protection and security as well as being sites of cultural formation. In this regard, Arjun Appadurai's contention that Palestinians are more concerned 'to get Israel off their backs than about the special geographical magic of the West Bank' (1996: 165) is incorrect. Many Palestinians attach considerable cultural and religious significance to areas within the West Bank, and view the region as a whole as forming the basis for the development of a Palestinian state. More broadly, their own territory protected by their own nation-state remains the goal of many liberation or separatist movements, and invariably this is viewed as the best way of preserving their culture or identity. Moreover, governments of established countries are ever vigilant when it comes to preserving their national culture and ways of life within their own territorial borders, and will pursue forms of cultural protectionism where necessary to ensure this end. Hence we should not ignore the persistence of territoriality in our globalizing age. This theme has been taken up by Jan Aart Scholte (2005), who stresses the continuing importance of territory in areas ranging from governance to identity, employing the term 'supraterritoriality' to express the idea that, while it is increasingly being transcended, territory is still present and embedded within supraterritorial developments.

What are we to make of these competing views on cultural deterritorialization? On this matter, John Tomlinson (1999a) is almost certainly correct in his observation that cultural deterritorialization is likely to be happening unevenly. In some instances, new forms of cultural territorialization or reterritorialization will often emerge as different cultural groups adapt to new circumstances such as migration, and bring with them reminders from their homelands, such as food, clothing and other cultural goods, as well as their former lifestyles and values. This is evident, for instance, in the Chinatowns that have emerged in numerous cities throughout the world since the nineteenth century, where ethnic Chinese migrants have carved out territories for themselves that architecturally and culturally resemble parts of China itself. Above all, reterritorialization can be seen as a response to the uncertainty generated by the disembedding of 'social relations from local contexts of interaction and their restructuring across indefinite spans of time–space' that Anthony Giddens has identified

(1990: 21). In other words, reterritorialization constitutes a search for a sense of home or place. Overall, therefore, it would seem that there are numerous processes going on with respect to culture and territory. This condition is captured by Jonathan Xavier Inda and Renato Rosaldo (2002), who consider that the processes of cultural deterritorialization and reterritorialization will be taking place simultaneously and continuously, and employ the neologism 'de/territorialization' to express this tendency. Nevertheless, there is a danger that the current stress upon mobility and flows in relation to cultural deterritorialization, and within globalization studies more generally, has exaggerated what is taking place at least at this current juncture, underplaying the continuing significance of territory or location. As we have seen, cultures do not necessarily require a stable territorialized existence (see Clifford, 1992), and numerous diaspora communities bear out this point, but such cultures do need to have histories and memories, and often these will be associated with particular places.

Transnationalism

What is transnationalism?

Continuing this investigation into how culture is moving in our globalizing era and the forms that it is assuming, attention will now turn to transnationalism. Despite being, and perhaps because of being, conceptualized in a variety of ways, transnationalism has gained considerable academic and popular currency in the recent period (see Kearney, 1995). To an extent this popularity may be due to the perceived inadequacies of internationalism, which continues to conceptualize the world in terms of nation-states and the extension or otherwise of national power, and thereby pays insufficient attention to the range of cultural forms, forces and tendencies that both extend beyond their borders and at the same time move within them. As Suzanne Gearhart (2005) has observed, transnationalism expresses something that is neither national nor international. But it is doing more than that: it is suggesting that something more is at work than just a binary tension between the global and the local. Transnationalism is effectively an acknowledgement that many contemporary flows are not truly global, and are simply anchored in more than one nation-state. Exploring this phenomenon therefore requires more contextualized and territorially situated analyses, and helps to explain why transnationalism is a subject area of particular interest to cultural theorists and anthropologists (e.g., see Eriksen, 2003). In contrast, many accounts within globalization studies pursue a more broad-brush approach, reflecting the territorially delinked nature of global flows and processes. However, from the transnational perspective, transcending national borders does not necessarily constitute globalization.

The developments facilitating globalization, such as telecommunications and transportation technologies, similarly contribute to forms of transnationalism. Indeed, transnationalism is generally viewed as part of the process of globalization, but also as an approach to studying it, and in this sense is considered to express the formation of new social spaces and new types of community and forms of human interaction, as well as the adaptations to these developments that are taking place within specific contexts. However, to complicate matters, forms of transnationalism arguably predate the modern and contemporary phases of globalization in the sense that diaspora communities, religious cultures and trading circuits, which extended across regions, could be found in the pre-nation-state era. This last point takes us to the heart of some of the criticisms that have been raised against transnationalism, namely the issues of definition and conceptualization, and more specifically how it differs from other cross-border movements. For example, what makes an immigrant community a transnational community? Critics have also observed that the vast majority of the world's population are not migrating and hence are not living transnationally, and even those who are on the move are not necessarily engaging in transnational activities. As a result, it is argued, the significance of transnationalism has been overstated. In response, some writers on transnationalism note that the continuing demand of global capitalism for cheap migrant labour is likely to ensure transnationalism becomes even more widespread in the future (Portes, 2001).

argument against transnationalism

Transnational communities and cultures

To return to the question of what distinguishes a transnational community, an important feature of transnationalism is that it offers migrant communities an alternative to assimilation, something that is evident in Richard Rouse's (1991) study of Mexican labour migrants in Redwood City, California, who maintain multiple interconnections with Aguililla, their home town in rural Mexico.[8] Such is the density of these connections that a transnational migrant circuit or community has emerged, stretching from the Silicon Valley to Aguililla. As Rouse puts it: '[t]oday, Aguilillans find that their most important kin and friends are as likely to be living hundreds of thousands of miles away as immediately around them' (ibid., 12).

Crucially, the technological developments contributing to global interconnectedness, such as phones, the Internet, email and planes, enable them 'to
maintain these spatially extended relations as actively and effectively as ties
that link them to their neighbours' (ibid.). Rouse concludes that the
Aguilillans constitute a 'single community spread in a variety of places'
(ibid., 13).

A similar story is evident in Peggy Levitt's (2001) study of the numerous
familial, civic and religious connections that exist between Miraflores, a
town in the Dominican Republic, and Jamaica Plain, a neighbourhood in
Boston, Massachusetts. Here the migrants participate in the political, social
and economic lives of both countries, creating communities that span
borders and blurring notions of origin and destination in the process. Levitt
succinctly encapsulates the transnational experience in the following
description: 'Because someone is always travelling between Boston and the
island, there is a continuous, circular flow of goods, news and information.
As a result, when someone is ill, cheating on his or her spouse, or finally
granted a visa, news spreads as quickly in Jamaica Plain, as it does on the
streets of Miraflores' (Levitt, 2001: 3). In other words, Levitt notes, it is not
necessary to migrate in order to be a 'transnational villager'. It is even possible for the Mirafloreños to share the same experience in both localities,
with the availability of Spanish-language CNN enabling migrants and non-
migrants to watch the same programmes simultaneously, including the
ever popular *telenovelas* (soap operas). More profoundly, such transnational
linkages and interconnections are also responsible for bringing about social
and cultural change. For example, the women from Miraflores have been
pushing for greater equality for Dominican women in their own society in
part because of the experience of their female relations and friends who
have migrated to the USA (ibid., 14).

While much of the early writing on transnationalism was centred upon
international migrants, the term has been extended to incorporate a wide
range of cross-border communities, identities and cultures. Thus, transnationalism is considered by its advocates to be manifested in a variety of
forms: business communities; religious and ethnic cultures; artistic,
scientific and professional communities; and regional civil societies and
identities. Transnationalism is also viewed as being at work whenever particular cultural forms (popular culture, music, fashions, cuisines, etc.)
spread across a number of nation-states. For example, Japanese popular
culture – in the form of games software, comics and animations, pop
music and television dramas – has enjoyed growing influence in East
and Southeast Asia (see Iwabuchi, 2002). The common theme of these

transnational cultural forms and communities is their obliviousness to national borders and identities, which for some writers means that they are undermining social constructions like 'the national' and 'the local' and in particular Benedict Anderson's (1983) notion of the 'imagined community' of the nation-state (see Hannerz, 1996).

The transnational and the national

It is certainly the case that transnationalism has a complex and often uneasy relationship with the nation-state and national cultures. Such uneasiness can be seen in the domestic challenges that some governments face from transnational communities operating within their national territory who have members whose loyalties clearly lie outside of their borders. For instance, in Central Asia and the Caucasus, transnational ethno-cultural affiliations have since the collapse of the Soviet Union complicated the process of nation-building and forging a national identity in the newly emerged nation-states (see Mehendale and Atabaki, 2005). However, transnationalism should not necessarily be viewed as a challenge to nationalism and the nation-state. To return to the example of Japan mentioned above, Koichi Iwabuchi (2002) detects a strong nationalist impulse behind the transnational cultural flows that are spreading Japanese popular culture to other parts of Asia. In a similar vein, there are instances of governments promoting and actively seeking transnational connections, including providing dual citizenship and dual nationality laws for emigrants, as a way of extending the influence of their respective countries. Indeed, transnational national communities are able to operate as sources of social solidarity and financial support for the homeland, sending back remittances, investing in their country, and so forth. For example, the Mexican government has especially sought to develop such linkages and promote 'Mexicanness' abroad more generally, and this may in part explain why it reacted so strongly against the US government's proposal to erect a 3,200-km fence along their mutual border in order to prevent illegal immigrants entering America from Mexico. In 2006, it is estimated that there were some 10 million Mexicans living in the USA, around 4 million of them illegally, and many send remittances to their families in Mexico thereby benefiting the Mexican economy. At a meeting held in Columbia in February 2006, Mexico and ten other Latin American states agreed a coordinated lobbying campaign against a tough US immigration bill that included the construction of the border fence, as well as seeking jointly to promote Hispanic migration.

Ultimately, whether transnationalism undermines the nation-states and national cultures is dependent upon the individuals involved in the particular transnational circuit or community. The extent to which individuals participate in transnational circuits or absorb the cultures of their host nations will in turn be influenced by their respective age, gender, class, occupational and other perspectives. In this vein, Aihwa Ong in *Flexible Citizenship: The Cultural Logics of Transnationality* (1999) emphasizes the variety of strategies employed by transnational Chinese investors, managers and professionals with regard to their work, investments and families in their dealings with the different nation-state regimes in the Asia Pacific region. The complexities of transnationalism hinted at here, and the sense that it is more than an expanded nationalism, have been highlighted in a number of recent works on this subject, especially in relation to debates about notions of nationhood and 'home' for transnational peoples. For example, *Searching for Home Abroad* (Lesser, 2003) is a series of studies of Japanese-Brazilians that highlights the difficulties involved in determining what constitutes 'home', especially in the contemporary period, and whether it is possible to have multiple homes. Japanese-Brazilians are a product of high levels of Japanese immigration into Brazil during the first half of the twentieth century, but more recently this trend has been reversed, with hundreds of thousands of Japanese-Brazilians relocating to Japan. As well as problematizing concepts such as home, diaspora and identity, with one study even questioning whether Japanese-Brazilians exist (Linger, 2003), the most striking theme emerging from this volume is the sense among many of the Japanese-Brazilians who have returned to Japan that they feel more 'Brazilian' there than they do in Brazil.

Finally, in linking cultural deterritorialization and transnationalism, Kennedy and Roudometof (2002) have noted that the deterritorialization of culture has transformed how we think about 'community'. Community is no longer predicated upon locality, though this is not to claim that the latter does not retain significance for the former especially in its symbolic or imagined form. Interestingly, Kennedy and Roudometof consider that globalization has given community in the form of transnational communities a new lease of life, and consider such communities to be 'almost destined to provide the most significant form of "community" in the future' (ibid., 24). However, while this may or may not prove to be the case, we should also not ignore the fact that globalization at least in its neo-liberal guise has also been harmful to communities and forms of community life throughout the world.

Conclusion: cultural flows and contexts

In sum, culture is a subject that generates considerable debate, and this is reflected in the existence of multiple conceptions and usages of it. Within globalization studies, contemporary globalizing processes and technologies are generally considered to complicate matters further by ensuring cultural flows travel more rapidly, transforming the relationship between space and time in the process, as well as encouraging more intensive and extensive forms of intercultural contact, which are developments that inevitably impact upon cultures and our experience of them. For example, such technologies facilitate the emergence of deterritorialized global networks, which in turn contribute to cultural mixing by paying little or no attention to geographical boundaries and cultural borders. More broadly, as we have seen, globalizing technologies along with advances in transportation, are widely viewed, as a result of the flows they are generating, to be contributing to cultural deterritorialization, transnationalism and other complex forms of connectivity. It means, for instance, that within territorial-based cultures and societies, multiple translocal cultures and societies exist.

However, it has also been shown that in relation to cultural flows we need to retain a critical perspective. We should not overemphasize the idea of cultures travelling, and neglect the fact that they require a degree of stability and regularity in order to be reproduced. Indeed, as we have seen there is criticism of the over-reliance upon metaphors of mobility in relation to this subject, perhaps reflecting the influence of cultural theory, with critics pointing to the dearth of empirical research.[9] Moreover, we must accept that when cultural flows are sporadic and meagre in nature, they are unlikely to generate meaningful cultural encounters and, it follows, have any significant impact. Alternatively, when cultural flows are a product of more powerful global forces such as media organizations it may actually provoke resistance, though again this may serve to limit their influence. When considering cultural flows we therefore need to investigate the cultural forms that are actually flowing and the sources generating them, as well as how they are being received.

Thus, while the implausibility of bounded cultures is now widely accepted, we should not overplay the idea of 'culture in motion'. In this regard, Jonathan Xavier Inda and Renato Rosaldo (2002) are correct when they maintain that culture is not simply 'free-floating'. As they put it, 'the deterritorialisation of culture is invariably the occasion for the reinsertion of culture in new time-space contexts' (ibid., 11). By this, they mean that 'cultural flows do not just flow etherally across the globe but are always rein-scribed (however partially or fleetingly) in specific cultural environments' (ibid.). This returns us to the notion of culture being reterritorialized, but it also reinforces a theme of this work, namely the importance of examining the contexts and locations in which global cultural flows are experienced if we are to gain an insight into the ways in which they are being reinscribed. In short, it is only by focusing upon how cultural flows intersect with par-ticular societies, regions and other localities, as well as with specific groups and sections of society, that it becomes possible to determine what is actu-ally taking place.[10] But we must recognize that as a result of our particular backgrounds or life histories we already possess cultural frameworks, which will shape our outlooks and inform our dealings with globalizing processes, including our encounters with other cultures and cultural flows. They will influence how we respond to sounds and media images from abroad, foreign cultural goods and products, and people from other countries moving into the areas where we live, as well as the other forms of global interconnectedness that constitute globalization. Naturally, these cultural frameworks are not static and will change as a result of our global encoun-ters. More importantly, the approach outlined here enables us to gain an understanding of the nature of the relationship between culture and glob-alization. In other words, by examining global–local intersections and how human agents are negotiating them, we will be able to trace how our cul-tural attitudes are both being informed by and in turn informing globaliz-ing processes. It is at these intersections that the various types of relationships which exist between globalization and culture emerge, recip-rocal, dialectical, reflexive, and so forth. Globalization and culture are, therefore, not separate entities; rather, they are mutually intertwining or interpenetrating sets of processes. Of course, how we engage with global-izing flows and processes will in turn influence the nature and future course of globalization. In short, culture can shape the trajectories of global inter-connectedness that constitute globalization, and vice versa.

Recommended reading

Arjun Appadurai's essay 'Disjuncture and Difference in the Global Cultural Economy' (1990) is regarded as something of a classic in this area. For an informative overview of sociological approaches to culture, see Diane Crane (ed.), *The Sociology of Culture: Emerging Theoretical Perspectives* (1994). An influential anthropological account of culture is James Clifford's article entitled 'Travelling Cultures' (1992). For comprehensive and informed accounts of cultural deterritorialization, see John Tomlinson's *Globalisation and Culture* (1999a), and Nikos Papastergiadis's *The Turbulence of Migration* (2000), while for up-to-date case studies of transnational affairs and experiences, see the journal *Global Networks*. Two useful volumes on migration, immigration and transnational spaces and cultures are Peter Jackson et al. (eds), *Transnational Spaces* (2003) and Ludger Pries (ed.), *New Transnational Social Spaces* (2001). For a range of case studies from different parts of the world on the meaning of 'home' to transnational peoples, see Nadje Al-Ali and Khalid Koser (eds), *New Approaches to Migration?* (2001).

3

Global Communication, Media and Technology

Global communication encompasses a range of technologies and mediums, and in considering this subject in relation to cultural globalization the focus here will be upon interpersonal communication, information exchange and the media. For some commentators, ICTs and the media are the motor of contemporary globalization, and consequently this chapter will seek to determine the extent to which recent developments in these areas constitute a transformation in human communication and connectedness qualitatively different from anything that can be found in previous eras. Hence, consideration will be given to the extent to which communication and media forms are genuinely globalized, the nature of the global digital divide, and whether we are witnessing the emergence of a network society. However, determining the extent of globalization in relation to the media and ICTs is made more difficult by the myriad of communication and information flows, and their differing velocity and extensity, something which in part is explained by the unequal spread of global telecommunications links and technologies. There is also the issue of what criteria we should employ in measuring the extent of global connectivity? Should they be based upon: voice traffic; ownership or access to ICTs; or, the actual usage of a given technology? In this vein, does a particular technology have to be found all over the world in order to be regarded as evidence of globalization?

While keeping the above points in mind, there is nevertheless evidence to suggest that in a number of areas in relation to electronic communication we are indeed becoming more globally connected. In this regard, for radio, according to the UN body the International Telecommunication Union (ITU), 95 per cent of the global population was covered by broadcasting services in 2002, while for television the figure was 86 per cent (Minges, 2006: 136). Likewise, the planet is close to achieving complete connectivity in the form of basic access to mobile phone telephone networks (ibid., 138). Further, according to the ITU, internationally between 1994 and 2004 the number of main telephone lines increased from 643 to 1,207 million; the number of mobile cellular subscribers grew from 56 to 1,758 million; the number of Internet users climbed from 21 to 863 million. As for international telephone traffic minutes (measured in billions), there was similarly a significant rise during this period: the figures for 1994 and 2004 were 57 and 145, respectively (ITU, 2006).

Media and globalization

The nature of media globalization

The worldwide increase in radio and television ownership since the 1960s has underpinned media globalization. According to *Screen Digest* (May 1998 issue), towards the end of the millennium there were over a billion television sets worldwide, though regional disparities in levels of ownership persist. For example, in 1996, Europe had 442 television receivers per 1,000 inhabitants in comparison with only 50 per 1,000 inhabitants in Africa (UNESCO, 1998: Table 6.5). One common global trend that is clear is the decline in the number of people watching public service broadcasting stations. This pattern is due in large part to the introduction of satellite and digital technology, which has led to a significant increase in the number of television channels, radio stations, broadcast programme hours and multi-television households, and has resulted in television viewing becoming a more fragmented and individualized experience. In this vein, many television and radio stations are using these channels to cater for particular tastes, cultures and ethnicities, and are effectively 'narrow-casting' rather than broadcasting. For example, in Germany such developments have combined to reduce the market share of viewing time for the public service corporation from 100 per cent in 1975 to just 39 per cent in 1995 (Mackay, 2000: 53). Watching television is therefore less and less a national community experience. This tendency is further encouraged by the rise of transnational television and the emergence of a number of regional television markets, such as in Latin America, the Middle East and Asia. Such markets are often centred upon an influential regional power, such as Brazil, Saudi Arabia and India, respectively, and facilitated by a common language; though, of course, regionalism is not globalism.

Media globalization has similarly been boosted by the emergence of a number of powerful multimedia giants such as Disney, Sony, Bertelsmann, General Electric, News Corporation, Time Warner and Viacom. The concentration of media ownership into fewer corporations and conglomerates is enabling these organizations to shape the leisure and entertainment industries through their capacity to finance, produce, market and distribute products for cinema and television. Chris Barker (1997) maintains that media TNCs are circumventing national regulation and thereby under-mining national regulatory environments, a trend that is reinforced by the market-oriented international regulatory regime the WTO and the ITU have established for media and communications. Concern is regularly expressed that these developments are leading to 'globalized' or homo-genized patterns of viewing, with the same formats for television programmes such as the news, soap operas, quiz shows and 'reality TV' being evident in countries throughout the world, as are certain television channels (e.g., CNN, BBC World, Cartoon Network, Discovery and Nickelodeon). More specifically, a frequently heard view is that the global media are American-dominated with the television schedules in countries in Europe, Latin America and elsewhere awash with US programmes and formats. In the case of the latter, as Susanne Schech and Jane Haggis (2000) have noted, Latin American 'soaps' (telenovelas) are ultimately just that – 'soaps' – and therefore are firmly within the tradition of US media culture.[1] In contrast, the US imports very few programmes: only 1 per cent of its commercial programming and 2 per cent of its public service program-ming (Barker, 1997: 49). Moreover, critics maintain that successive US administrations have sought to control the international regulatory frame-work of the culture and information industries in order to ensure their own cultural exports have ready access to the markets of other countries. In order to achieve this end, they argue, the USA has employed the language and ideology of the free market to criticize what it claims are the protec-tionist policies of some national governments. More broadly, it is also the case that the dominant media organizations are all Western corporations, with the notable exception of al-Jazeera, which ensures that the world's news agenda is largely Western-driven and -focused. These organizations are able to influence international news agendas, and are often accused of presenting partial accounts of current affairs, of marginalizing serious news journalism, and of eroding public debate both globally and nationally (see Habermas, 1984).

On the political Left, such developments are construed as a form of media imperialism that is spreading Western and/or American capitalist values and economic power, and are reflected, for example, in the spread of commercialization and the growth of cross-border advertising (see Mattelart and Siegelaud, 1978; Schiller, 1979). However, the standard criti-cism of this approach is that it assumes non-Western audiences are simply passive and unable to read media texts and messages. As Marian Bredin (1996) discovered in her study of aboriginal communities in northern

Canada, foreign programmes can actually reaffirm indigenous values and identities, as indigenous peoples employ their histories and cultural outlooks to negotiate what they are being presented with on their television screens. In fact, all members of a television audience are engaged to a varying extent in actively constructing their own meanings as part of a process of self-understanding and self-definition. Invariably, individuals will interpret media texts and other cultural products from the perspective of their own cultural histories (Sinclair et al., 1996). Moreover, we should reflect upon how important television actually is for us, and whether television programmes are really capable of undermining indigenous values. In this regard, John Tomlinson (1991) stresses how television viewing is incorporated into our lives as simply one of the activities we undertake, while the nature of our interaction with this medium is shaped by our own dispositions and personal circumstances, all of which raises the issue of the nature and quality of television programmes. In relation to this theme, the media imperialism thesis takes insufficient account of the variable quality of US programmes and hence in some instances limited appeal, nor how broadcasters often employ them as schedule fillers while at the same time prioritizing domestic products (Barker, 1997). It is also the case that there are countervailing flows of television programmes moving from Latin America or Australia to the USA, for example (Mackay, 2000). Imperialism is therefore an inadequate concept to describe contemporary media patterns and processes. However, it should be noted that the response of some writers to such a contention is 'electronic colonialism theory', which focuses upon how the global media influence our thinking and actions, especially in relation to our behaviour as consumers (see McPhail, 2006).

Media globalization? The sceptical perspective

Sceptics raise numerous challenges to the claim of media globalization (see Hafez, 2007). Some writers stress the extent of local resistance to global media empires (e.g., Thussu, 1998). Most importantly, despite Western media MNCs increasingly broadcasting in national languages, their presence outside of North America, Europe and Australia, remains fairly limited. Moreover, programme distribution is restricted by the fact that programme rights are subdivided, rather than sold globally, in order to maximize income (Sparks, 1998). Even CNN, despite its international *modus operandi* – it is available in over 200 nations – is ultimately an American news network, and on occasion has been criticized for toeing the Washington line, an association that has curtailed its global spread. Above all, it is stressed that governments

retain the ability to subject international media organizations to national regulation. Moreover, television companies and radio stations remain nationally
oriented and will often examine international events through a national
prism, and consequently their output is unlikely to generate international
interest (Tomlinson, 1997b). Furthermore, public service broadcasting has
not disappeared, and in a country such as the UK it remains in reasonably
good health despite increasing pressures from commercial stations and the
plethora of new television channels (Mackay, 2000).[2] Related to this point, it
is noted that despite having entered an era of satellite television, national
television viewing patterns have not undergone a revolution and global television does not yet exist (Sparks, 1998). In this regard, with some notable
exceptions, such as US television dramas and comedies, people will generally watch domestic television programmes when given the choice.

A global audience and public sphere?

The existence or otherwise of global audiences and a global public sphere is
also an important determinant of the nature and extent of media globalization. In the case of the former, satellite technology and mass television
ownership ensure that major events such as the Olympics, the World Cup
and the Live Aid concerts, as well as episodes such as the tsunami disaster of
late 2004, the toppling of Saddam Hussein and the death of Diana, Princess
of Wales, attract worldwide television audiences, enabling a significant proportion of the human race simultaneously to have common cultural experiences. However, from the sceptical perspective, these events and episodes
are occasional events and exceptional historical episodes, and therefore are
unlikely to sustain the sense of universal fellowship necessary to build mass
global audiences. More importantly, television viewing is ultimately an
experience where we are placed at a distance from the actual event or
episode, reliant upon the production skills of the programme makers, and
this will often serve to diminish our levels of engagement.[3] In short, how
effective is television as a medium for generating mass global audiences?

   As for the issue of a global public sphere, international crises, such as the
recent war in Iraq, can and do generate considerable international media
attention and global debate. But again these are one-off episodes that by
themselves are unable to sustain a global public sphere. Indeed, in the case
of the Iraq war, massive international opposition was unable to prevent the
USA and its allies launching their invasion, suggesting that both existing
institutions and the media were incapable of providing the type of global
forum able to shape international decision-making. However, perhaps so

great is the diversity that exists within the world that a global or transnational sphere of public debate will always be difficult to attain. Lastly, Jean Baudrillard (1983) addresses this subject from an entirely different perspective, arguing that transmissive technologies, and the flows they produce, have led to the media blurring the line between fantasy/simulated reality and the real world. The media are in fact, he maintains, generating an entertainment-driven 'hyper-reality', and consequently has effectively given up on its communicative function.

A global press?

With regard to the newspaper press and print journalism, there are some signs of globalization, notably the expansion of global news agencies, such as Bloomberg, Reuters, Associated Press and Agence France Presse. Global and transnational news organizations can also be seen to be shaping domestic politics and political agendas. For example, in the UK, the News Corporation's ownership of newspapers such as the *Sun* – which is part of the Rupert Murdoch media empire – ensures that he has an influence upon British domestic politics, especially in relation to the issue of Europe. Ultimately, however, the notion of a global press is undermined by the absence of genuinely global newspapers, which is a reflection of the particular medium. It is simply much easier for media images and radio waves to shoot around the world in comparison with newspapers; though, of course, the former are reliant upon the construction of the necessary technological infrastructure in order to be able to travel in this way. The *Financial Times* is one of the few newspapers, along with the *Wall Street Journal*, that aims to sell globally, but circulation outside of the UK was 130,000 in 2000 and its readership base is narrow and confined mainly to affluent business people (Mackay, 2000: 67). In addition, newspapers tend to take a more overtly national perspective than television in their coverage of the news. Of course, international news in both tends to be conflict- and disaster-driven, which raises the issue of how accurate an impression people are getting of other countries. But to continue with the print media, it is essential to recognize the different forms that it takes. For example, compared to the national orientation of many national newspapers many magazines and journals, such as *Cosmopolitan*, *Newsweek*, *Time* and *The Economist*, are designed to have international appeal (Mowlana, 1997). Moreover, most national newspapers now run Internet websites, which enable a global audience to access the news coverage they are providing. In a sense, therefore, small international circulation figures need not necessarily preclude an international or global reach.

Media globalization: an assessment

As was touched upon above, the nature of the medium and the type of cultural product are important determinants of the extent to which they are globalized. For this reason, the nature and form of films, music and still photography ensure that they can be reproduced relatively easily and found all over the world. Popular music, for example, has traversed the globe as a result of its user-friendly products (records, cassettes, CDs) and its dissemination via radio and more recently digital music players, though global media corporations such as PolyGram, Time Warner, Sony and EMI have also played a key role in the worldwide distribution of music. Radio, as a result of its use of wave-frequencies and relatively cheap production costs, was able to transcend borders before any other electronic media. And radio is arguably the one medium where a global product exists in the guise of the BBC World Service, which, because of its history, stated impartiality and provision of programmes in English and thirty-two other languages, does attract a truly international audience, though critics still view it as a Western institution especially as it is funded by the British government. Moreover, in 1997–8 the number of listeners to the BBC globally was only 138 million people, a figure that is actually declining due to increased competition from other sources (Hendy, 2000: 23). Of course, the global spread of radio as a whole is limited by the fact that it cannot be subtitled. Ultimately, however, 'radio' is actually constituted by numerous intertwining tendencies: local, national, regional and global or international. Thus, local and regional radio stations have created wider awareness of particular local and regional identities, though as is often observed the format and content of radio programmes actually look remarkably the same all over the world.

Overall, while there are powerful forces like media TNCs driving media globalization, and developments facilitating it, notably the global trend to deregulation, its continuing unevenness is ensured by factors such as the extent of cultural and linguistic diversity in the world, unequal access to media technologies, the existence of different media systems, the sheer number of local and national radio stations, newspapers and television channels, and the regulatory role performed by states. A crucial determinant of media globalization is the nature of local reaction to global media, which will be contingent upon our particular circumstances and contexts. A further contribution to the unevenness of media globalization is that states differ in their ability to control media TNCs and impose regulatory regimes, which means that there are considerable variations worldwide in the number of imported programmes and other products. In sum, media globalization should not be conceived of as an established condition, but as an ongoing project that is being contributed to by numerous processes and multilateral flows, not all of them global in reach, which are generating complex interactions within different contexts. All of this necessitates multi-level analyses of the subject.

Globalization, communication and technology

The evolving nature of global communication

Global communication has been aided by a number of technological advances in the contemporary period. In particular, the Internet, email, fax, mobile phones and text messaging have made it much easier to communicate with different parts of the world. The rapid and massive expansion of information on the Internet enables unprecedented and instantaneous access to information and has resulted in a rise in the international exchange of data.[4] Moreover, recent technological innovation is leading to the merging of different forms of mediated communication, enabling us, for example, to gain access to the Internet, email and receive news and information services via our mobile phones. In addition, there has been considerable progress in relation to telecommunications infrastructure, with the effective globalization of fibre-optic cables and satellite and digital technologies facilitating social and cultural interaction across borders, regions and continents. In 1997, there were 30 million kilometres of fibre-optic cable in the world (Whitehouse, 1999), but by the end of 2001 this had risen to 45 million kilometres. Researchers have also been mapping the growth of voice paths on key global telecommunications routes. For example, the number of transatlantic voice cable paths increased from 22,000 in 1986 to 1,264,000 in 1996, while the number of transatlantic voice satellite paths increased from 78,000 to 710,800 for the same period (Staple, 1996). In this vein, digital technology constitutes a major leap forward for global communication, with digitization able to translate information into a universal binary code, making it possible to convert information between different communication media and then transmit it via digital networks. Similarly, broadband technology enables greater data traffic capacity, and is being introduced at such a rate that it is considered to be one of the fastest ever expanding technologies: worldwide, the number of broadband connections took off during 2004 and reached around 100 million towards the end of that year (BBC, 2004), all of which has meant that worldwide data flows and voice traffic are rising, with the latter increasing by 13 per cent a year. During 2007 over 300 million people worldwide accessed the Internet through high-speed broadband connections, contributing to the spread of video websites such as YouTube and social networking services such as MySpace and Facebook (Wray, 2007).

Mobile communication

Mobile phones have been a major contributor to the increase in voice traffic and there has been a dramatic growth in both their ownership and usage since the 1990s. In June 2006, the two billionth GSM (Global System for Mobile Communications) phone was connected. What is most remarkable about this statistic is that it took 12 years to sell the first billion mobile phones, but only two and a half to sell the second, with more than 80 per cent of the growth coming from developing countries. Interestingly, the recent dramatic expansion increase in GSM connections now means that mobile phones are the first communications technology to have more users in the developing world than the developed world, partly because mobile phone companies are designing affordable products for these newly emerging and potentially huge markets. Mobile phone technology also offers additional benefits for poorer nations. For instance, the Worldwatch Institute has argued that mobile phones will help to narrow the information gap that exists between developed and developing societies. In particular, mobile technology facilitates greater access to the Internet, enabling the less well-off to make wireless connections to the Web without having to purchase PCs (BBC, 2003). Lastly, it is highly likely that so-called 3G or third-generation mobile technology, which provides high-speed mobile services for video streaming, photo messaging and other multimedia functions, will lead to the continued growth in mobile phone usage.

The Internet and global connectedness

Another important way in which contemporary ICTs have contributed to a more globally connected society is through the Internet. By 2002, most countries were connected to the Internet, and during the last five years of the previous millennium, Internet traffic was increasing by 86 per cent a year (Kogut, 2004). The arrival of the Internet has also been confirmed by the growth in the number of Internet websites. In 1995, there were fewer than 20,000 sites, but by 2002 the number had risen to over 36 million.[5] The reason for the global spread of the Internet lies with the development of the World Wide Web, which recently has shown further signs of significant expansion. According to the monitoring firm Netcraft, in the year to October 2005 the Web enjoyed its biggest year of growth to date, expanding by more than 17 million sites. As well as overcoming the barriers of physical space and national borders that restrict the ability of people to interact and communicate, the continued expansion of the Internet may in time ensure that the formation of online communities and transnational networks becomes the norm, and not just behaviour pursued mainly by activists, migrants and the technically-minded.

For many, the Internet is more than just about connecting with others; it also provides a forum for expressing their personal freedom, enabling them to role-play and try out new identities within chat rooms, while at the same time maintaining their anonymity (Turkle, 1995). However, before we rush to proclaim that the Internet has permanently changed human behaviour, more tangible evidence is required over a longer period of time in order to demonstrate this point, especially given that the Internet as we know it only emerged in the 1990s. For example, we would need to investigate whether Internet usage is reducing the amount of time that we spend on other activities, such as watching television. While some research has been undertaken into this very issue – a study conducted by Stanford University in 2000 detected some evidence that the Internet was leading to a reduction in the amount of time allocated to watching television in the USA (Nie and Erbring, 2000) – at this stage there is insufficient data of this type to be able to reach any firm conclusions. In particular, we need more information to determine whether Internet usage is leading us to invest in virtual relationships at the expense of time spent on our 'real' social relationships, such as friendships and families. Indeed, to what extent are we using the World Wide Web to become globally connected and to interact with new cultures and peoples?[6] Moreover, the persistence of different types of digital divide (discussed in the next section) means that not everyone has ready access to the Internet.

The impact of blogging

A significant contributor to the growth of the Web has been the rise of blogging. Blogs, or web-logs, are self-published sites on the Internet that cover a myriad of topics and provide alternative citizen-based sources of information and entertainment to traditional news and media organs. In particular, human tragedy episodes, such as Hurricane Katrina in New Orleans and the 7 July 2005 bombings in London, generate the most blogging and this is undoubtedly because it provides a means for people to recall their own experiences and to articulate their feelings towards such events. The growth in blogging has been aided by the setting up of free blogging services, such as those provided by Movable Type and AOL Journals, and by companies such as Microsoft and Google providing users with the tools to publish their blogs, and more recently with the latter installing its own blog search engine. As a result, the blogosphere, the universe of weblogs, has expanded rapidly, and on average is doubling in size every six months. According to Technorati, a blog search and indexing site, during 2006 a new blog was created every second, or, expressed another way, between 75,000 and 80,000 were being set up every day (Arthur, 2006). In the USA, blog growth has been especially notable. According to a survey conducted by the Pew Internet and American Life Project, blog readership rose by 58 per cent in 2004, and around 8 million people had created a blog by the end of that year (BBC, 2005a). What is perhaps more significant with regard to the continuing vitality of this phenomenon is that the expansion of blogs has not just been confined to the Anglocentric world of the USA and the UK, but can be found in China, France, South Korea and Japan. Moreover, such has been the interest in blogging that media organizations and companies are moving into this area, attracted by its potential to reach new audiences and customers, respectively.

However, we should remain wary about becoming caught up in media hype surrounding this phenomenon, as it remains the case that the majority of Internet users are not actively engaged in the blogosphere. For example, even in 2004, the year that blog reading really took off in America, more than 60 per cent of online Americans had still not heard of blogging. This point is equally applicable in the UK, where a survey conducted in September 2005 found that seven out of ten British citizens did not know what blogging meant or entailed (BBC, 2005b). A survey conducted by the British Market Research Bureau revealed that, for the first quarter of 2006, the percentage of UK Internet users actually publishing or contributing to a blog was no more than 2 per cent, and no more than 10 per cent were accessing a blog more frequently than once a month (Lelic, 2006). Moreover, with regard to the global picture, many blogs have a short-term lifespan, with those that remain active, defined as having been updated in the past three months, constituting no more than half of all blogs (Perrone, 2005). However, such short-termism is understandable, given that many blogs are created in response to particular events or episodes whose impact will inevitably fade over time.

The individualization of media and communication

Returning to the issue of the media, the ICT developments described here are transforming how people obtain their news and entertainment. In particular, young people are increasingly getting their news from sources other than mainstream news and media outlets such as television and newspapers. A poll conducted by Globescan in Brazil, Egypt, Germany, India, Indonesia, Nigeria, Russia, South Korea, the UK and the USA, between March and April 2006, revealed that the 18–24 generation in these countries are taking advantage of the Internet to gain their news from a range of sources and enjoy comparing and contrasting news reports. Indeed, for one in five in this age range, online sources were their first choice for news, with sources that bring together various news sources such as Google News becoming especially popular (Hermida, 2006). More generally, people no longer expect simply to read newspapers, watch television and go online as a one-way process in which they remain essentially passive, but choose to participate in these media via such means as discussions forums, and to post their own stories and to comment on the content and quality of programmes on bulletin or discussion boards. Interestingly, the mainstream media are increasingly incorporating user-generated content into their reporting, especially when it comes to events like those in London and New Orleans described above, where such material provides them with both first-hand insights and a range of perspectives on these stories. The cumulative effect of these developments is a change in the nature of the relationship between the producer and consumer, such as the journalist and the reader, and arguably the boundary lines are starting to blur as aspects of the media become genuinely interactive. Likewise, while radio and television broadcasting is spread globally by the Internet, it is also fragmented by the emergence of podcasting, as more and more people customize their consumption and individualize schedules for their own convenience.

The spread of e-democracy

Internet websites, bulletin boards, chat rooms, RSS (Really Simple Syndication) feeds, email, instant messaging and blogging are arguably contributing to a new public sphere of debate, providing a forum for ordinary citizens to air their views and one that is difficult for governments to control. In particular, by facilitating worldwide communication and increasing information flows, the new technologies make it harder for a state to control information for its own ends and for authoritarian governments to monitor the activities of their opponents. Similarly, the success of the Zapatista movement in Mexico has been attributed to it bypassing 'official' media organizations and presenting its case to the world direct and unmediated via the Internet. New social movements and interest groups use the Internet to foster the development of transnational virtual or electronic communities and to act as democratic forums for discussion. Indeed, the Internet and email facilitate the building of a new type of community, making it more possible for like-minded people to communicate and interact, though critics question whether e-communities can be considered proper communities in that they do not require direct interpersonal contact. In reality, of course, global social movements are sustained not only by ICTs, but by a combination of this technology and many of its members actually meeting face-to-face at venues throughout the world, something that is facilitated by cheaper air transportation. The new technologies can also help to revive flagging democratic processes by providing additional means by which people can vote in elections. Moreover, this so-called 'push-button democracy' or electronic direct democracy provides new ways for political parties to contact and engage with the electorate, as well as holding out the prospect of enabling more referenda on a greater range of issues, all of which can facilitate citizen input into the legislative process and help to ensure governmental decision-making is more in tune with public opinion. But the Internet also provides opportunities for new voices to be heard, for minority and radical opinions to be articulated, and for breaking free from the dominance of the public debate on the part of major political parties.

However, when reflecting upon the liberating and democratic potential of new information and communications technology, we should not overlook the numerous bodies deploying this technology to collect information about us, ranging from government agencies to marketing organizations monitoring our lifestyle and consumption patterns whenever we go shopping and use the Internet. Moreover, we ourselves spend much of the time using the Internet for personal rather than community-oriented purposes, notably searching for information and shopping online. In this vein, while virtual communities are an obvious manifestation of global connectivity, they can also be forums where some of the more unsavoury elements of human behaviour can be seen, such as lying and personal abuse (just like 'real life' in fact!), a point that even Howard Rheingold (2000), the champion of the virtual community, has acknowledged.

The sceptical viewpoint

Overall, it is clear that developments in information and communications technology have significantly contributed to patterns of transnational and global interconnectedness. However, Paul Hirst and Grahame Thompson

(1996) question the impact of these technologies and they consider the introduction in 1837 of the telegraph and underground cables to be a more pivotal moment in the history of international communication. For Tom Standage, this was the 'Victorian Internet', which ensured that '[a]ttitudes to everything from newsgathering to diplomacy had to be completely rethought' (1998: 1). Writers who are sceptical about some of the more extreme claims made by globalizers do not deny that recent developments in information and communications technologies are shaping the ways in which we communicate with each other, but stress this is an evolutionary process, rather than a revolution. In this regard, with the exception of the rapidly industrializing countries in East Asia that are integrating into global communication and information networks at a remarkable pace, world telephone distribution patterns have remained relatively unchanged for a hundred years (Tehranian and Tehranian, 1997). Similarly, sceptics argue that we need to acknowledge the ways in which national societies can shape global and transnational phenomena both with regard to technology but also other areas of social and economic life, such as markets. For example, in *The Global Internet Economy* (2004), a series of studies devoted to studying the evolution of the Internet especially in relation to business, the common theme that emerges is the different ways in which it is evolving in particular societies, reflecting the specific conditions within those countries, such as national systems of law and regulation. It leads the editor to conclude that, despite the title of the book, 'the global Internet economy has not yet arrived!' (Kogut, 2004: 437). Such findings also serve to balance claims that national governments are unable to control or influence the Internet, and that the primary consequence of advances in global communications and information technologies is the enhancement of the power of MNCs and TNCs to the detriment of national sovereignty (Schiller, 1995). Finally, perhaps the most telling argument against the notion of global communication is that it is undermined by the persistence of inequalities in relation to access to information and communications technologies, a matter that will now be addressed.

The digital divide

The global digital divide

The so-called 'digital divide' refers to the unequal access to ICTs and would seem to present a fundamental challenge to Marshall McLuhan's conception of the 'global village' (McLuhan and Fiore, 1967). There are two notable senses in which a digital divide is said to exist. The first is internationally or globally between states, and the second is within states.[7] With regard to the former, Africa is less heavily endowed with both ICTs and supporting infrastructure in comparison with industrialized regions such as Europe and North America, a situation entailing many African states and peoples being less tied into global communication networks. In this vein, access to the Internet in some regions of the world is more limited than others, though in some instances this is also due to forms of political and / or religious control, a point that is applicable to certain states in the Middle East and Central Asia and the Caucasus. As a general rule, therefore, while Internet usage has risen significantly in the West and is increasing in many parts of Asia and Latin America, in regions such as the Middle East and Africa it has and is not. For example, in India, the number of people using the Internet rose from 4 million in 2000 to 23 million in 2003, though it remains a largely urban phenomenon and expansion is hampered by poor telephone connections and low bandwidth.

From a global perspective, in spite of representing less than 20 per cent of the world's population, roughly 90 per cent of Internet users were based in industrialized countries in 2003, though this figure masks considerable differences between countries within the developed world (*Guardian*, 2003). France, for example, has considerably fewer Internet users and households with PCs than the USA. In the case of Africa, it was home to only 1 per cent of Internet users even though it makes up 19 per cent of the world's population (ibid.). Again this is unsurprising given the limited number of telephone lines in Africa in comparison with other continents.[8] To cite a frequently mentioned example: Manhattan has more telephone lines than the whole of sub-Saharan Africa. Africa as a whole is faced with considerable variations in Internet usage, with the vast majority of users being in South Africa. African access to global electronic superhighways is further hindered by the fact that the continent has considerably fewer computers and mobile phones than other continents. However, the number of mobile phone subscribers in sub-Saharan Africa has risen from 72,000 since 1995 to 25.5 million in 2005 (Vasagar, 2005). And there have been attempts to ensure that it no longer remains the least-connected continent, notably through the construction of an undersea fibre-optic cable around the whole continent, which is intended to transform high-speed communications within Africa and integrate it into the international telecommunications network. There are therefore some positive signs for Africa in relation to this area.

In a similar vein, the picture is more complex for Latin America than was indicated above. While Internet usage has grown, it is uneven: Argentina,

Brazil and Mexico are 'online' and are the countries in which more than 80 per cent of the region's users reside, but it follows that other Latin American countries are not so well connected (Tran, 2000). Looking beyond Latin America, according to the ITU, statistics on Internet usage worldwide are flawed and this may in turn mean that the global digital divide may not be as wide as is often claimed. The problem lies, it maintains, with the inadequate data-gathering mechanisms and procedures of many developing nations. This was borne out by the fact that when their governments were presented with the findings of the ITU's own research many were surprised by the number of people that were online within their own countries (BBC, 2003). But putting aside questions and disputes over the reliability of data, there is little disagreement that improved access to the new technologies is vital for developing societies, and may enable some of them to skip or at least speed up stages of their development, especially as information (knowledge) and communication (networking) are important sources of wealth generation in the contemporary period and lack of access to them will almost certainly see such societies fall further behind.

Domestic digital divides

As for the digital divide within societies, in the early years of PCs and the Internet, numerous studies indicated a common pattern to this particular type of division, at least within the industrialized world. In essence, those first taking up the new information and communications technology and connecting to the Internet tended to be as follows: males, 18–24, white, suburbanite, with good incomes and university educated. It was therefore possible to detect educational, racial, gender and age divisions in relation to the Internet, with white men under the age of forty especially dominating the usage of this technology in post-industrial societies (Eisenstein, 1998). For example, in 1998 the number of female Internet users ranged from only 9 to 20 per cent in different European countries (BBC, 2000a). In the USA, the extent of the digital divide has generated enormous comment dating back to Bill Clinton's presidency, during which he called for Internet access and usage to become as common as telephone usage as a way of addressing this problem. As is the case in many other Western societies, the differences in levels of computer and Internet use in America have run along racial, educational, rural–urban and income lines. For example, white Americans have traditionally been much more likely to own a home computer than African Americans and Hispanics, and therefore have greater access to the Internet. Similarly, only 53 per cent of

American Indians living on reservations had access to basic telephone services in 1999 (Anderson, 1999).

However, as the Internet has spread and gained in popularity, the pattern described above has generally become less marked within developed societies (see Chen et al., 2002).[9] In particular, with Internet access increasingly available at libraries, workplaces and cybercafés, researchers are paying more attention to actual usage. It is in this area that divisions can still be detected, with those on lower incomes (in the main late adopters of the new technology) generally going online for fewer hours per week than other social groups, and more likely to stop altogether (Katz and Rice, 2002). But crucially the issue of Internet usage mirrors and reinforces existing social divisions and is therefore inextricably bound up with factors such as education, income, family background and neighbourhood (Warschauer, 2004; van Dijk, 2005). In other words, the digital divide is not simply a technological ill.

Broadband and the digital divide

A clearer manifestation of the digital divide is the unequal access to broadband, and this applies not only within societies, where there is often a tendency for broadband to be concentrated in urban rather than rural areas, but also between them: 93.9 per cent of Internet users in South Korea had broadband access in 2003 compared to only 18.3 per cent in the USA (ITU, 2003). In contrast with the slower and more restricted access afforded by dial-up connectivity, broadband provides high-speed and continuous online availability, and there is evidence that this is enabling people to explore a greater range of Internet applications and become more creative in their Internet usage. In the USA, for instance, research undertaken as part of the Pew Internet and American Life Project suggests that broadband is the single most significant determinant of Internet use, and more influential than factors such as age, gender and education (Horrigan and Raine, 2002). In the future, therefore, an important determinant of whether the digital divide narrows or widens will be the level of access to broadband. On the face of it, broadband is simply a technological determinant of the digital divide, but invariably there are social, political and economic factors underlying its unequal distribution. Thus, with regard to the USA, numerous commentators have noted that its problems lie with the lack of public promotion, whereas many governments in parts of Asia and Europe have been actively pushing and investing in broadband for social and domestic purposes (e.g., van Dijk, 2005).

There is also a competition factor behind the availability of broadband. As Mark Warschauer (2004) has noted, as a general rule in places where competition between service providers is considerable, the introduction of new broadband services tends to be quicker. Interestingly, and perhaps tellingly, in South Korea a competitive market does exist. More optimistically, Jan A.G.M. van Dijk (2005) makes the point that compared to other technological innovations, the digital divide may not be as enduring with regard to broadband access, as the shift from no connection to becoming connected is bigger than the step from narrowband to broadband, especially as the latter can offer a range of audiovisual services that are likely to have widespread appeal.

Addressing the digital divide

Accompanying the digital divide, there are additional disparities and anomalies surrounding global communications technology. Notable among them is the fact that the USA has unilateral control of the Internet's domain name and addressing systems. In 1998, the US Department of Commerce created a private not-for-profit corporation known as the Internet Corporation for Assigned Names and Numbers (ICANN) to take over this role. However, an increasing number of national governments are calling for more influence over the Internet, maintaining that ICANN's role encroaches upon their own sovereignty and that its supervision of the Internet is ultimately subject to veto by the US Department of Commerce. The US response to such charges is that its position is a product of the history of the Internet, which saw it lead the way in establishing much of the existing infrastructure, and that under its custodianship it has provided stability for the Internet while overseeing its continued expansion. Criticisms of the US role were aired in the months leading up to the UN-sponsored World Summit of the Information Society held in Tunisia in November 2005, and concerns were expressed that the World Wide Web could fragment if this matter were not resolved, with some countries deciding to go their own way. In the event, the summit agreed that ICANN will continue to technically manage the Net, but a new Internet Governance Forum (IGF) would be formed. However, critics maintain that this solution effectively means US governance of the Internet continues.

There are other issues that need to be addressed in relation to this whole area, such as the fact that the World Wide Web is an English-language-dominated phenomenon. In December 2003, at the opening of the first UN summit on the digital divide, the former Secretary-General Kofi Annan argued that with 70 per cent of websites in English, 'local voices' were being crowded out. Similarly, there are regular complaints from governments and citizens alike in both the developing world and in Europe that much of the content of the Web is American, a problem which is considered to arise from the influence of US Web servers and search engines. However, as will be discussed in the next chapter, there are changes afoot with regard to these areas both in the sense that other languages are emerging on the Internet, but also and most notably with the expansion of the Chinese content of the Web as a result of the dramatic growth in Internet usage in China. According to the government-run China Internet Network Information Centre, the country's online population is doubling every six months, and by the end of 2004 it had more than 20 million broadband subscribers (Twist, 2004).

Lastly, we should not overlook the considerable efforts being undertaken to narrow the digital divide. For example, the One Laptop Per Child campaign has led to the development of the sub-$100 clockwork laptop computer. Likewise, a handheld, battery-operated alternative to PCs, the Simputer (short for simple computer), has been designed in India. In this vein, the open-source movement provides services and information as public rather than private goods (and hence without charge), such as the Linux operating system and OpenOffice (which provide free alternatives to systems offered by Microsoft), its own browser, Firefox, as well as the online encyclopedia *Wikipedia*. Moreover, organizations such as the World Bank and the UN are seeking to tackle the digital divide and spread ICTs to developing countries – with the UN attempting to connect every village in the world to the Internet by 2015 – though progress is slow, especially with regard to who will pay for the construction of the information and communications infrastructures.

A network society?

The network society of Manuel Castells

Whether developments in information and communications technology are leading to a global network society is an issue that has engendered considerable debate. Manuel Castells (1996) is the theorist most associated with the network society, which he maintains is composed of a number of inter-related elements, including capitalism or rather informational capitalism and resistance to capitalist globalization, but crucially it is ICTs that have facilitated this development and enabled networks to coordinate their activity. Castells contends that networks are distinct from other forms of social organization and have become the dominant organizational mode, transforming the different sectors of society in the process. As he puts it: '[n]etworks constitute the new social morphology of our societies, and the diffusion of networking logic substantially modifies the operation and outcomes in processes of production, experience, power and culture' (1996: 469). For Castells, the emergence of the network society is the cumulative effect of three independent processes: the information technology revolution of the 1970s; the restructuring of capitalism and statism in the 1980s; and the social movements of the 1960s and 1970s, especially feminism and environmentalism (Castells, 1997b: 7). In particular, he emphasizes how ICTs have ensured the rapid circulation of increased information flows around the world and, as will now be shown, changed the relationship between time and space.

Castells: 'timeless time' and 'the space of flows'

In the manner of Giddens and Harvey, Castells articulates notions of 'timeless time' and 'the space of flows', arguing that we employ ICTs to eliminate the sequencing of time. For example, we accumulate time through information collection so that the past, present and future appear in the same hypertext, thereby eliminating the 'succession of things' (ibid., 11). Likewise, time can be annihilated through instantaneous communication between different parts of the world. The space of flows refers to the possibility of practising simultaneity without territorial proximity: of a network of places or nodal points being connected around one common, simultaneous social practice – ranging from financial markets to global social movements – via electronic circuits. Indeed, Castells identifies three layers of material support that constitute the space of flows. The first layer, a 'circuit of electronic impulses', is formed from 'microelectronics, telecommunications, computer processing, broadcasting systems, and high-speed transportation – also based on information technologies' (1996: 412), and facilitates and coordinates simultaneous practices within a network. The second layer is composed of 'nodes and hubs', such as the global cities and national, regional and continental economies that go to make-up the global financial system or the networked places within advanced manufacturing firms (i.e., intra- and inter-firm linkages), which as well as being spatially dispersed are 'hierarchically organised according to their relative weight within the network', though such hierarchies can change over time as the nature of the activities and functions performed by the network evolve (ibid., 413). The final layer 'refers to the spatial organisation of the dominant, managerial elites' – in other words, their interpersonal connections and networks – 'that exercise the directional functions around which such space is articulated' (ibid., 415).

The network society as a new social epoch

For Castells, the challenge to the network society lies with 'resistance identities', notably in the form of ethnic groups and fundamentalist religious movements. In spite of such counter-tendencies, Castells believes the informational networking that ICTs facilitate binds the network society and in so doing creates a new social epoch. Thus, the network is the organizational form of the Information Age, establishing a different type of informational structure, one which is sustained by the Internet (Castells, 2001). Hierarchical and bureaucratic institutions such as the nation-state cannot match the organizational efficiency, dynamism and flexibility of networks evident in the difficulties that countries face in dealing with international criminal networks. Ironically, if governments want to tackle such networks they will have to function as networks themselves, operating as nodal points, coordinating their activities and pooling their information, all of which entails power being shifted from political institutions to the flows and cultural codes embedded in networks. However, as will now be discussed, Castells's thesis has attracted criticism.

Manuel Castells: critical perspectives

To begin with, while Castells presents an extraordinary amount of material, he has been criticized for failing to provide an in-depth exposition of networks, for insufficiently differentiating between them, and for not properly demarcating the relationship of networks with other organizational forms. It is therefore claimed that this central feature of his work is under-conceptualized (Urry, 2003), and for some writers Castells's networks remain at the level of metaphor (Nas and Houweling, 1998). In a similar vein, Robert Holton (2005) argues that Castells presents a generalized treatment of networks that has insufficient empirical data. It is a criticism that carries all the more weight because Castells sets great store by the fact that his theory, though broadly drawn, has empirical applicability (Stadler, 2006).

Another general criticism of Castells's thesis is that in its emphasis upon metaphors it pays insufficient attention to the issue of power, decision-making and the forces driving the network society, and indeed ignores the fact that networks emerge out of and stretch across societies, inevitably mirroring existing socio-political formations. In this regard, actors such as communications technology MNCs and TNCs, national governments, legal institutions and international trade organizations have significantly determined the global dissemination of information and communications technology, which in turn has influenced the trajectories of network formations. An important aspect of this control has been the ownership of intellectual property rights in relation to information technology and knowledge, notably the WTO-administered Agreement on Trade-Related Aspects of Intellectual Property Rights (TRIPS), which seeks to establish intellectual property standards for the global knowledge economy (Drahos and Mayne, 2002).

Peter Drahos and John Braithwaite (2002) believe that current rules concerning intellectual property are the product of coercion by developed countries (specifically the USA and to a lesser extent the EU) and powerful corporations which directly benefit from a state of affairs that they describe as 'information feudalism'. Thus, copyrights, patents and trademarks have protected layout designs and served to restrict access to computer software programmes and the algorithms that underpin digital technologies, resulting in many developing societies struggling to pay fees and royalties on these informational resources. If Drahos and his co-writers are correct, such intellectual property regimes will not only generate new forms of inequality and hinder development in the 'third world', but also have profound implications for the formation of a globalized information society because such a society is ultimately dependent upon access to and the sharing of information and knowledge. To continue with the power theme, from the Marxist perspective – interestingly a tradition from within which Castells began his academic career – even allowing for the changes that networks introduce to organizational forms within societies, they remain underpinned by capitalism and are operating within a capitalist global order. It follows therefore that in a substantive sense the network society differs little from previous epochs. However, Castells would undoubtedly respond to such points by arguing that he does take into account both the importance and the persistence of capitalism, and he has done so by articulating the notion of 'informational capitalism' – based, as mentioned previously, upon the information technology revolution of the 1970s and the restructuring of capitalism and statism in the 1980s – which is a more flexible, efficient and, geographically speaking, globally complete form of capitalism (see Castells, 1996). Nevertheless, as Frank Webster (2002) has observed, there is perhaps an unresolved tension in Castells's work between his emphasis upon the emergence of a new type of society and the continuation of capitalism. Of course, to take a broader view, while it is essential to identify the power relations and economic forces that underpin networks we should not discount the role of human agents participating in these organizational forms, many of whom will be doing so for non-economic motivations, such as for cultural and personal reasons.

Castells's association of information flows and mobility with elites, which, as mentioned previously, is the third layer of material support that he identifies as constituting the space of flows, arguably leads him to underplay the extent to which ordinary citizens are able to participate in such flows, and are not simply confined to 'the space of places'. In this vein, the ability of social movements and NGOs to influence the agendas of network elites, and in some instances to have an input into policy-making, complicates his notion of the hierarchical nature of the networks. Although again in fairness to Castells, in a later interview he acknowledged that given that the space of flows is materially based upon the new ICTs, a wider cross-section of society, 'wishing to do all kinds of things, can occupy this space of flows and use it for their own purposes' (Castells and Ince, 2003: 58).

Lastly, an additional attraction of Castells's theory is that it hints at the unevenness of globalization, and indeed he has written of the 'imperfect globalization of the network society' (2004: 23). He recognizes that not everyone is involved in networks. Similarly, he describes how networks adapt and are self-reconfigurable – expressed another way, the functions performed by particular nodes can increase or decrease in importance – as part of an ongoing process. Castells also acknowledges that the influence of technology is contingent upon its interaction with human agents in particular settings, something which leads Darin Barney (2004) to speculate whether it is more appropriate to conceptualize network societies rather than *the* network society.

Interpreting contemporary connectivity

Many writers contend that technology is the major contributor to globalization, especially in the areas of media and communication (e.g., Ohmae, 2005; Strange, 1990; Wriston, 1992). In the cases of Walt Wriston and Kenichi Ohmae, they maintain that technology has dictated the nature of contemporary business and banking, and in turn led to the emergence of the global economy. However, in focusing upon technology there is always a danger of lapsing into a technological determinism and neglecting other processes that are contributing to globalization, such as capitalism and modernization. In order, therefore, to ascertain the influence of technological innovation upon cultural globalization, it needs to be considered both in relation to these other dimensions, but also in the sense that technology is intertwined with them, and addressing, for example, the extent to which capitalism is providing the momentum behind the rapid diffusion of ICTs, especially as profit-maximization is likely to be the primary motivation behind the emergence of global communications technology and media organizations. But the globalization of communication has also been aided since the late 1980s by the end of the Cold War, the privatization of telecommunications in some countries, and an international trade liberalization regime that has facilitated the spread of the market economy. Furthermore, to evaluate properly this issue would require considering those forces – such as certain political movements and religious, national and ethnic traditions – employing technology to hold back those aspects of globalization they deem detrimental to their own causes.

To express all of this another way, and to focus specifically upon the concern of this chapter, namely the contribution of global communication, media and technology to cultural globalization, we should recognize that ICTs and global media do not operate in isolation but emerge out of and are engaged with by human societies, and this reality significantly determines the nature of their impact. In short, such technologies are always mediated by individuals and groups that are operating within particular social contexts; they do not have direct, automatic or inevitable effects. Indeed, a number of studies suggest that many people are appropriating the new technological innovations, such as the Internet, to fit in with and facilitate established patterns of behaviour as well as maintain existing social relationships (e.g., see Kogut, 2004). This conception of how technologies are operating will also help us avoid viewing them as having a momentum of their own, one that human beings are simply swept along by, powerless to resist – a tendency that can be found in some technological accounts of globalization. As has been indicated here, one of the defining features of contemporary ICTs is that in a variety of ways they are leading to greater individuation, providing citizens with greater autonomy and choice, especially when it comes to the media. However, as we have also seen, people are using these technologies to participate in different types of networks, and hence are also engaged in forms of community practice and formation. 'Networked individualism' is the term that has been employed to encapsulate such behaviour (Wellman and Haythornwaite, 2002). Finally, if we really want to determine the impact of technology upon globalization, which lack of space precludes us from doing here, this issue would have to be considered in relation to the influence of other technologies, such as transportation, and not by simply concentrating upon information and communications technology as has been the case here.

When considering this subject area in relation to cultural globalization we also need to recognize that there have been other important moments in the history of communication and information technology that have significantly contributed to forms of connectedness across the globe, notably the development of the Gutenberg press in the Middle Ages, which was based upon a technology called 'movable type' and invented by Johannes Gutenberg in 1448 – if we overlook the fact that the Chinese had thought of printing first in the eighth century. The significance of this invention was that it facilitated the spread of different forms of literature across Europe, including the Bible, and in doing so facilitated the Renaissance, the Reformation and the Enlightenment. Printing was therefore a major contribution to human interconnectedness and in time to the evolution of globalization, but crucially it emerged in the premodern era. Alternatively, perhaps we should view the technological developments in communications of the modern era as the primary contributors to globalization? Important among these, alongside the telegraph mentioned earlier, would be the introduction of the telephone (1876) and the wireless (1895). There are also historical precedents for the media TNCs of our time in the form of the publishing houses and international news agencies that emerged in the USA and Europe in the nineteenth century. On balance, however, while the origins of global communication can be traced back to the nineteenth century and arguably much earlier, as the statistics presented here suggest, the everyday flow of communication and information on a global scale is a feature of our time. The recent advances in ICTs and other developments within the communication industry, therefore, mark a qualitative change in the nature, volume and territorial extent of global connectivity.

Yet when evaluating the extent of global interconnectedness that communications and information technologies are facilitating, we should keep in mind South Africa's President Thabo Mbeki's observation that '[o]ver half of humankind has never dialled a phone number' (Lynch, 1997: 253). Moreover, at the start of the new millennium, of the world's population of more than 6 billion more than 4 billion people remained untouched by the IT revolution and barely 2 per cent were linked to the Internet, which is an indication of the enormous amount that needs to be done in order to overcome the global digital divide. In other words, it is possible to overstate what is taking place in relation to global communication, media and technology, and to get caught up with talk that we are living in 'an information age', 'communications revolution' and a 'global network society'. Since both worldwide ownership of ICTs and the reach of media flows remain uneven, global communication should not be construed as universal communication. However, as we have also seen, this is a rapidly changing area, and even since the year 2000 Africa and other developing regions have become more globally connected. There is also an established position within technology studies that as new technologies are disseminated to the point of saturation their costs invariably fall in order to attract further users. However, by way of a caveat to this optimism, for developing countries to take advantage of any reduction in costs many have to confront major infrastructural problems in order to gain access to these technologies, a point that is also applicable to some rural regions in developed societies. Furthermore, it should be noted there are, to use Pippa Norris's term, 'cyber-pessimists' who argue that, by dint of being at the start of the ICT revolution as well as having established communication networks in place, the early innovators are always likely to maintain their lead in this area (see Norris, 2001). There are also continued claims that the ultimate effect of technological advances, such as the Internet, will be to introduce new inequalities and exacerbate existing ones; this view is not simply confined to those opposed to globalization, but was also the opinion of roughly half of the 1,000 business leaders surveyed prior to the Davos World Economic Forum in 2000 (BBC, 2000).

In short, the inextricable nature – at least at this juncture – of many of the debates surrounding ICTs and the media is an indication of how difficult it is to determine the contribution of these communicative forms to cultural globalization. What can be said with greater certainty is that while technology may or may not have driven globalization, it has nevertheless provided much of the infrastructure for it to evolve. In this respect, the disembedded networks integrating different parts of the world that ICTs help to sustain are an important component of global interconnectedness. But to repeat, to understand how media and communications technologies and the flows that they generate are contributing to globalization, then we need to examine how they are being mediated by individuals and groups within different contexts.

Recommended reading

Given that there are so many books and articles on the areas of global communication, media and technology, a number of the works recommended here have been chosen specifically for their critical rather than celebratory tone. Manuel Castells's (1996, 1997a, 1998) influential trilogy of the information age is widely regarded as a classic on this subject. There are a number of informative works on the digital divide that explore both its nature and its social and political effects, as well as proposing practicable ways of moving beyond it (see Norris, 2001; Servon, 2002; van Dijk, 2005). For an accessible and up-to-date introduction to global communication and the media, see the second edition of Thomas McPhail's *Global Communication: Theories, Stakeholders, and Trends* (2006). Useful introductory works on other areas covered in this chapter include: on blogging, Kline and Bursetin (2005), on radio, Hendy (2000), on global and transnational television, Barker (1997) and Chalaby (2005) respectively, on the Internet, Wellman and Haythornwaite (2002), on mobile communication, Katz and Aakhus (2002), on virtual communities, Jones (1998); Smith and Kollock (1999) and on the media and globalization, Rantanen (2005).

4

Globalization and Global Culture

One of the major debates surrounding cultural globalization concerns whether we are witnessing the emergence of a global culture. It is an issue that attracts both academic and popular interest, though academics tend to be more sceptical of such a notion. Here the intention will be to determine whether such a culture exists, and, if so, the form that it is taking. The chapter will examine four areas in relation to this subject. It begins by describing the ways in which globalizing processes are potentially contributing to cultural homogenization, outlining a number of different conceptions of global culture in the process. The second section focuses upon the work of Roland Robertson, who provides a perceptive insight into the interrelationship between globalization and global culture, and in particular highlights the complexity of global–local dynamics. The third section offers a critique of global culture, arguing that such a concept is based upon a misreading of contemporary developments as well as resting upon the flawed notion of globalizing processes having particular effects or consequences. In the final section of this chapter, in line with the general emphasis of this work upon recognizing the plural nature of globalization, the case is made for conceiving of global culture as global cultures.

Globalization and cultural homogenization

For some commentators there are aspects of globalization – notably in the areas of communication, the media and the economy – that are considered to be having a homogenizing effect. It is argued that new information and communications technologies, improved transportation, and the emergence of a global media and powerful MNCs means that the world is becoming a smaller place, local cultures and traditions are struggling to survive and cultural difference is being eroded (Hamelink, 1983). This is reflected in the frequently heard comment that city centres across the globe are looking increasingly similar. The same major retailers, banks and other financial houses, fast-food restaurants and advertisement billboards can be found in all of them. In this vein, certain consumer products and brands can be found in countries throughout the world, the same films are being shown at cinemas, and many of the same programmes can be seen on our television screens. Ulrich Beck describes this cultural convergence in the following manner: 'In the villages of Lower Bavaria, just as in Calcutta, Singapore or the "favelas" of Rio de Janeiro, people watch Dallas on TV, wear blue jeans and smoke Marlboro . . .' (2000: 42). The concern of critics is that it is eroding cultural authenticity as well as encouraging similar aspirations and greater uniformity of lifestyles (e.g., Crick, 1989).[1] As a result of these developments, it is claimed that cultures and societies are confronted with powerful homogenizing pressures to the extent that it is possible to talk of the existence of a global culture, often viewed as a form of cultural imperialism (Mattelart et al., 1984; Schiller, 1989, 1991). However, the form that this global culture is taking and the forces driving it is a source of considerable debate. It has been variously articulated as Americanization, McDonaldization (Ritzer, 1998) and westernization (Latouche, 1996), with some theorists arguing that it is motored by capitalism or the combined forces of modernity. Such views will now be considered, beginning with the conception of global culture as Americanization.

Cultural homogenization as Americanization

As well as the USA being the most powerful country in the world and able to exert considerable international influence, it is noted that many of the leading media-entertainment conglomerates, such as Time Warner, CBS and Walt Disney, are American. As we saw in chapter 3, the USA exports significantly more television programmes than any other country in the world. Indeed, the issue of US global media domination has been discussed for some time, notably in the McBride Report, which was published in 1980, and led to UNESCO urging measures be taken to address this matter. More generally, outside of the USA concern has long been expressed about the omnipresence of American popular culture. Alongside television programmes, efficient global distribution companies and networks have ensured that US films, news organizations, software programmes and other products can be found across the globe. Moreover, American brands (Levi-Strauss, Burger King, McDonald's, Pepsi, Coca-Cola and Pizza Hut), music, street fashions and other aspects of its popular culture continue to enjoy considerable international appeal and influence. The USA also leads the field in the area of information technology, and enjoys certain advantages over its competitors. In particular, by being there at the start of the information revolution, the USA and its corporations have been able to shape information systems and processes (Nye, 2002).

However, the conception of global culture as a form of Americanization is problematic for a number of reasons. To begin with some of the most powerful studios in Hollywood, such as Columbia Tristar and Fox, are owned by Japan's Sony organization and the Australia-based News Corporation. More importantly, given the complex nature of corporate ownership in the contemporary period, it is debatable whether we should be too preoccupied about the national origins of corporations and conglomerates. As for the issue of US global media domination, while American news and media organizations, such as CNN, are extremely influential, they do not determine the news agendas of other countries. In this vein, the extensive international news coverage that issues such as Guantánamo Bay and the abuse of Iraqi prisoners by US soldiers receive would suggest that America as a whole, and Washington in particular, struggles even to shape the international news agenda. Moreover, the emergence of a media organization such as al-Jazeera, and the launching in France of CII (International Information Channel) – dubbed the 'French CNN' – in 2005, is perhaps an indication that in the future there will be a greater range of perspectives upon global affairs. It is also the case that the international media, in all their myriad of forms, have an impact upon American society. This was apparent in the few days leading up to the 2004 presidential election, when there was much speculation in the country about the extent to which a message released at the time by Osama bin Laden via the al-Jazeera news network would influence the final outcome. Furthermore, American cultural dominance is not even complete within the USA. There are countless television channels and radio stations within the country that broadcast in a foreign language, such as Spanish and Japanese, and are geared to particular ethnic or cultural groups.

There are also aspects of American culture that do not enjoy international appeal. In this regard, American political ideas, such as the minimal state and individualism, are far from universally attractive. Likewise, there appears to be something of a backlash against American cultural influence in many parts of the world, which may well restrict its future spread. This phenomenon has been noted by numerous commentators, who cite reasons ranging from envy of American power to the unpopularity of the George W. Bush administration (see Sardar and Wyn Davies, 2002). Indeed, such has been the spread of anti-Americanism that in September 2002 the US State Department organized a conference to address this phenomenon. Even Western governments, such as the Canadian and French governments, have pursued polices designed to resist what they consider to be forms of American cultural hegemony, especially in the area of popular entertainment. Such anti-Americanism may in part be a response to the number and volume of American cultural products that are exported abroad, but there is frequently an element of cultural reductionism at work. In other words, anti-Americanism is invariably based upon a particular conception of what American culture *is*, and that this culture is both uniform and stable, and, as will be shown later, neither of these things is the case.

Cultural homogenization as McDonaldization

Aspects of globalization, such as the spread of MNCs and TNCs, are also said to be contributing to another manifestation of global culture, namely 'McDonaldization'. This notion was first espoused by George Ritzer (1993) to describe 'the process whereby the principles of the fast-food restaurant are coming to dominate more and more sectors of American society as well as the rest of the world' (ibid., 19). Ritzer is working within the Weberian tradition: the German sociologist Max Weber maintained that modern societies are driven by principles of rationality, calculability, predictability and efficiency. For Ritzer, such principles are employed by McDonald's, but also by other businesses and modern institutions generally. The cumulative effect of these tendencies is the standardization of contemporary life, and as such this model is a more complete form of cultural homogenization than Americanization.

However, the McDonaldization thesis is not without its critics. In particular, it discounts the existence of variations of this model as well as different modes of organization and business cultures and practices. And regional and national variants do indeed persist, as do different styles of organizing corporations and modern institutions – such as can be found in, say, France, the UK, Scandinavia and Asia – reflecting local conditions or contexts. Some of these models enjoy considerable external cultural influence, notably Japanese management methods, elements of which companies in both Europe and America have incorporated or imitated (Elger and Smith, 1994). Indeed, what has been termed 'Toyotism' or the Toyota paradigm, involving the 'just-in-time' or *kanban* system of work organization and quality control circles, is often seen as an alternative to the Fordist model of industrial organization that first emerged in the USA.[2] Of course, in reality, companies will employ a variety of methods and ideas, drawn from a range of sources and adapted to local conditions in order to suit the purposes of their particular businesses, all of which runs counter to the notion that there is a universal business culture or set of principles for organizing modern institutions, whether this be McDonaldization, Fordism, Taylorist scientific management, Toyotism, or some other model.

Cultural homogenization as westernization

The origins of conceiving global culture as westernization could be said to date back to the period of European colonialism and the imposition by Europeans of their own institutions and practices upon their colonial subjects. This included establishing or promoting the nation-state, the wage-labour system, market economies, European legal-systems and conceptions of property ownership, languages and, in some cases, parliamentary democracy within their colonies. And, arguably, forms of Western cultural domination persist under contemporary globalization. For example, ICTs and transnational media have helped to spread the English language, which is now spoken by about a quarter of the human race. While it faces a challenge from Mandarin Chinese on the Internet, English is nevertheless the *lingua franca* of globalization. This is a legacy of British imperialism as well as a consequence of America's post-war domination of international affairs. English is therefore not only the language of commerce, but of international politics, diplomacy and science, reflected in its usage within the UN, the World Bank and the International Monetary Fund (IMF). Above all it is the main language of computing and global communication.[3] Furthermore, Abram de Swaan believes that with English established at the hub of the world language system it is likely to continue to spread because 'people tend to learn the language with the greatest communication value' (De Swann, 2001: 188). The negative aspect of this phenomenon is that in parts of the world the spread of English poses a threat to other languages, with some linguists forecasting that over 90 per cent of languages could die out during this century (Wurm, 1996). However, David Crystal (2003) suggests an alternative scenario to the universalization of English, noting that, when a dominant language spreads, new varieties evolve, which in the course of time could become mutually unintelligible. But if this does occur it is likely to be in the distant future, and in any case it is not in the interests of people learning English for them to learn a version that is unintelligible to other speakers as this would defeat the whole purpose of learning a global language.

Beyond the issue of language there is also a sense that global culture is dominated by Western values and ideologies. Non-Western critics argue that they are being encouraged to consume not only Western goods but to buy into Western lifestyles, especially the emphasis upon individualism. This is reinforced on the part of Western governments by their attempt to push their particular conception of human rights upon the non-Western world, using both their economic power and their dominant position within the institutions of global governance, such as the UN, to achieve this end. Indeed, Western individualism is said to permeate the UN Declaration of Human Rights and is championed by Western governments irrespective of its appropriateness for non-Western societies, which are often more religious and community-based. Similarly, it is often claimed that those institutions set-up to deal with global trade, aid and development, such as the World Bank, World Trade Organization (WTO) and the IMF, are promoting essentially a Western conception of modernity and modernization. In other words, they are founded upon a notion that there is a right way to develop and a distinct sense of what constitutes economic and political development, namely the establishment of liberal democratic, market-based societies. This is reflected in the structural adjustment policies imposed by these institutions upon many developing societies during the 1980s and 1990s, in which financial loans were dependent upon their respective governments implementing reforms that allowed the extension of the free market. The cumulative effect of such an approach is that it places pressure upon non-Western societies to take a particular path to development, and hence operates as a form of cultural imperialism.

A number of objections are raised against the concept of westernization. To begin with it implicitly conceives of globalization as a modern phenomenon in the sense that it is a position dependent upon the rise of the West, a development dating from the sixteenth century onwards. This perspective therefore overlooks the non-Western contributions to globalization that can be found by recognizing and examining its premodern history. Likewise, if we focus exclusively upon westernization in our own era we run the risk of neglecting other forces contributing to globalization, such as Asianization, Japanization or Islamization. Moreover, we need to take into account that Western societies are becoming more culturally diverse and pluralistic, which raises the issue of what we mean by Western culture and westernization (a point that is returned to in the third section), while the notion that international institutions are disseminating Western cultural values implies that those people working within them are unwitting agents in this process, and ignores the fact that within these forums there is considerable debate over policy, as seen in the recent rethinking over structural adjustment policies. In fact, international organizations such as UNESCO are generally sensitive to and seek to avoid charges that they are perpetuating Western cultural hegemony, an attitude that can even be found among some Western governments – although this may in part stem from feelings of guilt about their imperial past.

Global culture and capitalism

Many writers, especially those on the political Left, consider capitalism to be the primary driving force behind cultural globalization, and in particular to be generating a global consumerist culture, a development encouraged by the mass media and the advertising industry. Global cultural consumption assumes many forms, but is especially evident in youth culture, popular culture, lifestyle politics and forms of symbolic consumption (see Miller, 1995; Shields, 1992). This position has a long academic pedigree dating back to the 1940s and the work of Frankfurt School theorists Theodor Adorno and Max Horkheimer, who emphasized how culture was commodified under contemporary capitalist conditions, whereby the production, volume and nature of cultural commodities are determined by their market value (Adorno, 1991; see also Lash and Lury, 2007). This means that the forms of cultural homogenization identified at the beginning of this section are, from this perspective, products of capitalist expansionism. Within this tradition there are a number of specific claims made in relation to the cultural impact of global capitalism, two of which will now be considered by looking at the work of Immanuel Wallerstein and Leslie Sklair, respectively.[4]

1 Immanuel Wallerstein: culture as the idea-system of the capitalist world economy

As we saw in chapter 1, from the perspective of world-system theorists, the world system is a capitalist world economy. Immanuel Wallerstein maintains that the world system is based on a particular logic, that of 'the ceaseless accumulation of capital' (1990a: 36). Hence from his perspective, capitalism is the engine that is driving globalization, though Wallerstein rejects this term, preferring the 'world-system' (2004: 93). As for culture, for Wallerstein, it is 'the idea-system of this capitalist world economy' (1990a: 38). However, Wallerstein is not articulating a conception of capitalist culture as a homogenous entity; rather he sees culture performing a particular role within the world system, namely that of perpetuating it by containing the 'contradictory tensions' that it provokes (ibid., 51). In essence, the different cultural ideologies (ranging from racism and sexism to universalism) and the battles they generate divert attention from the economic divisions which underpin capitalism, and hence play a role in disguising the exploitation and inequality of the world-system (Holton, 1998: 171–2). Universalism establishes the myth that the system operates for universal benefit, while racism and sexism create hierarchies that enable capitalism to divide and rule. For Wallerstein (1990a), the paired ideologies of universalism and racism-sexism (anti-universalism) operate to undermine anti-systemic resistance, and it is for this reason that he describes culture as the ideological battleground of the modern world system. Indeed, capitalism is the main beneficiary from the confusion surrounding the whole concept of culture.

However, Wallerstein has been criticized for presenting a conceptualization of culture as derivative of the world system and of reducing it simply to ideology (Boyne, 1990). In other words, capitalist economics dominates culture and defines its purpose or, at the very least, shapes the parameters within which it will operate and function. But such a conceptualization of culture struggles to explain the eruptions of cultural fundamentalism that we have witnessed in the recent period, as well as the culture of protest against capitalist globalization that has emerged, both of which challenge capitalist culture. Thus, Wallerstein's account underestimates the ways in which culture can be used as a form of resistance. Moreover, as was touched upon in chapter 1, Wallerstein's world-system is criticized for ignoring the premodern cultural or civilizational processes and developments that contributed to globalization (Friedman, 1995). In sum, Wallerstein's world-system theory is charged with being a political economy model that pays scant attention to culture, and in its focus upon global structures and the unitary logic of the system neglects human agency. From the perspective of cultural theorists in particular, Wallerstein does not take culture seriously.[5]

2 Leslie Sklair: the culture-ideology of consumerism
Leslie Sklair (2001, 2002) similarly pursues a structuralist approach to this subject, and seeks to demonstrate that global capitalism shapes and defines both the world and globalization. In particular, Sklair is concerned with the global system and the way that it works, arguing that it is founded upon transnational practices, which operate in three spheres: the economic, the political and the cultural-ideological. Furthermore, each of these practices is characterized by a key institution: the transnational corporation, the transnational capitalist class, and consumerism, respectively. We can see from these spheres that culture is once again associated with ideology, as well as of course economics, and consequently it is denied any independent existence.[6] In this regard, one of Sklair's central claims in relation to cultural-ideological transnational practices is that consumerism

contributes to the survival of capitalism because it seeks to convince the majority of people that such a lifestyle offers them fulfilment. To paraphrase Sklair, the culture-ideology of consumerism provides much of the glue that holds the global system together: 'Without consumerism, the rationale for continuous capitalist accumulation dissolves' (2002: 116). The function performed by consumerism also reveals that the global capitalist system is engaged in an on-going process of sustaining and reproducing itself, something that Sklair believes is especially evident in the attempt to extend capitalist relations to countries in the developing world.

Global culture and modernity

As we have seen, many sociologists consider globalization and by extension global culture to entail the worldwide spread of the processes and forces of modernity, such as capitalism, rationalization, democratization, liberalism and industrialization (e.g., Giddens, 1990; Spybey, 1996). In other words, it is the modernization of the world that we are witnessing. For this reason, some of the forms of cultural homogenization outlined here, such as McDonaldization and westernization, are regarded as part of this tendency. Often underlying these drives is the association of modernity with progress and hence something that all peoples and countries would want to aspire to, an attitude that arguably can be detected in early modernization theory through to Francis Fukuyama's 'end of history' thesis (discussed below). Modernity, from this perspective, is inherently expansionist. Or, as the Mexican poet and critic Octavio Paz has more eloquently put it, all cultures are 'condemned to modernity' (Berman, 1983: 125).

But we need to be careful about our usage of the terms 'modernity' and 'modernization'. Anthony King (1995), for instance, makes a distinction between the humanities' understanding of modernity/modernism and the social sciences' understanding of modernization, arguing that the former are essentially Euro-American concepts – 'grounded in a spatially restricted historical temporality' (1995: 115) – and the latter is a largely American term. Moreover, in the case of modernization, King claims that social scientists after the Second World War conceived of it as having an international dimension, and hence as moving beyond the geographical limits established by modernity and modernism. And at the risk of complicating matters even further, it should be noted that, within the broad distinction that King makes, different conceptions of modernity and modernization can be found. For example, with regard to modernity, some sociologists identify a period of 'high' or 'late' modernity in relation to the changes

[handwritten margin note: What does that even mean?! "Modernization" ⊃ modern is current & is ∴ always itself but what it consists of right now is not what it will always consist of.]

ushered in by globalization. This approach seeks to incorporate what is perceived as our more reflexive era, resulting from the challenge to tradition and traditional authority from a globalizing modernity. In a post-traditional era, a concomitant of the greater individual freedoms that we enjoy is that the certainties and stabilities of the past are diminished, and we are therefore increasingly on our own as we enter a more insecure phase of human history. Again this condition is variously conceptualized, with Ulrich Beck (1992), for instance, maintaining that we are now living in a 'risk society'. From this perspective, modernity is a reflexive modernity, a theme that is returned to in chapter 7.

However, Martin Albrow (1996) challenges the association of globalization with modernity. He maintains that not only are the modern and the global different epochs, but more significantly we have moved beyond modernity and entered a global age, a development reflected in the challenge to rationality and the nation-state as the primary basis of action and social organization. Albrow insists that in part the reason this transformation is not widely recognized lies with the language of modernity. Being modern suggests being up-to-date and new, so how can we move beyond this condition, and indeed why would we want to do so? From this perspective, Francis Fukuyama (1992), a writer who believes a liberal democratic global order constitutes the future for humanity, remains trapped within the mindset of modernity. As Albrow puts it, modernity has 'transfixed the intellectual imagination' (ibid., 9), and this may explain the attachment of some writers to notions of 'late' or 'high' modernity even though its time has passed. For Albrow, the supplanting of modernity with globality is evident in the damage done to the global environment; contemporary weaponry with its potential for global destruction; the impact of global communication systems; and the rise of the global economy. Interestingly, the fifth way in which Albrow believes globality has taken us beyond the assumptions of modernity concerns what he terms 'the reflexivity of globalism' whereby individuals and groups now refer to the world as their frame of reference for their outlooks and beliefs (1996: 4). This is therefore not a reflexive modernity, but a reflexive globality.

Roland Robertson: social theory and global culture

The global-human condition and the interpenetration of the global and the local

Roland Robertson (1992, 1995), a leading writer on the sociology of globalization, emphasizes the significance of the encounter between the global and the local as part of a broader attempt to promote the cultural realm within globalization studies, a subject area that traditionally has had a strong emphasis upon economics and politics. As a result, rather than emphasizing structure and system, his approach is more centred upon human agency and identifying what is effectively a social and phenomeno-logical condition – a global-human condition, as he terms it. This condition is a product of a lengthy historical process and is constituted by four 'forms of life' (selves, national societies, the world system of societies and humankind), which are in constant interaction with each other, are transformed in the process, but crucially inform the way that we perceive the world. For Robertson, globalization therefore refers to the coming together of these different forms of life. However, he considers the metaphor or model of the 'global field' is a more accurate conception of the global rather than viewing it as a unified global system or a unitary global culture (1992: 26–9). From this starting point, Robertson believes there are certain shortcomings with the concept of 'globalization' – under-stood by him to describe both 'the compression of the world and the intensification of consciousness of the world as a whole' (ibid., 8). However, as suggested above, this does not mean that he overlooks the local within his conceptualization of globalization. For Robertson, global-ization 'involves the creation and incorporation of locality, processes which themselves largely shape, in turn, the compression of the world as a whole' (1995: 40). In other words, there is an ongoing process whereby the global and local, the universal and the particular, combine so that the local is pro-duced by, or is at least an aspect of, globalization, a point that is returned to below (ibid., 30). But Robertson goes further, suggesting that the global and local interpenetrate to the extent that 'glocalization' is perhaps a more appropriate concept to describe this condition. In short, this interpenetra-tion of the global and the local ensures they are not discrete cultural enti-ties, but a syncretic mix containing elements of both (Holton, 2005).

All of the above means that during the course of our everyday lives we exist with a sense of both the global and the local in our minds. To act simply in terms of the global would be to operate in too abstract a manner. Rather, we relativize by making sense of the global and reproducing it within our own particular contexts, shaped as we are by local cultural influences. The universal is therefore particularized. And it is not only indi-viduals that relativize in relation to the global – this tendency can be found in institutions, religions and national societies, for example (Robertson, 1992: 29) – while globalization ensures that we are undertaking such con-textualization more frequently because its processes throw together the global and the local more often. From Robertson's perspective, this also helps to explain why in the recent period we have witnessed a rise in nationalist, regionalist and local forces, leading to 'collisions between civilizational, societal and communal narratives' (Robertson, 1992: 141). This fragmentation is a product of the greater amount of interpenetration and relativization that is taking place in the contemporary period, as well as the growing consciousness of the world as a single community and the potential challenges this poses. There is, therefore, sameness and difference, homogeneity and heterogeneity, at work. Consequently, Robertson (1995) maintains, we must move beyond debates about global homogenization or heterogenization. While these simultaneous tendencies 'can and do collide in concrete situations', it is not a question of either/or, but of recognizing that they are complementary and interpenetrative (ibid., 40).

The universalization of particularism and the particularization of universalism

Robertson does not deny the existence of globalized discourses or general world-views, nor is he claiming that we are not influenced by the global. Indeed, social life is informed by global discourses about the nature of the world and our place within it, and, as we saw in chapter 1, he believes this tendency can be traced back to the ancient Greeks (Robertson and Inglis, 2006). Moreover, he recognizes the existence of global culture, though, to repeat, this is not of the unitary variety and it emerges from the interplay between the particular and the universal, the local and the global. More specifically, there are processes at work encouraging the 'global creation of locality', evident in the form of the locally orientated International Youth Hostel movement, the worldwide spread of suburbanization, and the tendency to promote internationally the rights and interests of native peoples in the form of global political movements and campaigns (Featherstone and Lash, 1995: 4–5). The plural nature of global culture is similarly reflected in the manner in which Japanese business and production methods have been adopted by other countries, and hence universalized. In each instance the local or the particular is universalized. Likewise, nationalism, and the national society that emerged from this ideology, developed in tandem with internationalism. The diffusion of the idea of the national society is therefore a form of institutionalized societalism, or, to put it another way, it marks the establishment of an international system of national societies (Robertson, 1992: 58). Indeed, for Robertson, 'the commitment to the idea of the national society is a crucial ingredient of the contemporary form of globalization' (1992: 112). He maintains that global culture is partly created from interactions between national societies (1992: 114). Therefore, the idea of global culture is now 'just as meaningful as the idea of national-societal, or local, culture' (ibid.). Above all, we should not conceive of global culture as existing above and beyond all localities, or of having qualities or properties that transcend anything that can be found within the units of a global system (Robertson, 1995: 34). Indeed, '[t]he global is not in and of itself counterposed to the local' (ibid., 35). For Robertson, the local is part of the global. In sum, there is a two-way process taking place involving the 'interpenetration of the universalisation of particularism' and the 'particularisation of universalism' (Robertson, 1992: 100). To return to the example of Japanese business and production methods in order to highlight this tendency, before they were universalized these cultural practices were forged from numerous global/external influences. Put another way, the universal was particularized before the particular was universalized.

Robertson, culture and globalization

If Robertson is correct then culture lies at the heart of globalization. This is because we are constantly applying our particular cultural frameworks during the course of our everyday interactions with the global. Robertson therefore challenges Anthony Giddens for simply equating globalization with modernity because it underplays the significance of the cultural realm, which includes the impact of race, ethnicity, nationalism and gender.[7] Likewise, Robertson is critical of Immanuel Wallerstein's world-system theory for not taking into sufficient account the heterogeneity and complexity generated by the processes of cultural globalization. For Robertson, such diversity emerges from the complex interaction of the four constituent elements that make up the global human condition. Such variety is continuously being produced and reproduced in our own time, and it is largely an aspect of the very dynamics that are often assumed to constitute homogenization (Robertson, 1995: 38). However, Robertson's thesis has been criticized for neglecting the structural dimensions of globalization, that is, for underestimating the political and economic forces driving globalization, and thereby devoting insufficient attention to the issues of power and inequality (e.g., Friedman, 1994). Moreover, it is claimed that his investigation into the global and the local, and the universal and the particular, is too abstract, especially given that he sets such store by what takes place when these forces meet and interact (Holton, 2005).[8] However, in relation to the theme of this chapter, as well as the broader concern of this book, one of the many strengths of Robertson's work is that he raises important questions not only about global culture but also globalization.

Globalization and global culture

Having examined particular forms of cultural homogenization in the first section of this chapter, in this section we will broaden the discussion by outlining the reasons why the linkage between globalization and global culture, in whatever form that culture may take, as well as the very notion of a global culture, are problematic.

Global culture: critical debates and contemporary developments

Within globalization studies it is possible to discern a number of different perspectives on the issue of global culture. While globalists consider it is appropriate to delineate the globalization of culture, for sceptics, such as Hirst and Thompson (1996), if a globalized economy does not exist then it is unlikely a global culture exists – though, as was stated earlier, Hirst and Thompson have been criticized for failing to provide an analysis of the interrelationship between culture and economics, and of neglecting the cultural dimension of globalization in general. In response, sceptics point out that the recent rise in tensions and conflict between different cultures at a global level would suggest that we are as far away as ever from living in a culturally homogenized world. Lastly, from a transformationalist perspective, the concept of global culture is unable to encapsulate the diversity and complexity of contemporary global cultural flows and the reactions they are provoking, ranging from cultural resistance to the establishment of new global networks (Held et al., 1999: 327).

A number of contemporary developments would similarly seem to run counter to the forms of cultural homogenization outlined earlier. In particular, the conceptualization of global culture as Americanization or westernization is premised upon a specific type of global order – one that is dominated by America and the West, respectively – when in reality this order is undergoing significant change. In this regard, Wallerstein (2003) believes that the erosion of US power is the defining feature of our age, a development dating back to the 1970s and the result of numerous factors, including America's relative economic decline. Indeed, America's demise phase is regarded by some commentators as an indication that we have entered a new phase – an era of globalization (e.g., Taylor, 2001). While we should not ignore the fact that the USA remains the dominant global power, it is the case that both it and 'the West' as a whole are today facing considerable challenges, most notably the spectacular growth of a number of Asian economies, with China and India threatening to become economic superpowers in the twenty-first century. As well as East Asia, a number of countries in Latin America are rapidly industrializing and becoming more integrated into global networks in the process. In fact, some of the constituent features of globalization, such as the spread of ideas and global communications technologies, have contributed to these changes, enabling non-Western societies to incorporate best practice and new technologies, and in some cases skip stages of development. So, whereas it took Britain almost 100 years to industrialize, this has been arguably achieved by some Asian economies in the space of 20–30 years. The cumulative effect of these developments is a blurring of the first world–third world distinction, paving the way for a more multi-polar world; this in turn has cultural implications, especially at an international level, allowing countries and regions outside of the West to enjoy greater cultural influence. Arguably, this is already happening, as alongside the spread of Asian business cultures and forms of work organization mentioned earlier, other Asian cultural products and practices have come to be globally disseminated, such as traditional medicines and medical treatments, cuisines, films (e.g., Manga films), martial arts, exercise regimes, software programmes and games, and Buddhist and Taoist philosophies. In particular, Eastern spirituality and therapies are becoming increasingly popular in the West.

Jonathan Friedman (1999) believes we are witnessing a major challenge to Western cultural identity. He similarly points to the 'rise of the East', but also to internal developments within the West such as multiculturalism and the fragmentation of nation-states as evidence of the decline of Western modernity and with it Western cultural hegemony. Friedman believes this is linked to changes in the world economy, which is undergoing 'declining hegemony, the increasing export of capital and the decentralisation of capital accumulation on a world scale' (ibid., 253). In short, we would seem to be returning to the multi-centred world of the thirteenth century identified by Janet Abu-Lughod. These developments are mirrored in the cultural realm, which is also undergoing high levels of decentralization or pluralism, such as the revival of ethnic and religious identities, reflecting diminishing Western cultural power and influence.[9] And for Friedman, symptomatic of the crisis of modern culture and identity is the heightened importance now accorded to cultural studies, hybridity theory and post-modern anthropology. Indeed, multi-centredness runs counter to the whole idea of a global culture because it is a condition marked by the absence of a single dominant power, and hence also of a unifying or homogenizing force. Quite simply, it is very unlikely that multiple centres would be generating the same or similar cultural forms.

Recognizing cultural complexity

Conceptualizing global culture as Americanization or westernization – and indeed assuming that it takes any particular form – is also unlikely to encapsulate the complexity of contemporary globalizing processes. Global cultural flows do not just, or even mainly, emanate from the USA or the West, for example. At any single moment images, symbols, ideas, advertisements, films and other cultural forms will be emanating from multiple sources and travelling in multiple directions across the globe, and many will have little or nothing to do with the West or America. For example, there are forms of cultural interaction taking place between parts of Africa and Asia as well as within these continents, and as we saw in chapter 1 this has been going on for many centuries. Moreover, the idea of westernization or Americanization underplays the possibility of cultural counter-flows in the form of food, fashion, religion, music, films (e.g., 'Bollywood') and other influences travelling to the West from other countries. The USA, for instance, has been assimilating new cultural influences throughout its history, something that is evident in its constitution, which borrowed much from European revolutionary ideas and ideals. In short, America is a 'cultural sponge' and consequently it is an ever-changing society (Nye, 2002: 242), a theme that is returned to below.

The numerous flows and interconnections that constitute globalization are therefore unlikely to be operating as a homogenizing force. In this vein, is it possible for any power to dominate global cultural flows and processes? The sheer volume of contemporary global flows of information, ideas and images means that they can no longer be monopolized, if they ever were, by any single country, region or corporation. Furthermore, by focusing upon global culture in a singular or unitary sense there is the likelihood of overlooking other forms and sources of cultural domination. For many cultural groups it is not Americanization or McDonaldization that threatens their cultural autonomy and identity, but a local influence or regional power. Tibetans, for instance, struggle to assert their Buddhist religious culture and identity as a result of China's attempted Sinoization of their country. Moreover, in the post-Cold War era, many of the states of the former Soviet Union have been attempting to reduce the level of Russian cultural and political influence within their societies. However, cultural pressures outside of the 'first world' are similarly a two-way process. For example, China and India are strong regional powers that exert considerable cultural influence upon neighbouring states, but are themselves not immune to countervailing flows. In the case of China, the cultural pressure and influence from neighbouring states comes notably in the form of Hong Kong and Taiwanese popular culture, from pop songs to karaoke singing, which are steadily permeating Chinese society much to the consternation of the Beijing government (Yang, 2004).

In relation to the issue of cultural complexity, it is questionable whether we should be thinking about this subject in terms of 'izations', such as Americanization, and the other varieties covered here. Peter J. Taylor (2001) believes that describing global developments in this way is problematical and should be avoided because it conflates process with end-state. Thus 'izations' imply inevitability and in so doing deny complexity and the possibility of alternative trajectories.[10] On a similar theme, an additional reason for being wary about asserting that global culture is Americanization or westernization or a product of global capitalism, and so forth, lies with the critical challenge these concepts now face. There is an increasing tendency within academia to 'anthropologize' concepts, to look at local experiences and consequently to articulate, for example, multiple modernities, capitalisms and, as we have seen, globalizations (Berger and Huntington, 2002; Wei-Ming, 2000). In general, there is now greater acceptance of different paths to and conceptions of modernity, such as Islamic and Asian modernities, and a view that the Western model may not be the only route to modernization, and may actually be inappropriate for some cultures and societies (see Eisenstadt, 2002), while recognition of the different types of capitalism, such as the Anglo-American, Scandinavian and Asian models, would seem to run counter to the idea of a global capitalism (see Albert, 1993). However, by way of a rejoinder to this particular point, we should not forget the role that money and power play in shaping contemporary globalization. Despite the existence of variants of capitalism, the principle of profit-maximization underlies them all and in this sense it is still possible to talk of a global form of capitalism. Moreover, some commentators play down the significance of different types of capitalism, insisting the Anglo-American neoliberal model predominates due to a combination of Anglo-American power, ideology, new communications technologies, and the support of international institutions such as the World Bank and the IMF. It is therefore possible to overplay the influence of local cultures in the face of such pressures. But if we are to pull all of this together and make a broad assessment of what is taking place in relation to capitalism in the contemporary period, then on balance there are likely to be both forms of homogenization and differentiation at work.

As well as being 'anthropologized', doubt has been cast about the accuracy and usefulness of the concepts being discussed here. It is increasingly recognized that 'the West' and 'America' are umbrella concepts encompassing and often subsuming considerable diversity within them. For example, it soon becomes clear when travelling across the USA that there are in fact many Americas. While in the case of 'the West', the degree of diversity is even more marked, with competing cultural flows travelling between the USA and Europe, as well as the cultural and political differences between them surfacing during the recent Iraq war (see Kagan, 2003).

Similarly, for hybridity theorists 'the West' and 'America' are cultural constructions formed from multiple and diverse sources. We saw in chapter 1 that the West has a rich and mixed cultural heritage, but this is equally applicable to the USA. For example, one of America's great cultural icons and exports, the pizza, is a product of generations of Italian immigration (Nye, 2002: 80). All of which raises questions about we mean by westernization and Americanization, and this in turn further undermines the notion that either constitutes a global culture. And from the perspective of hybridity theorists, who generally conceive of contemporary globalization as a period of accelerated mixing (e.g., Nederveen Pieterse, 2004), should we really continue to use artificial constructs like 'the West' under such conditions? In other words, contemporary globalizing processes introduce greater heterogeneity into concepts that are already of dubious validity. In this regard, it is often claimed that we are witnessing a blurring of 'the West' and 'the East' as cultures intermingle and regions become less distinct. However, the hybridity thesis can be overstated. Concepts such as 'the West' may well be artificial creations, but this does not mean that there are not dominant themes or tendencies within them that have coalesced over time. Furthermore, within any cultural encounter there will often be stronger influences or forces that predominate, and this is evinced on a global scale by the fact that Western societies do not experience the same level of external cultural bombardment as non-Western societies.

The global and the local

Another criticism of focusing upon global culture in relation to cultural globalizing processes is that it ignores the multiple ways in which such a culture – allowing for a moment that it does exist – can be indigenized, and even rejected and resisted. It assumes that 'locals' are simply passive recipients of such a culture, rather than playing a role in actively shaping it. For this reason, there is increasing recognition within globalization studies that the global and the local are engaged in an ongoing interaction.[11] It is an encounter which involves human agency and does not simply entail dominance on the part of global cultural and structural forces. As we have seen, Roland Robertson espouses the notion of glocalization to indicate the way in which the global and local interact and inform each other. Glocalization or global localization, 'a global outlook adapted to local conditions', was originally a concept popular within Japanese business circles, as Robertson himself has acknowledged (1995: 28). It gained international recognition when Sony adopted it as a marketing strategy, and is now employed by major corporations across the globe. In essence, companies are seeking to adapt their products to the tastes and sensibilities of local markets. For example, MTV broadcasts Chinese music in China and Hindi pop in India (Eckes and Zeiler, 2003). And even McDonald's, the supposed great cultural homogenizer, is similarly sensitive to local cultural conditions, and in adapting its outlets to reflect the contexts in which they are operating demonstrates a degree of flexibility that further undermines the McDonaldization thesis (e.g., see Watson, 1997). While reflecting the growing acceptance that the global and the local are engaged in an ongoing process of interaction, some writers emphasize the possibility of cultural flows moving from the local to the global, and informing the global in the process (e.g., Cvetkovich and Kellner, 1997). Again, there is perhaps some evidence of this tendency on the part of McDonald's, which now places greater emphasis upon healthy lifestyles and selling salads and fruit in their restaurants – although this shift may be due to the international criticism McDonald's has received, such as the film *Super Size Me*, rather than being the result of the companies engagement with local cultures.

Despite the recent emphasis upon glocalization, this does not mean that the global–local encounter is necessarily an equal one. It will often be the case that indigenous cultures are in the main responding and adapting to foreign influences. In fact, there would not be a global–local dynamic were it not for the more powerful external forces, such as MNCs and TNCs, generating cultural flows and ensuring such encounters. To continue with this theme of power in relation to the global–local encounter, we should not overlook the possibility of overarching power structures and systems shaping the nature of this interaction. In this vein, to return to the point made above, it is still capitalism and capitalist principles that are motivating MNCs and TNCs to establish firms and outlets in different parts of the world, as well as leading them to adapt to local markets. Indeed, there is also arguably Weberian rational calculability at work in the sense that MNCs and TNCs such as McDonald's have calculated that being locally orientated in their business dealings is the most efficient way of enhancing profits.

Finally, we need to consider whether it is now actually possible to be a 'local'? Given the intensity and extensity of contemporary cultural flows, are there any places in the world that have not yet to some extent been permeated by globalizing influences? What therefore does it mean to be authentically 'local'? And if the local no longer exists, does this mean that all is global? Ulf Hannerz (1990) hints at this by noting that local cultures are increasingly interconnected so that they form a global discourse of locality. However, we can go too far with this theme. While almost everywhere in the world is to some degree informed by global forces, we should keep in mind that, in general, people's everyday experiences and behaviour are conditioned by their immediate environment and personal life-histories. This highlights the crucial point concerning the relationship between the global and the local. Put simply, for dominant or homogenizing forces to exist they must spread their influence and be reproduced in new areas, but in doing so they interact with the local, where it is likely their form will to an extent be altered within these particular contexts.

A global culture or global cultures?

So, are we witnessing the emergence of a global culture? In brief, the answer is that this is unlikely both now and in the foreseeable future. Indeed, given the extent of human cultural diversity perhaps 'culture' is too strong a word to employ at the global level, and it is perhaps more likely that if current patterns continue we will simply see more people developing an ability to think beyond the local and particular and gaining a sense of being in the world. Ultimately, however, in order to determine whether a global culture exists or can emerge, we again need to think about what we mean by culture. In so doing, it is worth reflecting upon whether our continued concern with identifying a unitary global culture is an indication of our nation-state mindset, one which is increasingly inappropriate in the contemporary phase of globalization. Thus the stability and shared experiences required for the formation of such cultures are at odds with both the intensity and sheer unpredictability of contemporary global flows. It follows therefore that we should not discuss global culture in the form that it assumes within national societies or religious groups. This is because we can never expect a global culture to exert the same hold upon us and our imaginations as our national and religious cultures (Featherstone, 1990). In this regard, Anthony Smith insists that, compared to national cultures, 'a global culture is essentially memoryless' (1990: 179). For Smith, there are no 'world memories' able to unite us all, and 'the most global experiences to date – colonialism and the world wars – can only serve to remind us of our historic cleavages' (ibid., 180). We are also likely to interpret world events through our national prisms, thereby precluding them from becoming world memories and the basis of a global culture. The socialization processes, common values and sense of group homogeneity that are required to ensure the development of such a culture are all missing, not to mention shared historical memories. Moreover, many of our global encounters will be of the virtual kind, conducted in cyberspace, and as a consequence are unlikely to be as meaningful as our local, 'real life', everyday experiences, which take place within the confines of particular national territories. For a global culture to replicate our national cultures, it would require a world state or at the very least more fully developed international institutions that allowed for forms of popular participation. In short, in comparison with our national cultures, we feel little or no attachment to a global culture as it fulfils no emotional or practical need for us. From Smith's perspective, given the continued relevance of national cultures, there is little prospect of this state of affairs changing in the foreseeable future. Smith goes further, arguing that 'the idea of a global culture is a practical impossibility' (1990: 171). This is because if we conceive of culture as 'a collective mode of life, or a repertoire of beliefs, styles, values and symbols, then we can only speak of cultures, never just culture; for a collective mode of life, or a repertoire of beliefs, etc., presupposes different modes and repertoires in a universe of modes and repertoires' (ibid.).

However, Smith's conception of culture is almost certainly influenced by his work on nationalism and national culture, and this leads him to perceive both culture and global cultural developments in a particular way. In contrast, the social anthropologist Ulf Hannerz, who has written extensively on the relationship between cosmopolitans and locals in the contemporary period, has a broader conception of culture and a different approach to this subject, identifying, as mentioned above, a world culture in the interconnectedness of various local cultures as well as in the development of cultures without anchorage in any one territory (1992b). For Hannerz, the world is not a single homogenized system of meaning and expression, yet it 'has become one network of social relationships, and between its different regions there is a flow of meanings, as well as of people and goods' (1990: 237). But again we can see how different academic backgrounds can come to inform perspectives on cultural globalization. Of course, in their own terms – that is, from their particular perspectives of what constitutes culture – both Smith and Hannerz are correct in their assessments of global culture.

A further obstacle hindering the formation of a unitary global culture is the lack of an 'other'. Culture formation and group solidarity are aided and enhanced when it is possible to contradistinguish with another cultural group, one which will be variously perceived as different, alien, of not belonging and as 'outsiders'. Assuming that Martians do not exist, in relation to global culture there would seem to be no obvious 'other' with which to make such a contradistinction (Featherstone, 1990). However, if we conceive of global culture in a particular sense, namely westernization, where arguably it is possible to identify an 'other' in the shape of those groups and societies who do not conform to Western norms and values, then in recent times Osama bin Laden and the al-Qaeda network could be said to perform this role: their actions are often presented by Western leaders as defying the international order – viewed from the perspective of the West as democracy, human rights and the rule of law – and hence they are accused of operating outside of civilized society. But as we have seen, the whole notion of westernization is not without its critics.

In short, there are numerous factors militating against the formation of a global culture, of whatever form or manifestation. In particular, given the complex ways in which globalizing processes are operating, including – if Roland Robertson is correct – the extent of the interpenetration of the global and the local, it is highly unlikely that a unitary global culture will ever emerge. As Mike Featherstone has observed, rather than thinking of global culture as a common culture, we should conceive of it as a field on which differences and power struggles are played out (1995: 14). While there are homogenizing pressures exerting an influence in the contemporary period, at the same time there are heterogenizing forces at work. This means that we should treat notions of Americanization, McDonaldization, and so forth, with considerable scepticism – although Ritzer et al. are likely to respond that they are merely seeking to delineate the dominant tendencies of our age rather than define absolute conditions. Yet even these tendencies will be critically interpreted, indigenized, and even rejected, as well as having to confront counter-tendencies. Hence, for some writers, the main consequence of the forces of cultural homogeneity is actually even greater differentiation and fragmentation (e.g., Axtmann, 1997).

A more productive approach to this subject would be to think of global culture in the plural as global – or at the very least globalizing – cultures. We are, for instance, witnessing the emergence of a number of global cultures in the contemporary period, including a globalizing Islam, Buddhism and Christian evangelicalism, a worldwide anti-globalization movement, a global environmental movement, a world music community and a global football culture. What these movements have in common, as well as their global reach, is that their respective supporters, devotees or adherents identify with a particular cultural form that marks them out from others. They therefore have something distinctive to become attached to and as a consequence their commitment to it is likely to be all the stronger. In other words, these global cultures retain a particularist dimension and this goes some way to addressing Anthony Smith's critique as well as his conception of culture. The notion of global cultures is also recognition of the fact that we inhabit multiple cultures, including those at the global level. For example, a Muslim will identify with the *ummah*, the universal community of Islam, which extends to all parts of the world, but he or she may also be interested in world football, and hence also be engaging with another global culture. This approach also means that we can view the forms of global cultural homogenization covered here, such as McDonaldization, Americanization and westernization, which certainly have spread across geographical borders and into new territories, as simply competing global cultures rather than constituting a unitary global culture. Indeed, conceiving of global culture in the latter sense is to ignore the sheer diversity that exists in the world, as well as being an unrealistic assessment of how contemporary globalizing processes are working. Further, by considering this subject in this way we are acknowledging that, while there is not a dominant homogenizing cultural power at work, this does not mean that homogenizing forces do not exist, and are being experienced and engaged with by peoples across the globe.

If we accept the existence of global cultures, we can better understand how the global and the local interact, especially in relation to the process of self-constitution. Put simply, if there were only a single global culture there would be the prospect of many peoples in the world rejecting it. With global cultures, in contrast, there will be some that we identify with and they will come to form part of our cultural outlook or frames of reference. In other words, alongside our local cultures, which of course inform how we perceive different global cultures, the global and specifically certain global cultures can also form part of the context in which we perceive and interpret the world. It means that subsequent global cultural flows will be interpreted in the light of this interaction between the global and the local as part of an ongoing process of self-constitution. The subject is therefore formed from the encounter between, or more specifically the interpenetration of, the global and the local.

In conclusion, this investigation into global culture has deliberately not been confined to the cultural realm, and has included, amongst other things, consideration of the global political order and the nature of the international economy. Culture is obviously inextricably linked with both power and money. All of this returns us to a theme outlined in the Introduction, namely that if we are to understand cultural globalization, we need to draw upon the insights of a range of disciplinary approaches. What has also become evident during the course of this chapter is that the divergent stances over the issue of global culture can again be traced to differences between academic disciplines. As we saw in the first section, the emphasis upon cultural homogenization (of various forms) and world systems tended to be strongest amongst sociologists and economists. In contrast, in the third section, the emphasis upon heterogenization and hybridity in relation to global culture tended to come from the cultural theorists and postmodern anthropologists. Once again, there would seem to be an aspect of cultural globalization generating a divide between the social sciences and cultural studies.

Recommended reading

Key works on the interrelationship between globalization and global culture are Roland Robertson's *Globalization* (1992) and M. Featherstone (ed.), *Global Culture* (1990). Leslie Sklair in *Globalization: Capitalism and its Alternatives* (2002) explores in detail the connections between globalization, capitalism and consumer culture. For concise and informative essays on the relationship between the world-system and culture, see Wallerstein (1990a) and Boyne (1990). Serge Latouche presents a comprehensive account of the different aspects of westernization in *The Westernization of the World* (1996). For the McDonaldization thesis and an informed criticism of it, see George Ritzer's *The McDonaldization of Society* (1993), and Barry Smart (ed.) *Resisting McDonaldization* (1999), respectively. And for a good introductory work that covers a range of areas and debates on the theme of cultural imperialism, see John Tomlinson's *Cultural Imperialism* (1991).

5

Globalization and National Culture

It is often asserted that globalization is eroding national cultures. This chapter will assess this contention, looking at the challenges confronting nation-states and national cultures in a globalizing era, such as the influence of global and transnational media, the impact of ICTs, patterns of global migration and the increasingly multicultural nature of many societies.[1] The views of Anthony Smith (1995) and Michael Billig (1995), who stress the continuing relevance of national cultures in our global age, will be examined, as will the influence that hybridization and hybridity theory are having upon this debate. But the chapter will begin by outlining some of the major theoretical perspectives on nationalism and national culture as well as associated critical debates. Overall, it will be shown that the globalization-as-threat-to-national-culture thesis is too simplistic a conception of what is taking place, based upon both an inadequate understanding of the nature of national culture and a flawed assumption that global cultural flows operate in a single or uniform manner.

Nationalism and national culture

Before examining how globalizing processes may be impacting upon national cultures, we need to consider the nature of such cultures, which includes being aware of the power relations at work in their formation. In this regard, national cultures have traditionally reflected the influence of dominant groups or elites within a society, which until relatively recently has meant that women and minority groups have generally contributed little to their development. This in turn has meant that national cultures and nations have traditionally been sites of cultural contestation. Reflecting this fact, a further analytical difficulty that national cultures present us with is that they are not fixed and stable entities; rather, they evolve over time, which merely adds to the difficulty of determining any influence that globalization is having upon them. Put simply, are national cultures changing because of internal transformations or because of external influences introduced by the processes of globalization, including a shifting global context? Alternatively, are these changes a product of the interpenetration of the global and the local? Furthermore, there are additional complicating factors when considering national cultures, notably the conceptual slippage that often takes place when writers discuss nationalism, nations, nation-states and national identities (see Connor, 1978).[2] This problem is exacerbated by a lack of consensus over the origins and nature of nationalism and national identity, reflected in the emergence of a number of different schools of thought on this subject. These have been termed 'primordialist', 'modernist' and 'ethno-symbolist', and to this list must be added the interpretations of writers who seek to move beyond traditional approaches to nationalism, which for the sake of analytical convenience will be categorized here as 'post-national'. In broad terms, these positions will now be sketched out.

The primordialist conception of nationalism

Primordialists believe it is possible to identify nations, national cultures and a sense of national loyalty as far back as the Ancient Greeks and other early civilizations (see Geertz, 1963; van den Berghe, 1979). From this perspective, nations are natural and universal, both an extension of kinship relationships and effectively an instinctive part of human behaviour in the sense that they fulfil a human need. Nations may disappear and reappear in the course of human history, but they are always there and as such cannot simply be invented (Kellas, 1991). As it will probably have occurred to the reader, if we are to accept this thesis much depends upon our definition of 'national'. More specifically, the 'national communities' of the ancient period are unlikely to accord with our contemporary conceptions of nationalism, and are nations only in a much looser or broader sense than we understand today. In this regard, the primordialist insistence that nations existed in antiquity is challenged by the fact that during this period there were strong countervailing forces at work, notably regionalism, migration, pluralism and cultural mixing.

The modernist conception of nationalism

Modernists, in contrast, maintain national cultures and nationalism emerged during a specific period in modern European history, the culmination of a number of developments, before then spreading to the rest of the world. For example, Benedict Anderson (1983) considers the emergence of print-capitalism in the late eighteenth century as pivotal in the development of nationalism because it led to different types of literature (books, newspapers, etc.) being disseminated throughout a country, enabling people to 'imagine' themselves as part of a national community engaged in a common experience, even though they were never likely to meet the majority of their fellow citizens. In a similar vein, Ernest Gellner (1983) identifies industrialization and the rise of 'industrial society', which surfaced in parts of Europe at the end of the eighteenth century, as significant moments in the history of nationalism. For Gellner, the connection between industrialization and nationalism stems from the fact that industrial growth is best facilitated by a particular type of culture and political system, namely, modern nationalism and the nation-state (Kellas, 1991: 42). In other words, industrial growth both necessitated and encouraged a common language and culture, a single currency, a common legal and educational system, and a centralized state to implement and coordinate these developments, all of which contributed to the formation of homogenous nations, subsuming the plethora of languages and local cultures and ethnicities that characterized feudal society in the process. Other writers consider nationalism was a calculated project, whereby nationhood and national traditions were 'invented' by elites in order to preserve the status quo and their own position (see Hobsbawm and Ranger, 1983). However, as many critics have noted, the problem with the modernist line of argument is that it struggles to explain the powerful emotive appeal of nationalism, and why so many have been prepared to kill for, and die for, their country (Kellas, 1991: 43). Indeed, it effectively implies that populations have been collectively duped and continue to be so. To paraphrase Anthony Smith: 'you can't invent nations where they don't exist' (1990: 180–1).

The ethno-symbolist conception of nationalism

Steering something of a middle path between these two schools of thought, ethno-symbolists insist upon the ethnic origins of modern nations. In this regard, Anthony Smith (1986) argues that nations have not been produced only by modern developments such as capitalism and industrialization; rather, they have their roots and origins in the *ethnie* (ethnic groups) of the pre-modern period. There is, therefore, within the ethno-symbolist tradition a strong emphasis upon continuity (Kellas, 1991). In other words, modern nations do not emerge from nowhere, but build upon and develop the ways in which members of an ethnic group associate. Ethno-symbolism, however, also has its critics. Ethno-symbolists such as Smith are accused of underestimating the differences between modern nations and earlier ethnic communities

(Özkirimli, 2000). In particular, it is claimed that the nature and structure of modern 'civic' nations cannot be found in earlier periods of history.

Post-national conceptions of nationalism

There have been additional criticisms levelled against these established approaches to nationalism, notably that they are Eurocentric (Chatterjee, 1986), gender-blind (McClintock, 1996), and assume cultural homogeneity and stability when in reality there is diversity and fluidity (Bhabha, 1990). What is common to 'post-national approaches', such as feminist and post-colonial accounts, is an attempt to move beyond the limitations and forms of exclusion upon which nationalism and the nation have traditionally been founded, that is, to problematize national cultures, challenge dominant constructions of the nation, and even to think beyond the nation itself (Özkirimli, 2000).

Writers engaged in the debate over the contemporary condition of national culture will often draw upon the particular theoretical approach to nationalism that best suits their own case. Hence for those commentators who consider we are witnessing the diminution of national cultures as a result of globalization, it accords with their thesis to point to claims that nations and nationalisms are modern constructions or inventions. If national cultures have not existed since time immemorial then it follows, it is argued, that we have been able to live without them in the past, can do so again, and indeed this is exactly what is now happening (Held and McGrew, 2002b). In contrast, writers who believe national cultures will survive in this global era point to their long histories and the ways in which they are embedded within both our societies and our imaginations. But this discussion will now turn to examining the particular ways national cultures are being challenged by the processes and developments that constitute contemporary globalization.

Globalization and the diminution of national culture

Global cultural flows and national cultures

There is now a substantial body of work insisting that global cultural flows are harmful to nation-states and national cultures. For example, taking as their starting point Appadurai's notion of 'scapes', Scott Lash and

John Urry (1994) argue that *mediascapes* are of greater significance than *ideoscapes*. In other words, in our postmodern era, it is the electronic dissemination and proliferation of images and information that are assuming greater significance than the ideas, ideologies, institutions and rational discourse characteristic of modernity, of which nationalism and the nation-state are an integral part. This is reflected in the fact that national governments no longer monopolize the flow of information. In this vein, the development of a transnational media would seem to have notable implications for nation-states and national cultures. For example, China has a tradition of authoritarianism and state control of the media, and hence would seem to be an example of a nation-state capable of controlling any outside cultural influences. However, as a result of the emergence of transnational media, which are starting to challenge the national media within China, Chinese society is being permeated by external cultural forces, not only Western but, as we saw in the previous chapter, from neighbouring states. In this regard, based upon a case study of Shanghai, Mayfair Mei-hui Yang (2004) identifies the makings of a transnational Chinese cultural identity that increasingly eludes state influence, all of which will make it harder, Yang argues, for the Chinese party-state to shape the national subject. The late Gerald Segal (2002), a respected writer on China, observed that the Chinese party-state has spent much of the last two decades fighting a rearguard action against external cultural influences.

Global cultural flows are also considered to undermine the national space. More specifically, globalization is viewed as paving the way for a more open conception of place and culture, challenging the bounded spaces of nation-states. This is achieved via the complex webs of global electronic media and information flows that create new areas of virtual space, allowing the development of virtual societies and virtual cultures, with little or no sense of national place or territory (see Jones, 1997; Woolgar, 2002). In particular, new information and communications technologies, such as the Internet and satellite television, are considered to pose a formidable challenge to national borders, reconfiguring our relationship with space, territory and identity in the process (Morley and Robbins, 1995). Such developments lead Doreen Massey (1994) to push for a 'progressive concept of place', insisting that the network of social relations, movements and communications or interactions that ties places together is not static, but must be viewed as a process. Furthermore, she maintains, places are not bounded entities but must be understood in their wider geographical context. In other words, it is its linkages to the 'outside' that help to define a place; for example, attempts to keep out those perceived as 'outsiders' can say a lot about a place. In a similar vein, Manuel Castells (1996) believes the emergence of the network society transforms the nature of social life by taking it beyond national boundaries. Also, Timothy Luke argues that transnational flows of capital, people, commodities, information and culture are generating a 'cyberspatial / televisual / informational glocality' fusing 'the local and the global in new everyday life-worlds' (1995: 91). Above all, he considers that the 'local and the global are commingling in new 'glocal' modes of production across and outside of national boundaries' (1995: 101). For Luke, today's already porous borders are being continuously permeated by global flows of goods, services and information and consequently being further eroded in the process. And such is the extent of the interdependence of societies and regions throughout the world that '[m]any institutions of existing nation-states are now a fetter upon the emerging glocal modes of production' (ibid.). As a result, 'the notion of "national interest" has less and less meaning in these glocal webs of interdependence' (ibid.). John Urry (2000) takes such ideas to their logical conclusion, arguing that the daily permeation of national borders by global processes and flows undermines sociology, which has traditionally been centred upon an examination of national societies, and necessitates the development of a sociology of mobility, one that is able to go beyond the borders of the nation-state.

Returning to the theme that people are bearers of culture, contemporary migratory flows are generally introducing greater complexity and heterogeneity to societies, leading to them becoming progressively multicultural and polyethnic. And this transition from ethnic to pluralist nations is engendering discussions about the appropriateness of employing multicultural rather than ethno-national models of community (e.g., Glazer, 1997), as well as contributing to the resurgence of ethnic nationalism, far-Right politics and racial violence in a number of countries (see chapter 6). How this relates to the debate about national culture is that it entails, following on from the point made in the previous section, national cultures being less homogenous and stable as a result of the growth of minority nationalities and arguably as a consequence less coherent and distinctive. In short, it becomes harder to discern unitary national cultures and hence to identify with them, a development reflected in debates about the crisis of national identity (e.g., Delanty, 1996; Rex, 1996). Moreover, the more visibly plural or multicultural nature of modern societies makes it easier for the free expression of our multiple identities. Under such conditions, our national culture and identity are less able to dominate and subsume our other identities and allegiances, becoming simply two of a number of mental constructs or imagined communities that we carry around with us. Indeed, to take a wider view in considering this issue, our private lives and attachments are invariably more meaningful to us than our national or public lives and allegiances.

Global cultural flows and the USA

The case of the USA bears out a number of the above points. For a start, it provides evidence of the complex effects of contemporary migration patterns because much of the debate in the USA is focused upon migration from regional as opposed to global sources. There is a particular concern with the number of illegal immigrants in the country – estimated to be about 11.5 million in 2006 or 3.6 per cent of the total US population – who are joined each year by between 500,000 to a million more, who mostly enter the country through the USA's long southern border with Mexico. As a result, more than three-quarters of illegal immigrants in the USA were born in Latin America, with a large proportion coming from Mexico. More significantly, the rate of unauthorized arrivals has steadily accelerated since the 1980s, with on average nearly five times as many illegal immigrants entering the country each year now as did so then. It is an issue that has aroused considerable feeling, and has provoked action on the part of anti-immigration and pro-immigration groups. On the part of the former, their activities have been channelled towards setting up Minutemen groups, who patrol America's borders, seeking to prevent illegal entry into the country. Moreover, the latter have organized a series of demonstrations against proposals to tighten immigration law, most notably the nationwide protest entitled Day Without Immigrants (1 May 2006), which entailed, among other things, a boycott of jobs in order to demonstrate how much illegal immigrants matter to the US economy. More broadly, the sense that the country is becoming more ethnically and culturally diverse because of immigration has provoked considerable discussion about the condition of the national culture and whether we are witnessing the 'disuniting of America' (Schlesinger, 1998).[3] Samuel Huntington considers that the USA was founded upon 'the twin bedrocks of European culture and political democracy' (1996: 61), encapsulated in the principle of equal rights for the individual, but sees this as now threatened by multiculturalism and an emphasis upon group rights. Huntington (2004) fears this will effectively lead to an internal clash of civilizations, serving to unravel the USA. In particular, he contends that current levels of Mexican and Hispanic immigration and, as he sees it, the limited assimilation of these immigrants into American society will in time weaken the national culture, and he would surely point to the release in April 2006 of *Nuestro Himno*, the Spanish version of the US national anthem ('The Star-Spangled Banner'), as supporting evidence. The problem with this stance is that it is predicated upon the notion that non-European ethnic minorities in the USA have less commitment to liberal democracy, thereby ignoring the considerable sacrifice many would have made to come to America, presumably because they were at least in part attracted to the American way of life and its associated freedoms. In contrast, Joseph Nye, Jr. (2002) has a more optimistic appraisal of the state of his nation, placing faith in the need for people to work but also in modern communications and media, which taken together necessitate a mastery of the English language as well as generating attendant homogenizing pressures. This means that newly settled immigrants have not only inducements, but also the means, to integrate into American society.

However, contrary to Nye, and looking beyond the USA, Jonathan Xavier Inda and Renato Rosaldo (2002) maintain that Western nation-states are less effective at exerting these homogenizing tendencies than they once were. Again, some of the developments particular to the contemporary phase of globalization are likely to be contributing to this pattern, notably national cultural flows having to compete with global cultural flows so that individuals are confronted with a never-ending stream of mixed messages. Similarly, as we saw earlier, global communication and information technologies make it more possible for the migrant and diaspora communities to stay in touch with their homelands, thereby arguably reducing the need for them to identify strongly with their host nation. In the USA, this is reflected in the emergence of what have been termed 'ampersand Americans', who hold on to dual nationality and in some cases seek dual citizenship, that of America and that of their homeland (*The Economist*, 2000). American identity in this instance becomes effectively a transnational identity (Kivisto, 2002). All of this has raised concerns in other countries and may in part explain why the UK government has recently introduced citizenship ceremonies for those wishing to become British citizens; why the Dutch government is trying to repatriate migrants who have been living in Holland for years; why the French government has passed new laws to ensure religious minorities assimilate into the country's secular culture; and why European Union states have been building 'Fortress Europe' in response to contemporary patterns of migration and immigration. In the case of the latter, such coordinated attempts to control migratory flows are an indication that national governments by themselves are unable to do so, and can perhaps be read as a further indication of their diminishing autonomy.

Globalization, the nation-state and national sovereignty

A further albeit indirect pressure upon national cultures could be said to derive from the challenges that different aspects of globalization present to the nation-state and national sovereignty (see Barry Jones, 2000; Holton, 1998; Mann, 1997). One such challenge is considered to come from the continuing evolution of the institutions of global governance. As the World Bank, the UN, the IMF, the WTO and the International Court of Justice assume a more prominent role in international affairs, they will increasingly constitute alternative sites of authority to that of national governments. Indeed, the decisions, policies and rulings of such organizations are intended to be binding upon nation-states. Similarly, the growth of regionalism and regional organizations, such as the EU, NAFTA (the North American Free Trade Agreement), ASEAN (the Association of South East Asian Nations), SADC (the Southern African Development Community) and MERCOSUR (Southern Cone Common Market) in Latin America, is often regarded as evidence of the erosion of national sovereignty. Most national governments now accept the necessity for regional cooperation if they are to remain significant players on the global stage, with some pooling their sovereignty by setting up regional institutions. Indeed, in the case of the EU, European economic and political integration is so far advanced that its potential to foster a pan-European identity, one which may in time come to challenge the national cultures of member states, is now a source of debate (see Hopper, 2004).

In addition to these external challenges to the nation-state, globalization may be changing the nature of the relationship between the state and its citizens. According to Gerard Delanty and Patrick O'Mahony (2002), we are witnessing the decoupling of nation and state and, it follows, of nationality and citizenship. They argue that while nationalism emerged from the connection between the political project of modernity (e.g., state formation and universal citizenship) and the cultural project of modernity (e.g., the forging of new identities), the connection between the two is being challenged in our globalizing era. There are now numerous ways in which citizenship is no longer exclusively defined by nationality. Most notably, with national governments increasingly recognizing international legislation and incorporating it into their own legal systems, especially in the area of human rights, citizenship is becoming divorced from nationhood. For Delanty this means that '[u]niversal personhood is coming to replace nationhood' (2000: 79). Arguably, we should start to think of citizens as sovereign in our global era, rather than collective bodies or institutions like the nation-state. On a more day-to-day level, there is now greater emphasis upon group or cultural rights within societies that are increasingly pluralistic and multicultural. This tendency manifests itself in many forms, ranging from affirmative action policies to religious groups, migrants and ethnic minorities becoming more assertive about their rights, as well as better organized to articulate their demands (see Soysal, 1994). In a similar vein, because they transcend or stretch across more than one nation-state, transnational processes, communities and circuits may serve to disrupt the link between nationality and citizenship, especially with regard to the degree of commitment of transnationals to a particular state and their readiness to pay taxes and participate in its electoral processes and civic community. It often leads nationalists to question the commitment of transnationals to their country, and Alejandro Portes has posed the question: 'what does it mean to have so many citizens who are, in a very real sense, neither here nor there?' (1996: 77). At the very least, transnationalism may in time entail a shift away from the traditional state-based notion of citizenship towards more flexible conceptions (see Ong, 1999).

Such external and internal challenges to the authority and status of the nation-state may be contributing to the growing disenchantment with national politics in many countries, evident in declining voter turnout and the rise of new social movements. What is relevant for this discussion is whether or not this more critical stance towards the nation-state – assuming that this is what is happening – is weakening our attachments to all things 'national'. For primordialists and ethnosymbolists, national traditions and 'ways of life' predate the emergence of the nation-state and therefore will persist and remain meaningful in people's lives irrespective of what happens to this institution, while from the perspective of sceptics, if globalization is in doubt, then some of the effects attributed to it in relation to nation-states and national cultures must also be questioned. In contrast, from the hyperglobalizers' perspective, evidence of the declining influence of the nation-state can be gleaned from the fact that it is no longer an exporter of culture. This contrasts sharply with its past history. Indeed, the consolidation of the nation-state in Europe was the prelude to imperial expansion in Africa, Asia, the Middle East and Latin America at the turn of the nineteenth and twentieth centuries and the cultural and political remoulding of these societies. Today, the role of disseminator of culture and cultural values is increasingly the preserve of private corporations. The only exception, at least if one conceives of globalization as Americanization, would be the USA. However, even in the case of America, as we saw in the previous chapter, it is still companies, such as McDonald's, Coca-Cola and Disney, rather than Washington, that are the primary agents of cultural dissemination. Moreover, a transnational media and the diffusion of communications technologies may in future allow ordinary citizens and non-state global networks to have a greater influence upon cultural trends and developments.

Global capitalist markets and national cultures

The globalization of capitalist markets may potentially foster cultural convergence by encouraging common ways of organizing economic and social life – a tendency with obvious implications for national cultures. Thus, the pressures of competing in a global market, the diffusion of best practice and industrial technologies, capital mobility and competition as well as the ability of MNCs and TNCs to establish an international division of labour and global communication networks are leading, it is claimed, to international convergence (Berger and Dore, 1996). This state of affairs is compounded by national governments having to observe international trade rules and agreements and deregulate their economies. Such arguments echo concerns of an earlier era, when it was feared that standardized industrial cultures, founded upon common organizational and working practices, were eroding local and national distinctiveness and contributing to the mass society. To an extent, globalization revives these debates because it describes trends that transcend national borders. Today, it is arguably not so much in the area of production that such tendencies can be seen, but in marketing and consumption, where there is now a greater emphasis upon brand names and labels (Klein, 2000). Corporate capitalism would therefore seem to be establishing its own globalizing culture and ideology. However, this point needs to be weighed against a number of studies that emphasize the continuance of local and national distinctiveness, including forms of cultural resistance, in the face of the ongoing march of global capitalism (e.g., Lowe and Lloyd, 1997). Further complicating patterns of cultural convergence is that new computerized technologies facilitate post-Fordist flexible manufacturing systems, enabling firms to tailor their products to particular markets and even to cater for individual tastes and lifestyles. Such individualization of consumption patterns would seem to run counter to the idea of cultural convergence, though of course ultimately people are still engaging in a common experience of consumerist capitalism. Whether it is cultural convergence or individualization, or both, that we are witnessing, neither phenomenon is likely to be in the interests of national cultures and nation-states, especially in relation to the formation of an active citizenry.

There is a further way in which an aspect of globalization may work against the nation-state and national culture. Again it concerns global communication and information technologies, which in this instance may help to revive the local as opposed to the national. Local foodstuffs, music, arts and crafts, regional languages and dialects, local customs and traditions have, via the Internet and the World Wide Web, the means for their wider dissemination and promotion. Even remote and little-known towns and villages are able to publicize their existence through this means, often as a way of attracting tourists and investment. Furthermore, those 'locals' who have left the area can keep in contact with their former home-towns or regions and contribute to their revival, most notably by buying their products. This is enabling various forms of local revival and expressions of localism when for so long they have been in decline. Indeed, it was often the spread of the national culture that subsumed local cultures and identities.

Finally, Timothy Luke (1995) presents an especially bleak assessment of the condition and future prospects of the nation-state. Drawing upon the work of Baudrillard, Luke portrays our age as one in which the modern/realist new world order of nation-states has been usurped by a set of postmodern/hyperrealist neo-world orders created by contemporary global flows. We have therefore moved beyond Benedict Anderson's (1983) imagined national communities to a world of virtual communities where history, reality and the social have been replaced by the hyperreal. Luke notes that this has considerable implications for politics, where attention shifts away from the domain of the nation-state to a hyperreal politics conducted largely by non-state actors in cyberspace. His claims therefore raise questions about where power lies and indeed what constitutes power in an era of neo-worlds? However, Luke presents the world as an essentially informationalized place and as such he presents something of an ideal type because, as we have seen, globally inequalities of access to information and communications technologies remain. Moreover, while noting that Luke is merely seeking to identify dominant tendencies rather than a definitive condition, he nevertheless may be underestimating the extent to which national governments and nation-states are still significant actors on the international stage, and even shape many global flows, a theme that is returned to in the next section.

In sum, the national communities from which national cultures emerge are more porous than ever before, permeated daily by different peoples, cultures, ideas, images and sounds. National governments are struggling to assert their authority and even to maintain their territorial borders – they lost the battle to erect borders in cyberspace some time ago. Further, some of the developments associated with globalization, and covered elsewhere in this work, such as cultural homogenization and cosmopolitanism, are considered to foster new cultural formations, networks and identities. Cumulatively, such changes present a range of challenges to nation-states and national cultures, leading some commentators to conclude that both are in decline. At the very least, it is reasonable to enquire what it means to be a 'national' in our globalizing era.

The persistence of national cultures in a global era

National rootedness versus global ephemerality

The claim that national cultures are being eroded or reconstituted by powerful globalizing forces is far from universally accepted. To begin with, critics argue it assumes that people who adhere to these cultures are passively acquiescent in this process, content to be swept along by global cultural influences. It is also the case that we inhabit numerous cultures at any one moment, and therefore being bombarded by images and information from around the world will not necessarily weaken our attachment to our respective national culture. As we have seen, many media MNCs and TNCs, who are major disseminators of global cultural flows, are adapting their products to suit national markets, suggesting national distinctiveness persists and national cultures retain their vitality. But a more fundamental objection is that national cultures are the product of shared histories and collective memories, and thereby are able to generate deep allegiances that globalizing processes will always struggle to undermine. Arguably, this point is equally applicable to those national cultures with relatively brief histories. In Africa, for example, the national cultures of many countries were forged out of a struggle against European colonial rule, undertaken by all sections of their society, a feat which generated its own cultural memories that helped to bind together the newly emergent nations. In short, from this perspective, national cultures have roots and substance compared to ephemeral global cultural flows. For this reason, Anthony Smith believes cosmopolitanism and regionalism, which are often associated with globalization, should not be viewed as resulting in the demise of nationalism. Quite simply, for Smith, national identity exerts 'a more potent and durable influence than other collective cultural identities', leading him to conclude that 'the chances of transcending the nation and superseding nationalism are at present slim' (1991: 175–6).

The notion that the increased migration is undermining national homogeneity has similarly provoked a critical response. For a start, patterns of contemporary migration are a source of considerable academic dispute. Hirst and Thompson (1996) stress that the majority of the world's population find it difficult to move for reasons ranging from the imposition of stricter border and immigration controls by advanced industrial countries to the passing of the 'frontier' societies, such as Australia, Canada and South Africa, which attracted huge numbers of people in the past. In truth, there is considerable variety in the extent to which people can move across borders, and it is closely related to a migrant's professional qualifications, wealth and status, as well as the nature of the state that he or she is seeking to enter. Hirst and Thompson also note that the period 1815–1914 was the greatest era for recorded voluntary mass migration, with episodes such as two world wars, the Cold War and the formation of new states doing much to disrupt migration in the twentieth century. However, there is an emerging consensus among migration scholars that post-war patterns of migration, especially since the mid-1970s, involve many more countries than in previous eras, with virtually every country in the world now importing or exporting labour (Castles and Miller, 1998). Most importantly, Held et al. (1999) highlight the complexity of contemporary migratory flows, evident in the emergence of new regional systems of migration, especially in Latin America, within Africa, and across South and Southeast Asia. Overall, they conclude that 'contemporary patterns of migration are more geographically extensive than the great global migrations of the modern era, but on balance are slightly less intensive' (ibid., 326).

Likewise, the claim that national distinctiveness is being eroded as countries become more culturally heterogeneous has been refuted. Nikos Papastergiadis (2000) contends that even when nation-states acknowledge the multicultural nature of their society, 'this representation of difference is projected only to confirm the greater image of the national culture' (2000: 113). He does not provide supporting examples, but South Africa, the USA and the UK would be possible instances of this tendency. Multiculturalism is therefore employed to complement and reinforce the nation. While Papastergiadis may slightly overstate his case, since multicultural or polyethnic societies at the very least ensure that national cultures are less homogenous, his arguments are a useful counter to the claims that we are witnessing their passing.

In this vein, we should not underestimate the extent to which people are willing to protect 'their' particular nation-state and national culture. Within a number of European countries, for example, there is concern about the impact that globalization and in particular immigration is having upon their respective national cultures, an attitude that is considered to be contributing to the re-emergence of the extreme Right. For example, in promoting cultural separatism and the right of people to their own national identity, the Republican Party in Germany and the National Front in France have seemingly struck a chord among sections of their respective societies. But concern over the fate of the nation-state and its culture in the contemporary period is not just the preserve of the extreme Right. Further defensive reactions to globalization are evident in the endeavours of many national governments to protect aspects of national life, such as their language, customs and culture, from globalizing forces and pressures. The French government is endeavouring to preserve the French language and music industry, and has attempted to restrict the number of American films that can be shown in France in order to protect its indigenous film industry. In Canada, the government has sought to limit the extent to which US culture industries can hold a stake in Canadian media and telecommunication industries (Held et al., 1999: 371). More generally, national governments throughout the world consider it to be an important part of their role to promote their respective national cultures both at home and abroad, through such measures as promotional videos, investing in their tourist industry, and educational and cultural exchange programmes.

National cultures are also arguably 'reproducing' themselves, thereby ensuring that we continue to live as 'nationals'. In this regard, Michael Billig in *Banal Nationalism* (1995) contends that we receive daily reminders that we are part of a nation, even though we do not always consciously register many of them. This process of reproduction includes such things as postage stamps, national newspapers, national flags on public buildings, airplane logos, maps, national flowers, national cuisines, architecture and, in some cases, a national language, as well as the more formal but less regular public ceremonies and holidays. Compared to these tangible everyday reminders that we are nationals, the rapid succession of images of the world that we see on our television screens, it is claimed, lack depth and meaning. Moreover, even international competitions, such as the World Cup and the Olympics, which are intended to bring nations together, often stir up patriotism rather than internationalism, as countries compete with each other. And to return to Samuel Huntington's concerns over American culture and assimilation, it is also the case that migrant and immigrant communities living within national societies, including the USA, will be similarly subjected to such 'nationalizing' pressures.

The international nation-state system

As for the nation-state, it may be in a healthier condition than its critics claim. While the growth of international law will to an extent circumscribe national sovereignty, it is nation-states through their governments that are responsible for signing and implementing such legislation. Moreover, nation-states played a pivotal role in setting up institutions such as the UN, the EU and the WTO, for which nation-statehood is a membership criterion, and most importantly these institutions are invariably used by governments as forums in which to promote their respective national interests. And despite all of the discussion about global flows and processes, the world is still shaped by an international nation-state system – a system of inter-nation-state exchanges – rather than globalization (Featherstone, 1990: 6). Above all, there does not appear to be a groundswell of international popular support for the further development of the institutions of global governance. In contrast, there has been an increase in the number of nation-states in the recent period, reflected in the expanding membership of the UN, which currently has more than 200 member states. Moreover, it is nation-statehood that many oppressed peoples and liberation groups of the world continue to aspire to, those that have achieved this end being unlikely to want to give it up. And nationalism and the pursuit of national independence continue to be a powerful motivating force and goal, either in the form of ethnic nationalism (witness the recent turmoil in the Balkans) or liberal nationalism (e.g., the other newly liberated states of Eastern Europe, such as Poland and Hungary). It would seem, then, that Lash and Urry (1994) overstate their case: ideas, ideologies and modern institutions such as the nation-state remain as important as information and image in the contemporary period. In short, from the perspective of those who are sceptical about globalization, the nation-state remains a key actor on the international stage, and looks likely to remain so for the foreseeable future.

However, if we are to glean a more accurate picture of the nature of the relationship between globalization and the nation-state, and in turn understand how it impacts upon national cultures, then we perhaps need to move beyond debates between globalists and sceptics. Most importantly, we need to take a historical perspective towards this issue. As we saw in chapter 1, the nation-state has historically facilitated globalization – and is indeed an expression of it in the sense that it is a universal phenomenon – but has also on occasions hindered its progress through erecting boundaries and borders and hence restricting cultural exchange. Inevitably, national cultures have been informed by this inconsistent relationship. Furthermore, if we apply this historical examination to the issue of sovereignty, in all likelihood the concept of national sovereignty existed for only a limited period in early modern Europe, and specifically following the landmark Treaty of Westphalia of 1648, when the degree of interdependency between states was low (Ferguson, 2006). Under contemporary globalization, as we have seen, new transnational actors, the continued development of international institutions, global flows of various kinds, and more intensive forms of interconnectedness and interdependence all constitute different types of challenges to national sovereignty. Yet this does not mark *the end* of national sovereignty. Rather, it is more accurate to think of sovereignty as a condition that is increasingly 'negotiated' between different actors on the international stage, including by national governments, but at the same time acknowledge that this has almost certainly been the case for some time (see Keohane, 1995).

Cultural hybridization and national culture

Hybridity theory provides a different insight into this debate about the condition of national culture in our globalizing era. For hybridity theorists, all cultures, including national cultures, are syncretic, formed through absorbing ideas and influences from a range of sources over time. Consequently, the notion of discrete and stable national cultures cannot be sustained, as cultures have always intermingled and borrowed from each other. This is evident, for instance, in some of the constituent features that define English culture, such as the patron saint (Saint George) and the English language. The former was a rather mysterious figure, but is believed to have originated from the Middle East, and the latter, already a hotchpotch of linguistic sources, arrived in England from northern Europe in the fifth century (Crystal, 1995). Indeed, English culture as a whole has been forged from numerous invasions, including those by Angles, Saxons, Vikings and Normans. Thus, national cultures are continuously evolving and incorporating new influences. In the case of some countries, notably Brazil, Mexico, Indonesia and Zanzibar, their hybrid origins and the hybrid nature of their respective national identities are openly acknowledged – something that would be difficult to deny given their experiences of colonialism – and in some cases even celebrated. More profoundly, from the perspective of hybridity theorists, social constructions such as nations and religions have served to conceal the hybridizing processes that are at work. It follows from this that advocates of national and religious cultures – or more specifically those who hold monocultural conceptions of them – are either failing to acknowledge their hybrid nature or are simply unaware of it.

As was discussed in chapter 1, writers such as Jan Nederveen Pieterse (2004) believe that accelerated hybridization, the increased mixing of cultures, is the defining feature of contemporary globalization.[4] If this is the case, then it has obvious implications for national cultures. And there would seem to be aspects of contemporary globalization that facilitate hybridity. As we have seen, the numerous processes that constitute globalization work to disrupt the relationship between culture and place. Thus, preserving cultures within distinct territorial borders becomes more difficult when these territories are permeated each day by cultural and information flows from around the world via modern communications technologies. Similarly, improved transportation and increased travel and migration, which are also a part of contemporary globalization, enable us to have a greater number of diverse cultural encounters and hence more opportunities for cultural mixing. Moreover, urban life in today's global cities makes it hard to avoid interacting with peoples and cultures from all over the world, whether in restaurants, cafés, theatres or cinemas, or simply through our ordinary everyday encounters and experiences (see Alsayyad, 2001). In sum, the developments and manifestations that we call globalization introduce greater mobility and fluidity into human societies, breaking down borders and boundaries in the process, and these are conditions favourable to hybridity.

However, the relationship between national culture and hybridization is more complicated than has thus far been presented. Two observations will be made to highlight this point. First, rather than just viewing national cultures as threatened by the forces of hybridity, we must also recognize the pressures that hybrid cultures face within the context of an overarching national culture and the extent to which they can be subsumed by that culture. Indeed, the hybrid encounter will rarely be an equal one between cultures nor is it likely to produce neat and immediately discernible outcomes, and in this regard we should keep in mind the theme of transculturality discussed in chapter 2, whereby cultures increasingly exist across cultures. In short, we need to consider the power relations that are at work when cultures interact and ensure that in focusing upon fluidity and mixing we do not overlook the existence of structures of inequality. Second, even allowing for the hybrid nature of national cultures, such cultures can surely come to stabilize and to endure, and in time become meaningful to their respective citizens. For example, in the decades leading up to the 1950s, the UK had a relatively homogenous ethnic and cultural mix, which in turn helped to produce a stable national culture revolving around certain common institutions and 'ways of life'. But for Nederveen Pieterse this should not distract us from the fact that national identities are still 'mélange identities' (2004: 33). From his perspective, cultures have always been 'overflowing boundaries', which are themselves 'provisional and ever contentious superimpositions upon substrata of mingling and traffic' (ibid., 100).

Criticisms of hybridity theory

As has probably become clear by now, hybridity theory has generated considerable criticism.[5] For a start, there is the issue of what is being hybridized in the hybrid encounter. Put simply, do discrete cultures have to exist for hybridization to take place? If so, does this not rather undermine the claim of hybridity theorists that all cultures are a mixture of borrowings from other cultures with overflowing boundaries? A further charge against hybridity theory is that most forms of cultural hybridization are superficial and fleeting encounters, and to embrace properly other cultures and to incorporate aspects of them requires commitment and time as well as empathy. People will indulge in forms of cultural mixing and experimentation, such as the growing number of Western citizens attracted to Buddhist teachings, but ultimately their hybrid experience is not so deeply rooted when compared to the hold that their national or even Western culture exerts upon them. In the case of the latter, for many people in the West, it is arguably their individual freedom that they especially value, as it is this that provides them with the opportunity to 'mix-and-match', culturally speaking. However, hybridity theorists respond to the charge that the hybrid encounter is a transient one with the question: who decides whether or not this is the case? Who is to say, other than the individual concerned, that a Spaniard practising Buddhism is not participating in a meaningful experience?

Accompanying criticisms of hybridity theory, doubts have been raised about the extent of cultural hybridization, both in the past and in our own time. Ideologies of exclusion, such as nationalism and social Darwinism, did much to shape the modern era, and inevitably served to restrict forms of cultural hybridization. More generally, there is a long history of governments endeavouring to protect their national cultures from hybridizing forces, ranging from limiting immigration to restricting the flow of foreign cultural products and ideas into their societies. In this regard, successive governments in Singapore have resorted to authoritarian state measures in order to protect what they consider to be their country's traditional culture and values. In the UK, a survey conducted in 2004 by the Commission for

Racial Equality revealed that more than nine out of ten white Britons have no or hardly any ethnic minority friends (Dodd, 2004). Many white people have simply moved out of inner-city areas, where immigrant communities are more likely to live, and this has obviously reduced the amount of cultural interaction. Consequently, London and some other cities are multicultural and cosmopolitan; other regions of the UK and especially rural areas, however, are not. While there is evidence that younger whites are 'mixing' more than older ones, the survey also found that the reverse is the case within some ethnic minority communities. Over 39 per cent of ethnic minority Britons under the age of thirty have friends who are almost exclusively from ethnic minority communities, compared to their parent's generation – that is, those over fifty years old – where the figure is only 19 per cent. These figures are all the more striking given the context of globalization, which is widely considered to be facilitating intercultural contact. Similarly, numerous European governments are expressing concern that many Muslims remain 'outsiders' in their societies despite having lived in their respective countries for a number of generations, although in most cases what really concerns European governments about this lack of cultural mixing is that Muslims and other ethnic minorities are not properly integrating into mainstream society and embracing their respective national cultures. In other words, it is cultural assimilation, not hybridization that they seek.

Hybridity theorists are unlikely to consider that the above examples undermine their case. As we will see in the next chapter, there has been a steady growth in the number of mixed-race couples and children in Western societies, which is perhaps the ultimate form of intercultural contact. Of course, this is only one type of cultural hybridization. Contemporary global cultural flows of ideas, images, films, sounds and symbols ensure that we do not have to be in close geographical and physical proximity to other people in order to experience aspects of their culture. Moreover, as mentioned previously, hybridity theorists contend that the national cultures into which some governments are endeavouring to integrate minority groups are already hybrid creations. Contemporary globalization is therefore merely hybridizing the hybrid, albeit at a more rapid rate (Nederveen Pieterse, 2004).

Globalization, national culture and complexity

As has hopefully become evident during the course of this chapter, there are strong arguments on both sides concerning the current condition of national culture, and the impact that globalizing processes are having upon it. Thus far, this issue has been presented as essentially a debate between those who are optimistic and those who are pessimistic about the fate of national culture, when in reality there is a more diverse range of opinion on what is a complex topic. A major reason for this complexity is that the encounter between the global and the national is taking place within different contexts. In other words, different types of state formation, as well as national cultures with different histories and in varying degrees of health, are being exposed to global cultural flows that are uneven in both their volume and reach. Inevitably, this means that such flows, which will be subjectively experienced and interpreted, will have a significant impact in some countries and regions, serving to erode national distinctiveness as a result, but fare less well in others, where they may even engender forms of national resistance. All of this means that, if we are to determine whether globalizing processes are undermining national cultures, then we will have to examine particular contexts and undertake specific case studies. Thus, the USA, as the world's most powerful nation-state, which may in part contribute to the generally high level of patriotism that can be found in the country, coupled with the fact that (as we saw in chapter 4) it is an important source of many global cultural flows, will have a different experience of cultural globalization compared to many Middle Eastern states that have briefer more fragile histories – for example, their right to exist being challenged by some Muslims in the region – and are the recipients of such flows.

When evaluating the impact of globalization upon national culture, we should also bear in mind that, from its inception, the nation-state has often had to take a prominent role in generating and maintaining national cultural unity, often marginalizing internal local cultures and identities in the process. In a sense, therefore, the external pressures presented by globalization today are part of a pattern, though of course we must not underplay the particular challenges that contemporary globalizing processes present to national cultures. Notable among these challenges are the forms of deterritorialization discussed in chapter 2, which arguably entail the linkage between national culture and territory not being as essential as it once was, given that it is now much easier to communicate with one's homeland from afar, as well as with fellow nationals wherever they may be in the world. Put simply, there is less of a necessity to live in one's own country in order to be a national. Furthermore, peoples of other cultures and nationalities increasingly inhabit our homelands, and despite the efforts of some nationalists and governments to preserve their particular cultural-territorial distinctiveness, cultural flows of images, symbols, sounds and ideas criss-cross national borders each day. And we have seen how such mobility and fluidity can serve to disrupt the national space. In this vein, there is the matter of how we conceive of our homelands from afar when they are actually undergoing rapid change, unless of course we hold on to a rather rose-tinted and essentially fixed or timeless conception of our national home that is characteristic of some expatriate communities.

Ultimately, however, it is only valid to consider national cultures as being threatened by global cultural flows if we conceive of such cultures as stable, immutable and homogenous entities. But if we view national cultures and indeed all cultures as conceptualized here – namely as protean and evolving forms or forces with permeable boundaries – then we will gain a more informed insight into the nature of the globalization–national culture dynamic, especially with regard to how the former contributes to the development of the latter. For example, in a relatively brief time, Indian restaurants have been incorporated into mainstream British culture. Indeed, 'going for a curry' is now an accepted part of British cultural life. In this way, at an unofficial or popular level, 'alien' cultures are decontextualized and absorbed into a national culture, contributing to its development rather than threatening its existence, a process that is possible because British culture is not an immutable entity, a point that equally applies to other national cultures (Axford, 1995).

The above example is perhaps also an indication that political elites will find it harder to construct and control national cultures in a globalizing era, a change reinforced by the decline in deference, greater individualism, and more critical media. All of this will ensure that any attempt by a government to shape the national culture will be greeted with a mixture of suspicion, cynicism and derision, with the New Labour government's failed attempt to promote 'New Britain' (through Britpop etc.) in the late 1990s an obvious case in point. But this change does not mean that we no longer have any cultural guides. In fact, we have new cultural elites: they are the style gurus, the pop stars and famous footballers, the magazine editors and designers, who are, if not dictating, then certainly informing and shaping popular tastes, although, crucially, the influence they seek to exert is likely to be for a transnational rather than a national audience. Likewise, many cultural products are no longer geared to contributing to the national culture. While, in earlier periods of history, music, furniture and architecture would often be designed to project a national style or be geared to catering for national tastes (though orientalism is an obvious exception), this is now rarely the case. Nowadays, the producers of these particular cultural forms are likely to have less allegiance to the national, draw upon a greater range of cultural influences from throughout the world in the creative process, and will invariably seek the widest possible recognition for what they have produced. It is appropriate to enquire, at least in the area of artefacts, and possibly in other areas, where the reproduction of national culture is taking place? Does this mean that national cultures will simply become memory museums? Will they come to be viewed as inherently nostalgic rather than as contemporary and progressive cultural formations? If this is the case, then their relevance will indeed diminish, especially to future generations. Of course, we should not overstate this point. There will be other areas of national life that will continue to contribute to the national culture, such as sporting successes, the deaths of important national figures, and notable public events and ceremonies. Nevertheless, it would seem that there are some aspects of national culture that are not reproducing themselves.

In sum, if we conceive of culture as a process – something that is constantly developing – then we will gain a clearer understanding of the interrelationship between globalization and national culture, and be able to appreciate that cultures, including national cultures, are multilayered and have evolved and collected influences, symbols, ideas and images over time. It is in this sense that global cultural flows are contributing to national cultures. To cite an oft-quoted example, and to remain with the Indian theme, according to surveys of eating habits in the UK, the British national dish is now chicken tikka masala. The globalizing processes at work here are obvious, and do not need to be set out. More importantly, this development will not necessarily displace the existing national cuisine, merely add to it. In other words, chicken tikka masala will take its place alongside roast beef, Yorkshire pudding, and fish and chips as part of the national culture, which will in turn be all the richer for it.

Recommended reading

There are a number of very good books on this subject area. For an excellent introduction to the relationship between globalization and the nation-state, which gives due consideration to the cultural dimension, see Robert Holton's *Globalisation and the Nation-State* (1998). Jean-Marie Guéhenno is a writer especially noted for articulating the view that the nation-state will struggle under conditions of contemporary globalization – see, for example, *The End of the Nation-State* (1995) – while in a number of works Anthony Smith has presented an informed case for the continuing relevance of national cultures in a global era (see, in particular, *Nations and Nationalism in a Global Era* (1995)). For essential works on hybridity theory and associated debates, see Jan Nederveen Pieterse's *Globalization and Culture* (2004) and an edited work by Avtah Brah and Annie Coombes entitled *Hybridity and Its Discontents* (2000).

6

Globalization and Cultural Conflict

This chapter will consider claims that aspects of globalization are generating forms of cultural conflict. It will begin by examining the work of leading writers who have made this connection, notably Benjamin Barber, Samuel Huntington, and Matthew Horsman and Andrew Marshall. The second section explores the possible ways in which globalization and related sociocultural and economic processes are contributing to cultural conflict in the contemporary period, while the third section of the chapter will investigate the interrelationship between globalization, global terror and religious fundamentalism, focusing specifically upon the al-Qaeda phenomenon. In line with the general emphasis in this work upon cultural complexity and plurality, and culture as process rather than bounded entity, many of the linkages made between globalization and cultural conflict will be challenged.

Globalization and cultural conflict

Globalization: Jihad versus McWorld?

In *Jihad vs McWorld* (1996), Benjamin Barber outlines two conflicting futures for humankind: that of jihad and that of McWorld. 'Jihad' entails a retribalization of the world, in other words, a world dominated by a plethora of fundamentalisms and ethnic nationalisms that are the antithesis of human rights, democracy and open debate. He terms this the 'Lebanonisation of the world', a condition whereby within national states 'culture is pitted against culture, people against people, tribe against tribe' (Barber, 2000: 23), and ethnic nationalism is omnipresent: 'the forces I identify with Jihad are impetuously demanding to know whether there will ever be a Serbia again, a Flanders again . . . or Catalonia again' (1996: 164). Should we continue along this path, all forms of social cooperation and civic mutuality will be damaged. The other future, McWorld, is based upon global networks of consumer capitalism. It is a world driven by communications technologies, pop culture and commercialism, in which organizations such as CNN, Disney, Macintosh and the BBC are key players, and there is an emphasis upon fast food, fast cars, fast computers and, in fact, fast lives in general. We have seen in earlier chapters that the forms of cultural homogenization and convergence suggested by McWorld are a concern for other writers. For example, the increasing similarity of shopping malls to theme parks has been noted by some commentators, a development termed 'McDisneyfication', whereby Disney theme parks have vast shopping facilities and shopping malls seek to entertain their customers (see Ritzer and Liska, 1997). Likewise, our televisions are both the medium through which we are entertained and the means by which we can carry on shopping, evident in the growth of shopping channels. We are confronted with fast-food chains advertising before movies begin, but also with multiplex cinemas with fast-food outlets.

As a result of such widespread commodification, the world becomes simply one huge 'entertainment shopping experience', transforming human beings and their lifestyles in the process. Indeed, within the developed world shopping has become a form of personal expression, relaxation, and even the basis of vacations. As Ritzer and Liska note, 'more Canadian package tours now go to the West Edmonton Mall than to Niagara Falls' (1997: 103). For Barber, such behaviour is the antithesis of democracy in that our energies are devoted to individualist patterns of consumption rather than public-spirited or community activity and political participation. Barber therefore presents two incompatible visions of the world, one that would support the notion of cultural homogenization, and the other that runs directly counter to it: '[t]he planet is falling precipitantly apart *and* coming reluctantly together at the very same moment' (2000: 23). And he foresees an ongoing struggle between these two forces, forces that for him are doing so much to shape our globalizing era and harm democracy. Thus, jihad and McWorld exist alongside each other in a dialectical relationship, which throws up all kinds of anomalies and absurdities: the French government regularly protests against and seeks to protect itself from Americanization, yet funds and helps to set up EuroDisney on the outskirts of Paris, for example.

However, Barber's thesis is problematic on a number of grounds. He conceives of globalization as global consumer capitalism, McWorld, when in reality there are different forces contributing to its contemporary form, including a globalizing Islam that has little to do with consumer capitalism. In this vein, Barber similarly neglects the varieties of capitalism that exist, simply assuming that there is one dominant *consumerist* form. Nor does he question how deep rooted our need is to shop and to consume. While shopping is a meaningful experience and has become a way of life for some people, many are not satiated by it and need more in their lives, as is evident in the growth of interest in religions and spirituality in general. As for Barber's discussion of the Lebanonization of national states as a 'possible political future', it is inaccurate in the sense that these forces have arguably always existed, resurfacing from time to time, depending on the particular state. The Basques, the Catalans, the Flemish and the Walloons, and the Québécois, for example, have a long history of seeking autonomy from their respective nation-states. Such Lebanonization or ethnic nationalism is therefore a phenomenon in its own right, the existence of which does not require a dialectical relationship with the forces of McWorld.

Globalization and tribalism?

While Barber identifies contrary and conflicting trends, Matthew Horsman and Andrew Marshall in *After the Nation-State: Citizens, Tribalism and the New World Disorder* (1995) seek to connect them, maintaining that globalization is contributing to forms of tribalism. They argue that individuals are retreating into communities defined by 'similarities of religion, culture, ethnicity, or some other shared experience' for reassurance and protection as a result of the fear and confusion generated by contemporary processes, notably globalization (1995: x). For Horsman and Marshall, such tribalism is evident in the reinvigoration of ethnic, racial and national identities, in the forms of exclusion and discrimination operating against minorities and immigrant groups, in the vitality of many separatist or independence movements, and in the rise of religious fundamentalism. Globalization and related processes will be examined in the next section, but for now it should be noted that a criticism levelled against their association with cultural conflict is that these are essentially background explanatory factors, and focusing upon them tends to encourage analyses that remain at a general and abstract level. It also assumes that globalization and associated processes are working in a particular fashion when, as we have seen, they are likely to be working in numerous and often contradictory ways at any one moment. In reality, there will be multiple reasons for people resorting to tribalist patterns of behaviour, many of which will have little or nothing to do with globalization, but will be contingent upon particular contexts and local conditions. Furthermore, even if we keep our investigations at the level of general explanations, there are a number of recent developments contributing to this phenomenon, such as the end of the Cold War and the introduction of democracy to new regions, which again are largely unrelated to globalization. Of course, any plausible explanation of the prevalence of cultural conflict must take into account the underlying processes of the contemporary period, and, to repeat, these will be addressed in the second section of this chapter.

Globalization and civilizational conflict?

Samuel Huntington (1993, 1996, 1997) maintains that during the Cold War the primary sources of conflict were ideological (communism versus capitalism) and economic, whereas in the post-Cold War period, conflict will be cultural, with a 'clash of civilizations' and traditions dominating global politics. More specifically, he envisages that the future of the world will be shaped by the interaction of seven or eight major civilizations: Western, Japanese, Confucian, Islamic, Hindu, Slavic-Orthodox, Latin American and possibly African. The most important conflicts of the future will occur along the cultural fault-lines separating these civilizations from one another. For Huntington, there are numerous potential flash-points in Central Asia, the Caucasus, the Balkans, the Middle East and the Mediterranean, many of which centre on tensions between Islam and the West. He therefore rejects Francis Fukuyama's (1992) contention that with a universalizing liberal democratic capitalism we have reached the 'end of history'. Instead, for Huntington, we are heading towards an increasingly particularistic world of civilizations in which differences will be heightened, not eroded. Moreover, because in comparison with ideological divisions, civilizational differences have deep historical roots, and hence are more meaningful to us, the potential for future conflict will be high. Huntington believes this is borne out by the fact that many of the top items on the international agenda are inter-civilizational issues, such as human rights, democracy and immigration. While we can change our political ideologies, we cannot change who we are, namely our ethnic, cultural and religious backgrounds.

With regard to globalization, Huntington believes it is exacerbating the clash of civilizations because the increased cultural interaction resulting from contemporary globalizing processes makes us more aware of our differences. He argues that '[t]he forces of integration in the world are real and are precisely what are generating counterforces of cultural assertion and civilisational consciousness' (1997: 36). For example, one of the developments associated with globalization, namely increased patterns of migration, has led both to the construction of so-called 'Fortress Europe', through a range of measures designed to restrict entry into the EU, and to calls in the USA to limit the numbers of new immigrants. Huntington considers this reflects a desire in the West to maintain ways of life and Western civilization. Globalization therefore reinforces civilizational cleavages. As he puts it, 'wars occur most frequently between societies with high levels of interaction, and interaction frequently reinforces existing identities and produces resistance, reaction and confrontation' (Huntington, 1996: 63).

Huntington's critics argue that civilizations – if they exist at all – are not discrete, monolithic entities; rather, they are internally diverse and complex, and draw upon a range of cultures, traditions and influences. In particular, he is accused of underplaying the extent of intra-civilizational conflict because it does not fit well with his 'clash of civilizations' thesis. Quite simply, if there are divisions within civilizations it is less likely that there will be conflict between civilizations (Harries, 1994). Huntington has also been criticized for underestimating the continued relevance of the nation-state in global affairs: national governments will act first and foremost in the national interest, rather than for some wider conception of a civilizational interest (Weeks, 1996). In this vein, there is scant acknowledgement within Huntington's work that people possess multiple identities and will have a range of allegiances. In sum, Huntington's thesis homogenizes, when in fact there is heterogeneity.[1] Furthermore, for some critics, such an approach fails to acknowledge that the processes and developments that constitute contemporary globalization are actually introducing greater hybridity, diversity and complexity. Indeed, given that Huntington is seeking to map our global futures he devotes surprisingly little attention to understanding the nature of globalization, and this is the concern of the next section.

Globalization and contemporary sociocultural and economic processes

The recurring theme of this section is that globalization does not exist in isolation, rather it both contributes to and is reinforced by a number of contemporary socio-economic and sociocultural processes. This investigation will begin by examining the ways in which these processes are arguably contributing to greater insecurity, and how this in turn may be generating forms of cultural consolidation and conflict. This particular discussion will focus mainly upon Western societies, though what is described below is increasingly applicable to other societies.

Insecurity and cultural consolidation

If globalization entails or is constituted by more intensive forms of global interconnectedness, then inevitably it overlaps and becomes intertwined with other major processes and developments of our time, such as detraditionalization and post-industrialism. 'Detraditionalization' is the term that sociologists have employed to describe the increasing challenge that traditional practices, institutions and forms of authority (such as the church, marriage, the family, schools, governmental institutions, the nation-state, local communities, trade unions, stable patterns of work, etc.) are facing in our late modern era (Heelas et al., 1996). Aspects of globalization contribute to this tendency in a variety of ways, notably through the extension of market principles. The spread of global markets, market values and consumerism not only ensures more of us are afforded greater choice, but also entails national institutions, political parties, religions and religious figures competing in the marketplace for our attention against other cultural forms and consumer products, thereby stripping away some of their prestige, aura and authority. In addition, emerging global systems of information and communication are displacing existing social and national structures, encouraging reflexivity by enabling us to see beyond these limited horizons (Lash and Urry, 1994; Urry, 2003). As we saw in the previous chapter, the authority of the nation-state may well be being eroded by globalizing processes. In this vein, the growing economic power of international financial markets and MNCs might make it more difficult for national governments to manage their economies independently and hence to perform many of their post-war functions, especially in the area of social-welfare provision. National governance is similarly challenged by the linkage that exists between post-industrialism and globalization. More specifically, the global ICTs that facilitate both tendencies have allowed post-industrial businesses in the West to relocate and outsource to low-wage economies in the developing world, setting up call centres and the like, and thereby contributing to globalization but at the cost of jobs in the developed world, a trend that Western governments – and of course trade unions – have been unable to prevent. For some commentators, such developments are undermining the ability of the nation-state to perform its traditional role as protector of its citizens, which may in turn weaken their attachment to it, thereby further eroding its authority. The cumulative effect of all of these processes is, it is claimed, that we are entering a late modern age, a period of reflexive modernization, in which freer from the traditions, constraints and patterns of authority of the past, we are more able to forge our own life-paths (see Beck et al., 1994).[2] As will now be shown, such a trans-formation has implications for culture and patterns of cultural conflict.

The condition that has just been described introduces both greater freedom and greater insecurity into our lives. The forms of protection, social solidarities and guidelines of the past are increasingly absent, dictat-ing that we must become more entrepreneurial and self-reliant, reflected in the turn to self-employment, home- and part-time working, people taking out private pension and health schemes, and the emphasis upon pursuing our own lifestyles. Clearly, some people are flourishing under contem-porary conditions: they are relishing the greater freedom and taking advan-tage of the enhanced opportunities to travel and to enjoy new experiences. For others, however, with forms of collectivism and sources of identity in retreat – such as workplace colleagues, unions and local communities – social life is more fragmented and insecure. Numerous writers believe such processes are leading isolated individuals to engage in forms of cul-tural consolidation (e.g., Bauman, 1996b; Beck and Beck-Gernsheim, 1996; Melucci, 1989; Wieviorka, 1994). They are retreating into their particular cultural or national group and rediscovering old certainties and patterns of collective behaviour in the form of ethno-cultural identities for reasons of security and community, and to attain a sense of purpose and meaning. Therefore, from the perspective of those involved, ethno-cultural revival and assertiveness, and even forms of racist activity, permit a form of social rebuilding and an escape from isolated individualism (Wieviorka, 1994). Thus, the turning inwards for protection is invariably accompanied by a turning against those perceived as 'outsiders', while, in this contemporary phase of globalization, more intensive and extensive patterns of migration ensure that we come across a greater number of so-called 'outsiders', which is leading some people to conclude that their own cultures are threatened and they are unable to control what is happening in their societies. Within the context of growing insecurity, more frequent encounters with strangers will often lead to competition and tensions between different cultural groups. In short, under such conditions greater contact with those of other cultures may simply remind us of how different we are.

With regard to the nation-state and national governments, as a result of the various challenges they are facing, there is now a tendency for people to turn to their particular national or ethno-national culture as opposed to their nation-state culture. In the case of the UK, for example, this pattern is evident in the trend towards people identifying with their respective Scottish, Welsh or English culture, rather than British culture. This is similarly a retreat into the security of sameness because the nation-state, as a product of the Enlightenment and the French Revolution, was founded upon the principles of universal citizenship. In contrast, recent ethno-cultural nationalisms are based upon exclusion rather than inclusion and democracy. Indeed, often a consequence of defending one's culture against external challenges is that the nature of the culture changes. Thus, in defending a conception of, say, 'Englishness' or 'Frenchness', the degree of ethnic and cultural diversity that exists within a society is played down or marginalized in the process (Tomlinson, 1997a). As Manuel Castells (1997a) has noted, contemporary nationalisms are 'resistance identities' in the sense that adherents feel threatened by globalization and associated developments. It is a national reaction that is in essence defensive, but one which is 'always affirmed against the alien' (ibid., 27). There is, then, a degree of rethinking taking place in relation to the nation-state and specifically over what people consider to be *their* national community, reflected in the difficulty that some nation-states are having in containing ethno-nationalist demands for autonomy and separatism, and leading some writers to question the future viability of the nation-state in its present form (e.g., Horsman and Marshall, 1995). Within Europe, for example, there is a trend towards the formation of more ethnically and culturally homogenous states, evident in the breakup of the former Soviet Union and Yugoslavia, and in the division of Czechoslovakia in 1993 into separate Czech and Slovak states. And separatist or independence movements remain, or have become, a significant force in the domestic politics of countries such as Belgium, Canada, Spain and India. Within the UK, Scotland and Wales now enjoy greater autonomy as a result of devolution. Of course, the most obvious examples of weak states struggling to contain ethnic and cultural tensions are in Africa, which has experienced a succession of civil wars and other such disputes. As Zygmunt Bauman has put it: 'Exit the nation-state, enter the tribes' (1993: 141).

Sceptics would contest this account of the contemporary condition of the nation-state. Hirst and Thompson (1996, 2000) maintain that national governments retain the autonomy to pursue substantive national economic and political management and, as we saw in the Introduction, question whether we are witnessing full-scale globalization in our own era. From their perspective, the nation-state remains a considerable force and, if anything, its powers and functions, especially with regard to the provision of services, have steadily increased in the post-war period, with the widespread introduction of the welfare state and national education systems, in particular, ensuring it continues to play a significant role in the lives of its citizens (also see Dunn, 1995; Holton, 1998; Mann, 1997 in relation to this area). While some governments are now seeking to introduce an element of privatization into their welfare states, notably in relation to health and pensions, levels of public spending have not, in general, declined. Moreover, when national governments blame globalization for difficulties that their countries are facing, such as downturns in their economies, it is a way of deflecting attention from their own performance. However, while these are valid points, perhaps what ultimately counts are our perceptions of globalization. Thus, the nation-state may continue to be a vibrant and significant force in the contemporary period, but if there is a growing perception that it is struggling because of the processes and tendencies that constitute globalization, then people are likely to look elsewhere for forms of security and meaning. Overall therefore, if this analysis is correct, we are witnessing the diminution of our national (nation-state) identities and concomitantly the revival of our older and less inclusive national identities, merely highlighting the contradictory effects of globalization.

In sum, contemporary globalizing processes appear to be provoking particularistic and parochial responses, expressed as forms of cultural consolidation and exclusion. However, we should recognize that it is only some people who are acting in this way, hence the national and regional variations, and that such behaviour is not necessarily a permanent condition, as our cultural identities and allegiances are constantly being reformulated in the ongoing interaction between the global and the local. Human beings also possess multiple identities, all of which will inform our behaviour in different ways, meaning that we are not just defined or dominated by our tribal loyalties. Furthermore, to return to a point made in the previous section, forms of cultural consolidation and conflict will often be due to factors that have little or nothing to do with globalization, with local circumstances likely to be especially significant. For instance, the resurgence of ethnic nationalism in the Balkans since the early 1990s is a product of factors such as the history and cultural dynamics of the region, as well as the role of contemporary political leaders, rather than a reaction to globalization. Once again, we can see that, in order to determine any influence that globalizing processes are having, we need to examine the particular contexts in which the global and the local intersect, although, needless to say, contemporary globalization, in the form of more intensive forms of global interconnectedness, provides the overarching context in which these developments are played out.

Cultural flows and cultural tensions

The more intensive global cultural flows that define our era may also provoke concerns because they ensure that we are daily confronted with 'the other', reinforcing in some instances ethno-cultural identities and differences. As Stuart Hall (1996) has observed, identity is forged in the relationship between us and 'the other'. Under conditions of contemporary globalization, this encounter does not have to be interpersonal and may consist simply of the images, symbols, ideas and sounds that we are able to experience from around the world without ever having to travel. Evidence of the tensions that this may produce can be seen in the attempt by Islamic governments to regulate, and even ban in the case of Iran, the use of satellite television receivers. In most cases, such controls are implemented in order to restrict Western and/or American cultural influence, which is perceived as a homogenizing force, although with regard to the government in Tehran they are also motivated by a desire to retain political control, especially as foreign satellite stations operated by exiles in the USA are considered to have played a role in the student protests of 2003.

However, it is the increased movement of people across the globe that has stimulated the most widespread cultural and political dilemmas in the recent period, leading to debates about identity and belonging, as well as creating new forms of exclusion. As Eric Hobsbawm has put it: 'Wherever we live in an urbanized society, we encounter strangers: uprooted men and women who remind us of the fragility or the drying up of our own families' roots' (1992: 173). In particular, 'jet-age migration', which as we saw in the previous chapter has led to many societies becoming more multicultural, is generating issues of how to incorporate new peoples and cultures into existing national societies, notably igniting debates about assimilation versus multiculturalism, as can be seen in the following cases.

1 Cultural tensions in France

In France there has been a long-running dispute over the wearing of Islamic headscarves in schools, culminating in French MPs voting by a large majority in February 2004 to ban these and all other overt religious symbols from state schools. The legacy of the French Revolution entails the French state seeing its task as defending republicanism and secularism and consequently always seeking to avoid providing official recognition of any religion. This matter goes to the heart of the French conception of citizenship, which is founded upon individuals rather than groups, cultural or otherwise. In short, a French citizen owes his or her allegiance to the nation and enjoys rights and liberties upon that basis. However, the French state's opposition to multiculturalism is considered by some commentators to be hindering the integration of France's Muslims. It is also seen as a background factor to the riots that spread from poor Paris suburbs to other cities across France in late 2005, although of course there were a number of factors behind these disturbances, and other groups were involved.

2 Cultural tensions in the USA

Similarly, in the USA there are ongoing disputes over the content of educational curricula in schools, colleges and universities that have resulted in a number of demonstrations and disturbances on campuses (see Chavez, 1996; Williams, 1996). This issue has often become polarized between supporters of multiculturalism and those concerned to promote an overarching American identity and civic culture. The former emphasize the right of young people to learn about their own particular ethnic or cultural background, with some arguing that American culture is essentially dominated by white Europeans, while the latter consider that the pressure to become Americans and to 'Americanize' is reduced by the promotion of multiculturalism in public life, especially in schools and colleges (e.g., Brimelow, 1995). As well as the educational curricula controversy, these different perspectives are being played out in debates over bilingualism and affirmative action policies. All of this has led some commentators to question whether America's 'melting pot' is still working or is even an ideal that the country should be pursuing, and more profoundly to speculate upon what it now means to be 'American' (Lapham, 1992). Indicative of this unease has been the rise of identity politics in American society, which in turn has been blamed upon the failings of assimilation (Shain, 1995). Some critics consider identity politics has generated cultural enclaves, leading to a decline in toleration and multiplying the potential for social conflict to the point where everyday life in the USA is a constant, low-intensity cultural war (e.g., O'Sullivan, 1996).[3] Identity politics is also considered to have harmed the democratic process because it has led to particular groups voting as a block to further their own interests, rather than taking into account the wider community. An alternative reading of what has been taking place within American society is that multiculturalism and the growing importance of identity politics reflect both a deeply held need to express cultural difference and a disillusionment with the form that assimilation has traditionally taken, namely the promotion of Wasp (white Anglo-Saxon Protestant) cultural hegemony (see Smelser and Alexander, 1999). Indeed, Richard Merelman (1994) considers identity politics and the recent instances of cultural conflict in the USA to be symptomatic of the decline of white / European ideological hegemony in American society. For Merelman, this development paves the way for more competition between different groups and for greater resistance by minorities to the power of the dominant group.

Globalization, multiculturalism and hybridization

However, as well as contributing to the development of multicultural societies, the processes of globalization can serve to disrupt such societies because, as we have seen, increased global cultural flows in their various manifestations may engender cultural hybridization. There is an understandable temptation for multiculturalists and in particular representatives of minority groups to play down or simply ignore the degree of diversity that exists within cultures as their position is predicated upon the notion that cultures are homogenous and discrete entities. To take the wider view, by facilitating hybridization, globalizing processes have the potential to undermine the case of all those who insist upon cultural and civilizational distinctiveness, of whatever form, highlighting, reinforcing and extending the degree of heterogeneity that exists within cultures, as well as generating new hybrid cultures. Alongside the everyday sampling and often subconscious assimilation of other cultures in the form of images, ideas and sounds that all of us are engaged in, one obvious visual manifestation of increased hybridization is the rise in the number of interracial couples and children of mixed-race parentage, especially within Western societies. In the UK, 'mixed race' is now the third largest minority group, and is set to become the biggest over the next decade, while in the USA, reflecting the extent of the changes, censuses now permit multiple identifications and social commentators talk of the 'generation EA' or 'ethnically ambiguous' (Arlidge, 2004). Ethnic ambiguity is increasingly evident in advertising and marketing, as well as in the entertainment and fashion industries. Celebrities such as Christina Aguilera and Tiger Woods are considered by firms to be able to sell their products because they are ethnically ambiguous, and therefore are likely to have wide 'cross-over' appeal, especially amongst the youth market, which is itself becoming more ethnically and culturally diverse. This may simply be the latest cultural trend, but it also reflects demographic changes in America and elsewhere, and the growth in the number of 'hybrids'. The wider political significance of this development is, as Nikos Papastergiadis notes, that hybrids have traditionally been viewed 'as lubricants in the clashes of culture', and as 'the negotiators who would secure a future free of xenophobia' (2000: 176).

Thus, such ethnic and cultural diversity, and indeed complexity, may work against the exacerbation of cultural conflict, for which a necessary prerequisite is distinctiveness and difference. Hybridity therefore challenges essentialism by destabilizing existing cultures and cultural identities, enabling us to recognize their complex and intertwined histories, and the ways in which each tradition has borrowed from each other, as well as other influences (see Nederveen Pieterse, 2004). In turn, the perception of other cultures as a threat, and the concomitant need to defend our own cultures, is reduced when we are aware that they are all the products of multiple sources. Hence, recognition and acceptance of hybridity can help us to see beyond the boundaries of our particular culture or tribe, and to recognize what we have in common with others. Indeed, from the perspective of hybridity theorists, cultural boundaries, cultural categories and other forms of classification inhibit us from exploring our hybrid roots and, it follows, understanding ourselves.

Of course, cultural complexity may itself provoke the fundamentalists for obvious reasons. But the condition of 'accelerated hybridization', if we accept that Nederveen Pieterse's (2004) description of the contemporary period is accurate, does raise questions about the future appropriateness of taking a militant stance in defence of a particular culture or ethnic group. Continuing this theme, is it possible that our mixed cultural heritages and multiple allegiances will eventually lead us to become resentful of people campaigning on our behalf for mono-cultures and mono-ethnicities with which we only partially identify? Being classified as belonging to a particular cultural group brings with it expectations of loyalty and adherence to group norms and values, which can restrict our behaviour (Appiah, 1994; Kuper, 1999). Put simply, our culture can hide our true self (Taylor, 1994). Nor is this solely a concern for individualistic Westerners. For example, practices such as arranged marriages that have become associated with particular cultures will often be deeply opposed by members of those cultures. In a similar vein, there are countless examples of people who carry out actions in the name of a particular culture, but their conduct merely serves to alienate members of their own cultural community. In this regard, the vast majority of Muslims are appalled by the actions carried out by extremists within their ranks.

Global ICTs, cultural mobilization and extremism

As we saw in chapter 3, an integral part of contemporary global cultural flows are the flows of information and communication. But these too can be, and indeed are being, used by cultural fundamentalists and ethno-nationalists for their own ends, notably for reviving and consolidating their respective collective cultural identities. Thus, developments in electronic media and communications technology, which facilitate the work of informal or non-state networks and organizations, are also serving to contribute to ethnic and cultural mobilization. It is enabling ethnic communities and nationalist groups to disseminate their message, paving the way for the establishment of worldwide support networks, especially amongst emigrant and diaspora populations who are able to maintain contacts with their 'homeland' (Richmond, 1984; Schlesinger, 1991). A further example of what Benedict Anderson (1994) has described as 'long-distance nationalism' is evident in the case of Hindu nationalism in India, which has received significant support and funding from some Hindus living in the West, especially in the USA and Canada (see also Appadurai, 1996). These practices are an expression of cultural deterritorialization – the cultures of emigrant and diaspora populations are separate from the places they inhabit – but also evidence of cultural reterritorialization, whereby ethnic communities and nationalist groups are seeking to promote the importance of attachment to their respective territories amongst all members of their cultural group or community wherever they live in the world. Such a project is therefore an indication of the continued association of culture and territory. In other words, within contemporary globalization it remains possible to *imagine* our community from afar.

As is well known, the Internet, the World Wide Web and electronic mail have been used to propagate extremism and hate. Such resources have been employed in a variety of disturbing ways, ranging from individuals engaged in Holocaust denial to groups supporting suicide bombers and kidnapping hostages. In particular, the new technologies have made it easier for extremists to operate with considerable anonymity, enabling them to disseminate their material, and to an extent circumvent national laws. National governments have hitherto found it difficult to monitor, control and successfully prosecute those engaged in such activities. On a more political level, far-Right groups are increasingly using the Internet to spread their message. For example, an annual report by Germany's intelligence agency on extremist threats, published in April 2000, warned that far-Right German groups had set up some 300 websites in order to promote their views and recruit new members (BBC World Service, 4 April 2000). Taking a wider view, it is in the area of political extremism and cultural fundamentalism that it is especially evident in what way the cultural aspects of globalization are intertwined with its other dimensions, such as the economic, the social and the political. This is because those people belonging to such groups and undertaking the type of activity described here are very often from marginalized sections of society and have most to fear from contemporary globalizing conditions, notably their jobs being relocated to another part of the world, and having to compete with newcomers, many of whom will be more skilled than they are.

Global communication and information technologies, as well as the emergence of transnational media, would also appear to be generating international cultural battles over ideas, images and 'ways of life'.[4] Indeed, Malise Ruthven believes 'the clash of civilisations, when it comes, will take place in cyberspace, not between armies or territorial blocs' (1995: 6). For instance, contemporary media and communications contributed greatly to the rapid spread of the controversy surrounding the Danish cartoons of the Prophet Muhammad in 2006, turning within a few days a local Danish dispute into a major international issue. In this regard, an interesting comparison can be made between this dispute and the row over Salman Rushdie's novel *The Satanic Verses* during the late 1980s, which led to the late Iranian leader, Ayatollah Khomeini, issuing a death fatwa against its author. The Rushdie affair took much longer to have any global impact, taking months rather than days to become a major international episode. There were clearly other factors at work behind the divergent impact of these two issues, most notably that the Danish cartoons appeared post-9/11 and in the context of the US government's 'war on terror', meaning that cultural sensitivities on all sides remained high. Nevertheless, the speed at which knowledge of the Danish cartoons spread from country to country in late January and early February 2006, so that they became *the* issue of the day, is an indication of the power and reach of modern communications and media. Moving beyond particular cultural disputes, the contribution of these forces to the compression of social relations across time and space is arguably evident in the rise of radical Islam, which has involved Islamist activists making extensive use of the Internet and satellite broadcasting, as will now be shown.

Globalization, fundamentalism and global terror

Globalization does not cause global terrorism. To insist upon such a connection is to conceive of globalization as a living entity with motives and political purpose, when clearly it is none of these things. Here the aim is merely to assess the extent to which its processes and manifestations are contributing to the increase in global terror, focusing specifically upon the al-Qaeda phenomenon. One of the major difficulties in writing about al-Qaeda, which emerged in 1991 and refers to a global database of supporters and operatives, is that in a certain sense it does not actually exist (Burke, 2003). Indeed, al-Qaeda is an ideology or world-view as much as it is an organization, and it has effectively become a cover name for disparate terrorist groups. In short, al-Qaeda resists neat definitions and categorization.

This is succinctly encapsulated by Jason Burke, who argues that Osama bin Laden and al-Qaeda 'are Millenarian, fundamentalist, reformist, revivalist, Wahhabi / Salafi and, at least in their rootedness in modernity if not their programme, Islamist' (2003: 39).[5] Al-Qaeda is also symptomatic of the struggle going on within the Islamic community over the future direction of Islam, with commentators increasingly referring to multiple Islams and even Islamisms.[6] Given the extent of this diversity, the subsequent discussion of al-Qaeda and Islam is inevitably conducted in broad terms.

Many Muslims, and not just the radicals and militants, associate globalization with Western or more specifically American economic penetration, which in turn is cited as a primary cause of the poor economic condition of many of their societies. From this perspective, globalization has allowed the USA and its allies to exert their economic power in the Middle East and elsewhere in the Islamic world, further enhancing it as a consequence (Falk, 1999).[7] Similarly, the cultural dimension to globalization is considered by many Muslims to threaten their own religious culture. From their perspective, it entails their societies being bombarded daily with images of Western lifestyles via television, films and advertisements, making it more difficult to preserve their own cultural distinctiveness and identity (see Mohammad, 2001). In short, there is a concern that globalization has meant the spread of consumerism and materialism, but also secularism and individualism, all of which are viewed as undermining the Islamic way of life and values. Ayatollah Khomeini warned of a 'black and dreadful future' for Islam and the Muslim people, a statement that was widely interpreted as a reference to the global domination of America's economic power and culture. And globalization itself has been viewed as one of al-Qaeda's targets (Talbott and Chanda, 2001). Hence, it was no coincidence that the 9 / 11 attacks were directed at the key centres of US power, and in targeting the World Trade Center, al-Qaeda struck at one of the symbols of globalization.

The rapid spread of ICTs especially the Internet is making it extremely difficult, if not impossible, for Islamic regimes to control the flow of information into their countries. In 2007, it was estimated that Iran had over 5 million Internet users, but Tehran is equally concerned about the prospects of counter-revolutionary activity carried out by Iranians living outside the country and over whom they have virtually no control. Indeed, there has been a dramatic rise in Persian-language blogging, with an estimated 46,000 bloggers inside Iran, and over 75,000 active Persian-language blogs worldwide in 2005 (Boyd, 2005). It means that Islamic governments can do little more than fight a rearguard action, as their citizens are presented with contrasting accounts of political reality. This was evident in the Iranian government's attempt at the end of 2006 to restrict online speeds in order to reduce the West's cultural influence in the country by making it more difficult for Iranians to download foreign music, films and television programmes (Tait, 2006). Moreover, global media organizations and technology ensure that Muslims are more aware of their generally poorer standards of living in comparison with people in the West, which is leading increasing numbers of them to migrate to Western societies. There are now around 6 million Muslims living in the USA, and in Europe the figure is roughly 16 million. However, Muslim leaders are concerned that those Muslims living in the West are attending mosques less frequently, and modifying Islamic teachings and prescriptions to suit their new environment and lifestyles, while the view of the fundamentalists is that Muslim communities in Western societies are living in *jahiliyyah*, the condition of ignorance and unbelief. Of course, globalization also means that the influence of *jahiliyyah* is spreading to Islamic societies, hence the need, from their perspective, for jihad. In this vein, the institutions of global governance – such as the UN, the World Bank and the IMF – are considered to be Western-dominated and a means by which the West can impose its values and practices upon Islamic societies, notably in the area of human rights and democracy.

Islamic globalization

However, globalization should not be thought of as alien to Islam. Islam is a global religion, and Muslims are part of a truly global community (the *ummah*). Furthermore, Islam has a history of empires and sultanates that only came to an end with the collapse of the Ottoman Empire, and many radical Islamists, including al-Qaeda and its associates, desire the return of the caliphate and the continued global spread of Islam. There is therefore a history of cultural deterritorialization and reterritorialization within Islam. Also, there is a sense in which aspects of globalization serve a useful purpose for Islam. The multiple forms of global interconnectedness, such as travel and modern communications and media, bring Muslims closer together and reinforce their collective identity, and almost certainly have contributed to the 're-Islamization' of Islam during the last three decades. In general, amongst Muslims there is a high level of awareness of the suffering of fellow Muslims in different parts of the world and inevitably the views of some within the *ummah* are shaped by this knowledge. This has echoes of Roland Robertson's conception of globalization as constituting the compression of the world, whereby events in one part of the world will have consequences for or be referenced against events in other distant parts. The creation of international Muslim and Arab newspapers and media, such as the television station al-Jazeera, has played an important role in this respect. While some of these sources have been accused of presenting partisan accounts and fermenting radicalism, it does mean that Muslims no longer have to rely upon Western news organizations such as CNN and the BBC for information. Media images of atrocities committed against Muslims, whether in Chechnya, Palestine, Iraq, Bosnia, Kashmir or elsewhere, foster a sense of solidarity and in some individuals a desire for revenge. All of this is extremely useful to extremist groups such as al-Qaeda. Indeed, radical Islamists use such film footage, which is circulated around the world in the form of videos and DVDs, as well as via Internet websites, for the purposes of recruiting new members to the global jihad.

Al-Qaeda and globalization

Al-Qaeda is noted for embracing many aspects of globalization. Most notably, as a global network it is heavily reliant upon many aspects of modern global communication. John Gray (2003) believes that in its organizational form, use of communications technologies and media awareness, al-Qaeda is very much a modern phenomenon. In particular, it utilizes the products of global modernity, such as the Internet, laptop computers, satellite phones and, of course, planes. Internet websites have been used by a number of Islamist groups for recruitment and organizational purposes, but al-Qaeda employs encrypted websites. As for media awareness, from the perspective of the al-Qaeda leadership, the attraction of committing atrocities such as 9/11 is that spectacular images in an era of global communication rapidly ensure a global audience. Indeed, the transnational media have aided al-Qaeda's cause, albeit unintentionally, by allowing video and audio messages from Osama bin Laden and other members of the al-Qaeda leadership to be relayed across the world. Alarmingly, there have been claims that the al-Qaeda network is exploring the possibilities of using global communication and information technologies to engage in cyberterrorism against the so-called 'network society'. Moreover, al-Qaeda and related organizations have themselves established elaborate global financial networks for raising and moving funds, generating money from a variety of sources, such as wealthy benefactors, and using Islamic foundations and charitable organizations as well as banks and companies to act as 'fronts' to finance their operations. As a result of the complex and fluid nature of international financial markets, and the sheer volume of financial transactions, national governments are having considerable difficulty in tracking down the financing of international terrorism. For John Gray, al-Qaeda is a 'by-product of globalization' (2003: 1).

In sum, the different developments that constitute globalization have enabled al-Qaeda to organize and sustain itself. However, if we really want to gain an insight into how globalization may have been contributing to the global terrorism pursued by al-Qaeda, it is necessary to understand the history of relations between Islam and the West. In this regard, globalization is perceived by many Muslims as simply the latest phase in a long history of Western attacks upon Islam, which for some dates back to the Crusades. In more recent times these attacks have been evident in the spread of European colonial rule throughout the Middle East during the first half of the twentieth century, the incorporation of the Islamic world into the Cold War, the support of Western governments for authoritarian regimes in the Middle East and Central Asia, and the West's involvement in the Muslim Holy Lands because of its need for oil. There is, therefore, a general sense within the Islamic world of being under siege from the West and of operating from a position of weakness (see Fuller and Lesser, 1995). It follows that the rise of Islamist and jihadist movements is in part a defensive response to these developments, reflecting a desire to hold on to the Islamic way of life (Halliday, 1996). Thus, it is when globalization is viewed or can be portrayed as a continuation of Western exploitation and injustice that groups like al-Qaeda benefit. Yet this connection between al-Qaeda and globalization needs to be balanced by a consideration, which unfortunately due to lack of space is not possible here, of the more recent internal problems afflicting Islamic societies, such as those of stagnant economies, authoritarian states, political corruption and burgeoning populations, as well as of the theological debates and political divisions that have been taking place within the Islamic community, all of which has facilitated the rise of al-Qaeda. Hence, to repeat, globalization must be viewed as a contributory rather than a causal factor in the rise of global terror.

Lastly, it is possible that al-Qaeda's campaign of global terror will influence the future course of globalization, making people more wary about travelling and moving to certain regions of the world as well as having a detrimental impact upon international trade and investment. For example, the US authorities have introduced stricter controls on the movement of people and capital into and out of America following the attacks of 9/11. This is not to suggest that globalizing processes will be halted or reversed by global terrorism, merely that their form will be affected by it.

And this issue relates to a wider academic debate about whether globalization will be held back by cultural divisions. Roland Robertson (1992) believes globalization provides the context in which civilizations assert themselves, and in effect discusses globalization as if it has already arrived. In contrast, the civilizational analyst Vytautas Kavolis (1988) emphasizes the continuing vitality of civilizations, as well as their distinctiveness and incommensurability, and hence is critical of globalization theory. Robertson for his part, while accepting the particularities of individual religions, emphasizes their relativization. In other words, globalization throws the different religious civilizations together and forces them to take account of each other, which helps to explain the current high level of civilizational and ethnic self-consciousness. This reinforces an important theme for Robertson that we visited in chapter 4, namely that 'globalisation involves the universalisation of particularism, not just the particularisation of universalism' (1992: 130).

Cultural conflict or cultural complexity?

The writers examined during the course of this chapter have, in their various ways, made connections between globalization and forms of cultural conflict. However, a common problem with their accounts is that globalization is largely treated uncritically, evident in the lack of reference to the relevant debates surrounding the subject. More importantly, there is little sense that globalization is a complex, incomplete and uneven process or set of processes, which will therefore impact upon different cultures and societies in a variety of ways. Consequently, the equating of accelerating global interconnectedness with cultural conflict is problematic, to say the least. Indeed, given the particular ways in which its multiple processes will be experienced and interpreted by different social groups and societies, each with their own cultures and histories, it is more likely that globalization will usher in greater heterogeneity and complexity rather than simply provoke conflict. Above all, globalization does not *cause* cultural conflict. While this may be one of the effects of its multiple processes, such an outcome will ultimately be determined by the nature of global–local dynamics within particular contexts. This is evident, for example, in the differing reactions of countries to becoming more multicultural as a result of a particular globalizing tendency, namely increased travel and migration. Thus, while the French state has rejected multiculturalism for historical reasons, an approach which may at least in part account for the major disturbances involving some of its ethnic and cultural minority communities in the recent period, in the UK, where multiculturalism has been a policy pursued by successive governments since the 1960s, there have been less overt cultural tensions during this time. Moreover, a BBC poll conducted in August 2005 revealed that 62 per cent of the 1,000 people questioned felt that 'multiculturalism made Britain a better place to live' (BBC, 2005). Nevertheless, another European country, Holland, arguably provides an example of the way in which globalizing processes such as migration are changing societies. Holland is historically a liberal country and noted for welcoming immigrants, but lately concern has been expressed within its society about the level of immigration – at the beginning of the twenty-first century more than 10 per cent of Holland's population of 16.3 million were 'non-Western' immigrants – and the perceived lack of integration into Dutch society of some Muslims, generating calls for much tighter immigration controls from some quarters. However, any influence that globalizing processes are having in eroding Holland's famed tolerance must be weighed against other factors, such as the murder of the Dutch film-maker Theo van Gogh in 2004 by an Islamic extremist, which created widespread concern about the state of the nation.

The interpretations of Barber et al. are therefore an overly bleak portrayal of global affairs. In this regard, one aspect of the more intensive forms of global interconnectedness that constitute contemporary globalization has been the further development of the institutions of global governance with some geared to promoting intercultural communication and dialogue. UNESCO, in particular, devotes considerable attention to this end, organizing international conferences, festivals, educational exchange visits, and encouraging the reform of school and university curricula along these lines. In a similar vein, a conflict-resolution industry has been evolving over a number of years, with organizations like the UN mediating between parties in disputes, as well as providing forums for expressing grievances. Furthermore, as we will see in chapter 7, there is a view that such institutions, along with the continued growth in the number and size of international non-governmental organizations (INGOs), may contribute to the formation of a global civil society that would offer an alternative to jihad versus McWorld.[8] Barber et al. are likely to respond that they are primarily concerned to identify broad trends and tendencies in the contemporary period, rather than addressing what is taking place within specific contexts. However, the consequence of their approach is that they tend to identify globalization as encouraging developments that go in only one or two directions when in reality, as we have seen, globalizing processes are capable of producing diverse responses contingent upon particular conditions or contexts and the nature of the interaction between the global and the local (Holton, 1998). In sum, while Barber et al. focus upon cultural conflict in relation to globalization, in reality, greater cultural complexity is more likely to be its defining feature, especially if we do not conceive of culture as immutable, and accept Robertson's claims about the interpenetration of the global and the local. Lastly, the common theme of writers that associate globalization with cultural conflict is that they see the global and the local existing in a dialectical relationship and as such have a particular perception of what globalization entails, and how it is operating. But, as the next chapter will indicate, some of the processes and manifestations that constitute globalization, as well as the reflexivity that lies at the heart of the interaction between the global and the local, can potentially lead to cosmopolitan outcomes.

Recommended reading

For works on globalization and the resurgence of ethnic nationalism, see Barber (1996) and Horsman and Marshall (1995). Samuel Huntington is the key writer in relation to civilizational conflict, developing his thesis in a number of articles and interviews, but the most obvious entry point into his work is his much-discussed book entitled *The Clash of Civilizations and the Remaking of World Order* (1997). Major works on reflexive modernization, reflexivity, and detraditionalization are by Beck et al. (1994), Lash and Urry (1994) and Heelas et al. (eds) (1996), respectively. For an assessment of potential societal implications of extremists using the Internet, see Susan Zickmund, 'Approaching the Radical Other: The Discursive Culture of Cyberhate' (1997), while in *Al-Qaeda: Casting a Shadow of Terror* (2003) Jason Burke presents an informative account of the cultural, theological and political background of al-Qaeda.

7

Globalization and Cosmopolitanism

In this final chapter, the relationship between globalization and cosmopolitanism is explored. It differs from previous chapters in the sense that the subject matter is addressed in a more speculative manner, with an attempt being made to think through the possible implications of more intensive forms of global interconnectedness in the contemporary period. The chapter begins by setting out some of the debates surrounding cosmopolitanism, as well as the approach that will be pursued here. It then proceeds to outline the ways in which some of the processes and manifestations that constitute contemporary globalization could potentially engender cosmopolitan attitudes and lifestyles. This includes evaluating the possible long-term effects upon individuals and societies of greater access to other cultures and traditions, through travel, migration and global communications and information technologies. It also will entail returning to some of the themes of this work, notably the emphasis upon the complex, plural and contested nature of cultural globalization. In this regard, the case made here in relation to cosmopolitanism needs to be counterbalanced by claims examined earlier in this work, such as the argument that globalizing processes are contributing to cultural conflict.

Before beginning this investigation, it is necessary to define the word cosmopolitan, which will be understood here as: '**1a** of or from or knowing many parts of the world. **b** consisting of people from many or all parts. **2** free from national limitations and prejudices' (*Concise Oxford Dictionary*, 8th edition, 1991: 260). As for how we become cosmopolitan, this matter is more complicated and will be addressed during the course of this chapter.

Approaching cosmopolitanism

Debates about cosmopolitanism date back to the ancient Greek Stoics. But in the recent period there has been a revival of interest in the subject that has generated a considerable literature covering a range of different areas. For example, cosmopolitanism is being discussed in relation to particular regions, such as Europe (Amin, 2001) and the Middle East (Zubaida, 2002), as well as cities (Sennett, 2002) and local neighbourhoods (Hiebert, 2002). Much of this work, although by no means all of it, has been shaped by the approaches of the political sciences, with the emphasis upon the development of ethical frameworks (Dower, 1998), world citizenship (Heater, 2003) and the institutions of global governance (Held, 2004). But this chapter, in line with the overall themes of this work, concentrates upon the sociological and cultural dimensions of cosmopolitanism, for which there is also an expanding literature (see Beck, 2000, 2002; Breckenridge et al., 2002; Tomlinson, 1999a; Urry, 2003).[1] By adopting this approach it will address the matter of what it means to be a 'cosmopolitan' in our globalizing era. The focus will therefore be upon citizens and individuals and the formation of cultural identities, rather than institutions, structures and legal and ethical frameworks. Indeed, a criticism of the emphasis upon the institutional framework or architecture of global governance is the underlying assumption that the peoples of the world will behave in a cosmopolitan manner, will take advantage of such structures and processes, and generally want to become world citizens.

However, the approach to cosmopolitanism pursued here is also likely to be challenged. For example, Martha Nussbaum (1996) views cosmopolitanism as a worldwide community consisting of all peoples, and for this reason champions the idea of a world citizenship. Yet the prospects for the establishment of world citizenship, a world state, and even properly functioning modes of global governance are remote at this stage, and hence any discussion of them must remain rather abstract. A further justification for adopting a sociological and cultural approach to cosmopolitanism is that, quite simply, cosmopolitanism is a multidimensional concept requiring a range of different types of analyses in order to comprehend it. In particular, in relation to globalization, cosmopolitanism ceases to remain an abstract notion, confined simply to academic debate. It becomes a lived experience for increasing numbers of people, and consequently more diverse and plural in nature. For this reason, some writers now discuss 'cosmopolitanisms' rather than cosmopolitanism (see Breckenridge et al., 2002; Clifford, 1992), a point returned to in the conclusion to this chapter.

Having outlined the approach to cosmopolitanism that will be taken here, in the next section we will look at ways in which some of the processes and developments that constitute globalization could potentially foster cosmopolitanism. Before doing so, it should be noted that such a linkage is likely to be challenged, especially by economists and those on the political Left, for whom globalization is inextricably linked to capitalism and the extension of capitalist markets. For instance, Peter Gowan, who does at least employ the term 'cosmopolitanism' in relation to globalization, nevertheless writes of a 'neoliberal cosmopolitanism', arguing there are powerful economic forces driving contemporary globalization and seeking to construct a global order that penetrates 'deep into the economic, social and political life of the states subject to it, while safeguarding international flows of finance and trade' (2001: 80). Such views are a useful reminder that there is a power dimension to globalization, but again this highlights how different academic disciplines have particular conceptions of this subject and often neglect its multidimensional nature.

Globalization and cosmopolitanism

Cultural connectivity and cosmopolitanism

There are aspects of globalization that foster or facilitate intercultural contact, and this could potentially engender cosmopolitan outlooks because it raises the possibility that understanding and even empathy might develop from greater familiarity with different cultures, societies and traditions. For example, as we have seen, contemporary population movements are ensuring that a number of societies are becoming progressively multicultural and multi-ethnic, and many people living within those societies are taking advantage of the chance to experience different cultures, ranging from trying new cuisines to religious faiths.[2] Others are engaging in forms of cultural hybridization, fusing or blending different cultures together, especially in the areas of music, dance, fashion and theatre, while the trend towards economic internationalization or globalization, depending upon whether one believes the perspective of sceptics or hyperglobalizers, is an indication that trade and business will be increasingly carried out beyond national borders, a development facilitated by global transportation systems. Such connectivity has in turn led to the rise of the 'border negotiators', the specialists able to deal with transborder disputes and problems of intercultural communication, such as international lawyers, diplomats, cultural specialists and other professionals, who are provoking discussion about whether their emergence is leading to the formation of transnational or 'third cultures' (Featherstone, 1990; Gessner and Schade, 1990). In a variety of ways, therefore, it is becoming more possible for growing numbers of people to behave as cosmopolitans. Furthermore, global communications and information technologies, the modem and the mobile phone in particular, are facilitating the stretching of social life across time and space, and this again means that intercultural contact is likely to be happening more often and more quickly in the contemporary period. All of this provides us with opportunities to think beyond our particular environments and societies, which in turn may foster new allegiances and challenge established loyalties. This does not mean that national mentalities and identities will disappear, yet it is widely believed that multiple identities, allegiances and citizenships will increasingly define our global age, leading to the blurring or overlapping of identities (Soysal, 1994). This trend is reflected in the formation of new identities, including hyphenated identities, such as 'Italian-American', 'British-Asian' and 'Polish-European'.

However, people will not necessarily become more cosmopolitan simply because they have more 'cosmopolitan opportunities'. In this regard, James Hunter and Joshua Yates (2002) identify what they term 'parochial cosmopolitans': people, especially business people, who travel widely but for the most part remain within the 'protective bubble' of their own culture, which prevents them from properly experiencing indigenous cultures. This type of cosmopolitanism, if indeed this is the appropriate term, is therefore of the shallow variety. Being on the move, as Ulf Hannerz has noted, 'is not enough to turn one into a cosmopolitan' (1990: 241). In this vein, much of the tourist industry is geared to ensuring clients enjoy relaxing and safe holidays, which entails confining them to artificial enclaves and in so doing limits meaningful encounters with 'the locals'. It is also the case, as we have seen, that the cosmopolitan opportunities facilitated by globalizing processes may serve to reinvigorate national cultures and identities, especially because of perceived threats to national traditions and ways of life. However, as will be shown in the remainder of this section, there are reasons to believe that national and parochial reactions will not necessarily be the dominant response to globalization. But before looking at this, a social phenomenon that has an uneven and uneasy relationship with cosmopolitanism will be explored, namely, the globalizing city.

Globalizing cities and cosmopolitanism

The emergence of globalizing cities, such as London, New York and Tokyo – and it has been claimed that there are a couple of dozen such cities in total (see Knox, 2002) – has implications for cosmopolitanism.[3] Their rise can be traced to, among other things, global migration, electronic communications and their role as the financial command centres of the world economy, all of which has contributed to their growth and enhanced their power, and in some instances led to a degree of detachment from the countries in which they are located. Indeed, globalizing cities offer to their inhabitants alternatives to the nation-state both in terms of sources of authority and identity. More broadly, they are an important element of the trend towards multi-level governance, which is itself a reflection of the erosion of national sovereignty (Delanty, 2000). Globalizing cities are perhaps also more in tune with contemporary developments than nation-states because they are arguably more tied into the flows and mobilities of globalization – although Brenner (1998) suggests the latter promotes the former in order to attract capital investment. For our purposes, globalizing cities are the places where many of the world's peoples will gather, as well as the points where the majority of the global cultural, communication and information flows both emanate from and descend upon, and as such are prime sites of cultural interaction and exchange. Indeed, one of the defining features of cities such as New York, London, Paris and Río de Janeiro is their cosmopolitan mixture of cultures and traditions. Moreover, globalizing cities are linked with other cities across the world via information and communications technologies and hence contribute to the formation of global networks (see Sassen, 2002). In fact, globalizing cities are frequently the pivotal or nodal points of cross-border networks – for Castells (1996) they are part of the second layer of the space of flows that he considers to be constituted by nodes and hubs – and consequently are playing a crucial role in encouraging forms of global connectivity, and not just in the economic realm.

However, this notion of globalizing cities as cosmopolitan places is likely to be disputed. While such cities are frequently the end points of complex, uneven and dynamic migratory flows – they are invariably the places that most migrants head towards on arriving in a country – this is not necessarily paving the way for cosmopolitan encounters between migrants and residents. Such interaction is precluded by the phenomenon of 'white flight', as the predominantly white upper and middle classes continue to move out of inner cities, especially in the USA and the UK. Likewise, many migrants will at least initially be doing menial and low-paid jobs and usually living in rundown areas, ensuring that they are effectively separated from much of the rest of the city and its inhabitants. In short, people are moving but not always connecting. Taking a different stance, Saskia Sassen (2000, 2001) believes global cities have emerged for economic reasons: they have become transnational centres of financial and service activity. She argues that, even in a world of decentralized economic activity, they are the places where economic and financial power are located. Globalizing cities, in other words, are a product of capitalism, not cosmopolitanism. In a similar vein, John Urry (1995) writes of cities of consumption displacing industrial cities. And, as is well known, extreme income inequalities can be found in many globalizing cities along with considerable economic and social deprivation, a condition exacerbated by the casualization of labour markets in the recent period. Even within Western societies, the standards of living in some urban neighbourhoods are on a par with certain countries in the developing world. Globalizing cities are therefore often places of social and cultural tension, as is evident in the formation of cultural and ethnic enclaves or ghettoes, and again these conditions serve to inhibit the spread of cosmopolitanism. Such divisions are reflected in the greater emphasis that is now placed upon surveillance within urban planning, notably in the form of 'gated' or 'fortress' communities. Interestingly, within urban centres these enclosed communities will often be the most globally connected, something that is made possible by contemporary communication and information technologies, and embodied in the so-called 'electronic cottage' phenomenon, which in some European and North American cities is taking the form of media enclaves or cyberdistricts. Manuel Castells (1993) believes 'the informational city', as he terms it, results in the primary urban dualism of our time, namely the division between a connected cosmopolitan elite and unconnected locals; the former is shaping city life, while the latter are largely excluded from such developments.

It is also the case that the most populous figure in any city, the stranger – cities are full of strangers – generally contributes little to cosmopolitanism. At any moment, a city is occupied by many people who are simply passing through, such as the tourist, the vagrant and the commuter, and consequently have little real sense of attachment to it and the people living there. Indeed, Zygmunt Bauman (1993, 1996b) goes further, arguing that the tourist and vagabond or vagrant are harmful to morality because they have no need to intervene in the moral debates of the places they visit or any moral responsibility towards the local population. From the perspective of indigenous inhabitants, as these travellers or tourists have no commitment to their society, borne out by the fact that they choose not to remain, there is little reason or opportunity to have a cosmopolitan encounter with them. Moreover, under contemporary globalization, the flows of people passing through our cities are generally more intensive, populations are more transitory, and the pace of life more rapid, all of which may be harmful to urban communities and the building of an environment conducive to intercultural encounters. In the end, however, the complexity of city life, the diverse global processes by which cities are being informed, and the myriad of groups and peoples involved in mediating these processes means it is difficult to reach any firm conclusions concerning the interrelationship between globalizing cities and cosmopolitanism. In this regard, Graham and Marvin in *Splintering Urbanism* (2001) present abundant evidence of urban fragmentation and secession, but nevertheless acknowledge towards the end of their book that forms of public mixing continue to be a part of city life. The varied accounts of everyday life in just one global city, London, which can be found in the volume edited by John Eade entitled *Living the Global City* (1997), again highlight the need to examine specific contexts when trying to determine how globalization flows and processes are operating, and more specifically being contributed to and participated in at these global/local intersections.

Popular cosmopolitanism

An additional reason why cosmopolitanism may not spread to all sections of society is that traditionally it has been the preserve of wealthy elites, and some writers consider this still to be the case. Today, broadly speaking, a distinction is often made between a middle-class cosmopolitan elite, made up of professionals, international business and media people, transnational politicians, managers and diplomats, who are defined by their mobility and participation in global networks, and a less mobile or even localized and territorially bound working class, whose outlook is at most transnational (e.g., Bauman, 1998a). In this vein, Jonathan Friedman (1999) identifies the emergence of another type of cosmopolitan elite, one that is constituted by intellectuals from cultural studies departments (hybridity theorists, postcolonial writers, and the like), who are, in his opinion, detached from the concerns of ordinary citizens.

Yet despite such views, there are aspects of contemporary globalization that may contribute to, or be seen as evidence of, the wider dissemination of cosmopolitanism. To begin with, some of the poorest groups within all societies are immigrant and diaspora communities, but many members will be bilingual or multilingual, possess hyphenated identities, and have a range of allegiances and loyalties beyond identification with their 'host' country (Appadurai, 1996; Cheah and Robbins, 1998). Many of them are therefore in a very real sense exposed to other cultures and influences and live in a cosmopolitan manner. Pnina Werbner (1999) makes such a point in relation to her study of Pakistani migrants, detecting a genuine and varied engagement with the different cultures and societies they are inhabiting, beyond the learning of languages, whether this is in North America, Europe or elsewhere, leading her to describe them as 'working class cosmopolitans' whose actions are carving-out 'global pathways'. Second, some of the developments and technologies facilitating contemporary globalization can similarly be seen as contributing to the popular spread of cosmopolitanism. For example, the global expansion of the airline industry and further development of jet airliners are leading to cheaper foreign travel and enabling more and more people from all sections of society to move around the world and experience other cultures – though we should not forget that Hannerz et al. are sceptical of the linkage between travel and cosmopolitanism. Such behaviour is underpinned by the individualization and consumption ethos of the contemporary period (chapter 5), which leads us to believe that we have the right to consume other cultures and places throughout the world (see Urry, 1995). Third, to repeat, it is possible to have a range of cosmopolitan encounters and experiences within the major towns and cities of our increasingly multicultural societies, including in our neighbourhoods, workplaces, schools and universities, where cultural communities overlap and intersect with each other (Hiebert, 2002). In our own homes, radio, television and the global music industry afford us access to new influences, in the form of current affairs and travel programmes and 'world music', for example. It is all part of what has been termed 'everyday cosmopolitanism' (Vertovec and Cohen, 2002). And it means that it is no longer necessary to travel to different countries in order to become involved with more than one culture, and hence to act in a cosmopolitan manner. All of this serves to blur the distinction that is often made between 'cosmopolitans' and 'locals', and would seem to raise doubts about Hannerz's contention 'that there can be no cosmopolitans without locals' (1990: 250).

Globalization, education and cosmopolitanism

A further reason for anticipating the spread of cosmopolitanism – and one that highlights the need to examine the political, economic and other sides to globalization in order to understand better its cultural dimension – stems from the way in which many national governments are adapting to globalization. More specifically, there is an emerging consensus among governments throughout the world concerning the necessity of providing well-funded education systems that lead to the highest standards, a development that has cosmopolitan implications. Education is increasingly regarded as a necessary prerequisite both for individuals to participate in our global age by providing them with the necessary skills and competencies, but also to enable countries to compete economically. In essence, if countries are to survive and prosper in a globalizing economy their respective citizens must be able to play a full part in what are increasingly knowledge-based economies. Tony Blair, the former British prime minister, was quite explicit about this point during his period in office, declaring: 'the increasing globalisation of the world economy means that the required levels of education and skills are now being set by international standards' (Blair, 1996: 78–9). But it is not just social democratic parties like New Labour in the UK that are thinking in this way; such attitudes towards education can be found across the political spectrum in countries throughout the world, and have even led to discussion about whether, encouraged by globalization, we are witnessing forms of political convergence between Left and Right (see Kelly, 1999; Sassoon, 1998).

The consensus over the importance of education to citizens and societies is reflected in the international expansion of higher education in countries across the globe, with one recent survey suggesting there will be more than 2 billion graduates in the world by 2025 (Norton-Taylor, 2001). What is relevant for this discussion is that education, especially higher education, has the potential to engender more critical, liberal and enlightened attitudes – a prerequisite of a cosmopolitan disposition – amongst its recipients. In general, the more educated the citizens, the more likely they are to question the claims of nationalists and national leaders, to challenge racial and cultural stereotypes, and to resist the essentializing of other peoples. They are also more likely to be aware of the constructed nature of many national traditions, including within their respective countries. No longer so constrained by a sense of national loyalty, these people are able to develop a broader perspective and to think beyond their national boundaries. Indeed, such attitudes are arguably contributing to the recruitment crises facing many national armies. Numerous studies also indicate that citizens are becoming more critical of their governments, with many commentators noting a diminution of trust in government and politicians, which may in part account for declining voter turn-out and membership of political parties, and a general sense of disengagement with national politics. Likewise, more and more domestic pressure groups and INGOs are scrutinizing the external ethical dealings of national governments, especially in relation to foreign policy, arms contracts, the environment, and trade with the developing world. All of this would suggest, to return to our definition of cosmopolitanism, that people are becoming freer from national limitations and prejudices.

An obvious riposte to such claims would be to point to recent international conflicts, which suggest both the persistence of 'traditional' non-cosmopolitan attitudes and that the media and communications revolution has not diminished our capacity to essentialize other peoples and cultures. Furthermore, the tendencies described here may still be mainly confined to modern industrial societies. It is also the case that not every national education system in the world is geared to the encouragement of critical thinking and the dissemination of liberal values. And in many countries, for a variety of reasons, many citizens in both the developed and developing world will still not go to university and hence not everyone will participate in the global expansion of higher education. Nevertheless, the developments described facilitate the emergence of a more educated and informed 'transnational' citizenry, increasingly willing and able to relocate to other countries for reasons ranging from work to personal choice. In this regard, Harold Perkin in *The Third Revolution* (1996) has mapped the emergence of a global professional society. In sum, it is education that provides individuals with the skills, professional qualifications and outlooks which both lessen their dependence upon their respective national states and enable them to act in a cosmopolitan manner.

Reflexive cosmopolitanism

In the previous chapter, reflexive modernization was discussed in relation to forms of cultural conflict; however, it is also a condition or epoch with implications for cosmopolitanism. To recap, writers such as Ulrich Beck, Anthony Giddens and Scott Lash (1994) consider our late modern age, which globalization has helped to shape and define, to be characterized by the loss of authority of traditional institutions, structures and forms, including government, the family, the church and the nation-state. This leads to greater individuation, in that we are more able to forge our own life-paths. We increasingly choose our own labels, identities, values and cultural associations rather than simply adopting those of our parents and the communities in which we were raised. Self-constitution and self-identity are therefore an integral part of reflexive modernization. This has implications for cosmopolitanism and the extent to which it is disseminated. As Samuel Scheffler has argued, cosmopolitanism entails 'that individuals have the capacity to flourish by forging idiosyncratic identities from heterogeneous cultural sources, and are not to be thought of as constituted or defined by ascriptive ties to a particular culture, community or tradition' (1999: 258). Thus, the cosmopolitan is a reflexive self-constituting subject, formed from numerous cultural experiences and allegiances. The cosmopolitan should not therefore be thought of as an autonomous agent free from attachments to particular places or cultures, allying only with world institutions, such as the UN. At the same time, globalizing processes further contribute to cosmopolitanism by affording us the opportunity to experience a greater range of cultural influences and traditions, to mix and match, in the process of self-constitution.

From a broader historical perspective, for Roland Robertson it is reflexivity that separates contemporary globalization from its earlier manifestations. This notion stems from his conception of globalization as entailing 'the intensification of consciousness of the world as a whole' (1992: 8). It means on one level, for example, that countries engaged in modernization will be aware of the models and paths pursued by other powers, and will have to make judgements and decisions in the light of this knowledge. Such reflexivity is similarly displayed by individuals – and for Giddens (1990) by modern institutions as well – having to mediate the intersection and interpenetration of the global and the local, resulting in a type of reflexive cosmopolitanism or 'glocalised cosmopolitanism' (Urry, 2003: 137). In other words, we incorporate ideas, images and symbols from around the world into our everyday lives so that they come to inform our outlooks and lifestyles, and in doing so we develop the capacity to think and act beyond our immediate surroundings, encouraging us to ruminate upon our place in the world and are actions within it. We therefore live with constant reference to the global. How we treat our local environment will have implications for the earth's ecosystem; the performance of our local and national economies will be related to the condition of the international economy; how our national football team is faring will be defined by the FIFA world ranking system, and so on. John Urry (2003) goes further, discussing reflexive modernization in relation to 'cosmopolitan fluidity'. For example, the speed and intensity of global flows mean that we know more about what is going on in other societies, a development that challenges the era of the nation-state, a time when 'the "other" society was almost always something to fear' (2003: 133).

Reflexive modernization has stimulated much critical discussion (see, for example, Alexander, 1996). In particular, whether people are actually displaying reflexivity and autonomy is a source of debate as we are born with identities and raised in communities and cultures that profoundly shape our outlook and behaviour. For this reason, some commentators believe that our national identities exert an especially strong hold over us to the extent that other identities often struggle to generate the same strength of allegiance and commitment. Moreover, even if we personally enjoy and benefit from the process of self-constitution, it will not necessarily entail a weakening of national loyalties. To claim this would be the case, John Hutchinson (2005) argues, is to ignore the extent to which shared myths and memories bind people to a particular nation, and to assume that people simply act in instrumental terms, although this point needs to be counter-balanced by the fact that globalization – for reasons ranging from the opportunities it can provide to the insecurity it can foster – is often considered to be generating greater individualism within modern societies.[4] Under such conditions the problem with belonging to a nation or national community is that it makes demands upon us, ranging from taxation to emotional commitment, and ultimately calls upon us to sacrifice our lives for it in times of conflict. Identification with a nation can therefore serve to curtail our autonomy. It follows, therefore, that in this context the supposedly weaker hold that our non-national allegiances and identities exert over us would have some appeal; since they place fewer demands upon us, we will have greater freedom to pursue our own lives, with little meaningful reference to collective groups other than those of our choice. In this vein, D.M. Green has noted, contrary to Hutchinson, that our political identities are becoming increasingly viewed in instrumental terms, a matter of preference rather than psychological necessity (2000: 85). If this is indeed what is happening, then in the future our identities will increasingly be formed by our interests.

To summarize what has been claimed thus far: improved levels of education for greater numbers of people, as well as the prospect of the emergence of the reflexive self in the late modern age, may help to lessen our allegiance to particular countries and national cultures. Therefore, far from stimulating the forces of nationalism and racism, some of the processes associated with globalization may well be helping to produce cosmopolitan citizens. In short, reflexive modernization and the greater individuation that it entails are a necessary prerequisite for cosmopolitanism.

The global need for cosmopolitanism

In their different ways the developments described so far challenge the cultural and political formations that may still serve to inhibit the dissemination of cosmopolitanism, namely nations and nation-states. While we saw in the previous chapter that some people are looking to their particular ethno-national group for forms of security and identification, behaviour that is the antithesis of cosmopolitanism, the broader socio-economic and cultural processes associated with globalization and identified here as potentially encouraging cosmopolitanism, as well as the lack of institutional buttressing from a nation-state, may mean that these local nationalisms will struggle to endure. They are perhaps a temporary and to an extent understandable reaction to the uncertainties ushered in by globalizing processes. Moreover, there is an additional sense that nations and nation-states are struggling to adapt to contemporary conditions, and it concerns the management of global issues such as the environment, development, trade policies, global diseases and health scares, population growth, people trafficking, nuclear weapons proliferation, international crime and terrorism. Global risks require cosmopolitan thinking and international solutions, and specifically the further development of the institutions of global governance, such as the UN, and transnational conceptions of justice, such as human rights regimes. Nation-states and national governments, in contrast, are not necessarily the most suited institutions for dealing with these problems as often they will be governed by the pursuit of their respective national interests. For Ulrich Beck (1999) our 'world risk society' must by necessity be a cosmopolitan place. All of this places greater onus upon the ordinary citizens of the world to behave in a more cosmopolitan manner, and there may be some evidence that this is beginning to happen, as will now be discussed.

To begin with, transnational media and global communication and information technologies, coupled with the higher levels of education discussed earlier, ensure not only a wider awareness of the problems described above, but arguably a greater proclivity on the part of many individuals to take an active interest in such matters and to address them. Moreover, the Internet and email make it easier for people to initiate global campaigns and networks geared to tackling these issues, which in turn can contribute to the formation of a global civil society (see Kaldor, 2003), a point that is returned to below.[5] And some individuals and groups would seem to be displaying signs of cosmopolitanism. For instance, environmentalists are increasingly challenging their respective governments because they believe their policies are harming the environment. While these policies may be in the national interest and of benefit to their own country, environmentalists will frequently take the global view, and many will be prepared to break national laws to make this point (Falk, 1995). Similarly, sociologists and even some national politicians are detecting a general diminution of patriotism and associated values, such as duty and loyalty, in the contemporary period. In other words, the maxim 'my country right or wrong' is being eroded by, for example, the increasing number of citizens prepared to challenge the legitimacy of their country going to war and of instances of civil servants leaking classified documents and former government ministers revealing state secrets. What is often motivating them is an ethical framework that extends beyond the confines of their particular nation-states. It is a consideration for the fate of other nationals, which translates as a concern for the fate of humankind. In this sense therefore they are acting as world citizens rather than as national citizens, as cosmopolitans rather than locals.

This transition may well be a consequence of some of the pressures acting upon nation-states and national cultures delineated in earlier chapters. Thus, the nation or the national is increasingly composed of numerous influences, an arena where the forces of cultural pluralism and solidarity encounter and compete with each other on a daily basis, entailing a loss of authority and a diminishing ability to exert a hold upon the imaginations of its citizens. Any notion that our national identity is our primary or defining identity is no longer sustainable: it must now compete with a plethora of identities for our attention, making it easier to be a cosmopolite. If this is indeed what is happening then we appear to be entering a new phase, marked by the passing of the high point of the nation-state and relatively homogenous national cultures. An alternative conception of what is taking place is that we are witnessing a return to a pre-nation-state past of polyethnic societies. In this vein, William H. McNeill (1986) emphasizes that polyethnicity is actually the norm in world history, whereas national ethnic homogeneity has been a relatively brief and unusual phenomenon. Irrespective of these particular interpretations, with regard to the wider claim being made here, polyethnicity and the lack of a distinct and unitary conception of the nation that it entails, is an especially suitable condition and environment for cosmopolitanism.[6]

Returning to the identification of contemporary manifestations of cosmopolitanism, more everyday or mundane cosmopolitanism is apparent in the boycotting of some fast-food chains and coffee houses for alleged or proven unethical practices, as well as the global growth of fair trade. According to the Fairtrade Labelling Organization, global sales of fair trade products climbed by more than a third in 2005 to £758 million ($1.38bn) (BBC, 2006). For environmental reasons, more and more people are seeking to purchase local produce, a trend that most supermarkets are now catering for. In addition, there is evidence that ethical rather than national considerations are influencing other areas of consumption, ranging from cars to pensions. Indeed, it is the act of weighing up the relative merits of the local, the national and the global that demands individuals behave in a cosmopolitan manner, and this is a further indication that a reflexive modernity can help to generate critical awareness and cosmopolitan outlooks and not simply a preoccupation with the self. In turn, this may partly account for the international causes that have emerged in recent years, such as the global campaigns addressing famine (e.g., Live Aid), poverty and the environment. It would seem, then, that in a number of important respects the citizens of the world have never been so ethically and globally aware.

All of this may indicate an emerging global consciousness, something that, as we have seen, Roland Robertson considers to be integral to globalization, and he coins the term 'globality' to describe 'the circumstance of extensive awareness of the world as a whole, including the species aspect of the latter' (1992: 78). And along with the examples mentioned above, developments such as the spread of the global market, global movements, the acceptance of unified global time, and the establishment of an international legal system (e.g., the International Court of Justice) encourage us to think globally and to *imagine*, to use Benedict Anderson's terminology, that we are part of a global community. In this vein, a global consciousness may contribute to and would be reinforced by the emergence of a transnational or even a global civil society. The latter, in theory, may evolve if the institutions of global governance continue to develop and gain enhanced powers, though national governments will continue to be obstructive. Moreover, the issue of unequal access to global communication and information technologies will need to be addressed in order to ensure that the majority of the citizens of the world are connected, and so that what Ulrich Beck (2000) has termed 'transnational social spaces' can emerge potentially facilitating the building of civil society beyond the nation-state. Similarly, the emergence of a global public sphere would contribute to this end, and, while cyberspace will help in this regard, it will also require global issues to become genuinely meaningful for people. Of course, looming environmental problems and international terrorism may ensure that this does indeed happen. Moreover, recent global events or episodes – such as the 11 September attacks upon the USA, the Iraq war and the tsunami disaster of late 2004 – were for some people more significant than domestic politics, and may in time come to form part of a collective global memory. However, a global public sphere also requires the establishment of genuinely internationally oriented news and media organizations, and, as we saw in chapter 3, currently most existing organizations have a national agenda to promote.

In summary, certain globalizing processes and developments may be encouraging some people to adopt a wider perspective and to act in a cosmopolitan manner. More importantly, some of the problems associated with globalization are ensuring that there is a global need for cosmopolitanism. Of course, as will be addressed later, the fact that there is a need for such thinking does not necessarily mean it will happen, and many people will still retain their national mentalities and outlooks.

Cosmopolitanism and the network society

The cumulative effect of increasing intercultural contact, greater emphasis upon education, reflexive modernization and greater individuation, and the problems confronting nation-states is that different types of demands and pressures are being placed upon individuals. New skills and coping strategies are now required: we are all having to become more independent, entrepreneurial and geographically mobile. There is also greater emphasis upon interpersonal communication skills and developing networks of contacts and associates. Although not everyone is living and operating according to these changes, it is possible to detect the emergence of what could be termed 'connected cosmopolitans', and not just among the young. They are well travelled, *au fait* with modern communications technologies and used to networking, and many will have developed extensive contacts both domestically and abroad. In short, they are well adjusted to operating within knowledge-based societies or economies.[7]

Ideas and information are key sources of wealth generation and societal development within knowledge-based economies. The development of such economies requires regular communication between and across societies, which in turn may lead to individuals forming new acquaintances and friendships in different countries. Although this exchange of ideas and information has gone on in the past, it is the current intensity and extent of such exchanges that make our own era different from earlier periods of history. In particular, universities are primary sites of cultural interaction and exchange, and becoming increasingly so. As well as lecturers attending international conference and students studying for degrees abroad, the formation of transnational information/policy networks and 'disciplinary communities' via the Internet has been an especially notable recent development (Stone, 2002). For governments, allowing their citizens to exchange ideas and share best practice is a productive way of improving material conditions within their respective societies. Indeed, even governments operate in this way, sending delegations abroad to learn from other countries. This makes it difficult for governments to control the activities of global policy networks, and to prevent their citizens from acting in a similar way.

Moreover, for a national government to try to prevent such activity would be to harm its own economy and society. There are numerous examples of societies isolated from the international community – notably North Korea, apartheid South Africa and Saddam Hussein's Iraq – falling behind comparable societies. Thus, while the motives behind these forms of global exchange might be selfish or nationalistic, they nevertheless facilitate cross-cultural and cross-societal dialogue and interaction, which in turn are further prerequisites of cosmopolitanism.

Global policy networks and the exchange of information are not just confined to academia and governments. INGOs and transnational advocacy networks (see Keck and Sikkunk, 1998), and even groups opposed to globalization, such as environmental and 'development' groups, are organized in this way. For Manuel Castells (1996) this is all part of the 'network society' that defines our age, characterized by the global diffusion of information: information flows are multi-directional and largely ignore national borders. Hannerz considers the global *ecumene* to be 'a network of networks' that draws individuals and groups into 'a more globalised existence' (1992b: 47). Above all, the openness and non-hierarchical nature of global networks encourage the formation of transnational public spaces and virtual communities, and hence facilitate sociality beyond the nation-state. The network society – if we return to our definition of cosmopolitan ('consisting of people from many or all parts of the world') – allowing for the fact that it can be used for non- or anti-cosmopolitan purposes, is in the strict sense of the word a cosmopolitan place. However, whether these developments can contribute to the formation of a truly cosmopolitan or world society is less certain. There is now growing recognition of the limitations of computer-mediated communication, especially with regard to how meaningful virtual societies and virtual communities are for the individuals involved. In other words, this type of experience cannot compare with actual or 'real-life' interpersonal contact and interaction, and is susceptible to various forms of abuse. Yet Internet-based communication has its defenders and advocates, and the electronic spaces it provides for forms of connectivity and sociality are considered to have cosmopolitan potential. In particular, with no face-to-face interaction, traditional hierarchies of gender, class and race are less detectable and hence less of an issue (Holmes, 1997). Barry Wellman and Milena Gulia (1999) maintain that when online communities are viewed in conjunction with other technological developments, such as telephones and planes, we clearly have got used to the idea that social relationships and social solidarity can exist without physical proximity.

To take a broader perspective, as well as being a useful disposition for participating in the global network society, an additional reason why we may witness the spread of cosmopolitanism is that, quite simply, it is good for us. A cosmopolitan outlook enables us to experience and learn about different cultures and societies, and therefore to expand our knowledge and widen our horizons. To be opposed to cosmopolitanism is therefore to impose limits upon our lives. Martha Nussbaum (1996) believes that cosmopolitanism facilitates self-knowledge because the more we know about others the better able are we to know ourselves. As suggested above, cosmopolitanism is also good for societies, since it enables them to incorporate new ideas and cultural influences, thereby facilitating their development and preventing them from stagnating and decaying. Of course, this general assertion of the benefits of cosmopolitanism is not directly related to globalization. However, as has been shown, there are aspects of globalization – such as global communications technologies and increased travel – that can facilitate cosmopolitan experiences. Indeed, to resist cosmopolitan pressures would entail individuals and societies trying to seal themselves off from the processes of globalization.

Where is the evidence of the spread of cosmopolitanism?

An obvious counter-argument to the case being developed here is that there is little tangible evidence of the spread of cosmopolitanism. Within Europe, for example, this impression is reinforced by the recent growth in support for far-Right parties and groups. However, electoral fortunes are a notoriously unreliable indicator of public trends. Arguably, of more significance is that a number of major long-term processes and developments associated with globalization – such as advances in communications and information technologies, increased travel, reflexive modernization, challenges to the nation-state and greater emphasis upon higher education – are able to generate forms of cosmopolitanism.[8] While we must not downplay or underestimate the dangers of the extreme Right, it would seem that historical trends are working against them. Indeed, the extreme Right's recent revival can be read as a rearguard action, an attempt to hold on to perceived boundaries and order in response to the change, unpredictability and fluidity ushered in by the processes of globalization. There is also a sense in which, in a globalizing era, all of us will have to change our attitudes and outlooks if they are not to become anachronistic. For individuals to refuse to adapt would be to place themselves at odds with the different forms of interconnectedness that define our age. The people who will flourish in our global era are likely to be those who are open to other cultures and traditions, and are able to learn from and draw upon them.

Who or what is a cosmopolitan?

From looking at the cultural and sociological aspects of cosmopolitanism, the conception of it as a lived experience has emerged here, something that becomes possible when we are able to look beyond our national cultures. However, becoming cosmopolitan does not mean giving up on our national cultures as cosmopolitanism is not an absolute condition. More specifically, our national identities and national cultures need not preclude the development of a cosmopolitan perspective – and given the prevalence of nationalism and the nation-state it is unlikely that anyone can ever be completely free from national attachments. One can still be Russian or Mexican, for example, and a cosmopolite. Becoming a cosmopolitan, and thereby open to other cultures and cultural experiences, requires being free from national limitations or prejudices, which returns us to the definition of cosmopolitan outlined at the beginning of this chapter. As long as we are not defined by our respective national cultures, there is the prospect of us developing a cosmopolitan disposition. As we have seen, globalization can facilitate this transition because its processes and manifestations enable us to experience a plurality of cultural influences and to gain multiple attachments and sources of allegiance. Furthermore, if we accept the hybridity case that the main consequence of globalization is to introduce greater messiness and reduce cultural distinctiveness, it should in theory become easier to transcend national borders. In sum, the world has become 'a gradual spectrum of mixed-up differences' (Geertz, 1980: 147).

To be cosmopolitan does of course entail more than just being free from national preoccupations. If this were the only criterion then the leadership and supporters of al-Qaeda would qualify as cosmopolitans because in their desire for a return of the Caliphate they seek an end to the nation-states of the Arab and Muslim worlds. There must, therefore, be additional elements to being a cosmopolite, two of which will now be mentioned. First, no culture, community or tradition – national or otherwise – must influence us to the extent that it inhibits the fostering of a cosmopolitan outlook. In other words, our sense of attachment to a single culture, group or society must not be so strong that it precludes our engagement with other cultures, groups and societies. Second, as well as being able to absorb other cultural experiences, cosmopolitanism must also entail a set of attitudes and values (see Held, 2004). Thus, a cosmopolitan will be concerned with universal standards of justice and human rights and be sensitive to other cultures in negotiating these common standards; have a sense of fellow feeling with the citizens of the world; be interested in equitable and participatory modes of global governance; as well as want to experience and engage with other peoples and cultures as equals. A further reason for making this point is that one reading of the cosmopolite is as simply a consumer of cultural experiences, a person (typically a Westerner) who passes through different societies with no stake in any of them, and by implication is detached from their fellow human beings. Jonathan Friedman has put this more succinctly, arguing that a cosmopolitan is 'participating in many worlds without becoming part of them' (1995: 78). In contrast, the position taken here is that rather than free-floating and maintaining their distance, and perhaps occasionally adopting a position of superiority, the cosmopolitan must be genuinely interested in the cultures and societies they encounter because to do so is to display their common humanity; that is, their cosmopolitanism.

It has been suggested here that becoming cosmopolitan is an eclectic process; we are not born cosmopolitans. Rather, we are born and raised in particular communities and our cosmopolitan outlooks emerge from synthesizing a range of influences, many – but not all – of which will originate in these communities, such as the education we receive. This means that the individual developing a cosmopolitan perspective will retain some allegiance to particular groups, such as families, friends and communities, and will have to balance a combination of demands and concerns – the universal and the particular/local – throughout their lives. In short, the cosmopolitan will be an expression or manifestation of the interpenetration of the global and the local. Furthermore, it should not be thought that our particular attachments and commitments are necessarily incompatible with cosmopolitanism (see Appiah, 1996). Our communities – as well as being sources of meaning and fulfilment – can potentially provide us with the universal values necessary to think and act in a cosmopolitan manner.[9] Indeed, a person who does not have any compassion towards the people that they have been raised with is unlikely to feel any towards humanity as a whole. Or, to put it another way, having an allegiance to the 'worldwide community of human beings', to use Martha Nussbaum's phrase (1996: 4), must inevitably include those belonging to my local or particular communities.[10] There is then an interrelationship between the global and the local when it comes to cosmopolitanism. In this vein, if I have children and raise them as tolerant and compassionate individuals, then this benefits both my particular community and humanity as a whole. And if my children have been raised and educated in such a way, then I would hope that they would not have a proclivity to make distinctions between the particular and the universal.[11] All of this reinforces the point made earlier about the role that education and the processes of reflexive modernization can play in fostering critical intelligence, which in turn may provide the basis for a cosmopolitan disposition and the possession of multiple allegiances and a plurality of concerns that go beyond universal–particular distinctions.

Conclusion

The concern of this chapter has been to explore the possible linkages between globalizing processes and the cultural and social dimensions of cosmopolitanism. It has not been claimed that increased cultural flows necessarily produce cosmopolitanism, but we have seen that there are a number of long-term processes associated with or by-products of globalization capable of stimulating cosmopolitanism.[12] Contemporary global developments, notably global migration, greater intercultural contact and interconnectedness, globalizing cities, global risks, reflexive modernization, higher levels of education, and of course increased cultural flows, all have the potential to generate cosmopolitan dispositions by affording us the opportunity to think beyond our particular cultures and communities. In this vein, the challenges that globalizing processes present to national cultures and the nation-state are arguably a necessary prerequisite for the attainment of attachments and allegiances beyond these formations.

However, we should not overplay the relationship between globalization and cosmopolitanism. In this respect, Jan Aart Scholte believes globalization has simply encouraged 'modest growth in cosmopolitan attachments' (2000: 5). More significantly, determining the spread or otherwise of cosmopolitanism is not an easy task, something that is reflected in the dearth of available data, and it is for this reason that the emphasis here has simply been upon delineating broad globalizing tendencies and developments with potential cosmopolitan effects. Pippa Norris (2000), however, has examined the data for cosmopolitanism that does exist, notably combining the 1990–91 and 1995–7 World Values survey, which draws upon evidence from 70 countries, revealing that in comparison with 'the world as a whole', people identified most strongly with their nation and locality or region, the figures being 15 per cent, 38 per cent and 47 per cent, respectively. But the survey also revealed a generational divide with those born after the Second World War being much more likely to see themselves as cosmopolitan citizens than earlier generations, indicating that 'in the long term public opinion is moving in a more internationalist direction' (ibid.,

175). Interestingly, Norris similarly highlights rising educational levels and growing urbanization as contributing to this trend. Nevertheless, such data are now more than a decade old, and to return to the argument of this chapter, cosmopolitanism should not be viewed as an either/or condition. That is, we are not either cosmopolitan or local, nor are we simply cosmopolitan or national. Rather, cosmopolitanism should be considered a cumulative process, marked by the gathering of cultural influences, allegiances and experiences, which accords with our ability as human beings to possess more than one identity. However, this also means that the validity of the connections made between globalization and cosmopolitanism is dependent upon the accuracy of one's understanding of contemporary globalization. As we have seen in previous chapters, the multiple processes of globalization are also capable of generating national and parochial reactions.

More intensive and extensive forms of global interconnectedness can both help us to think beyond our nation-state, but also remind us of our attachment to it, especially in a rapidly changing world. Cosmopolitan feelings will always have to compete with the, arguably, stronger pull of our communitarian attachments; this is certainly the view of Anthony Smith, who believes a cosmopolitan culture will be shallow, lacking in roots, in comparison with our existing 'deep' cultures (1995: 24). For the foreseeable future therefore local and national allegiances will continue to resonate with many people, although, as has been suggested here, this is not necessarily an obstacle to the formation of a cosmopolitan perspective, which it has been contended should be viewed as a process of self-constitution. It is only when our particular allegiances inhibit us from collecting these experiences and properly encountering other cultures that it becomes a problem in relation to cosmopolitanism.

Ultimately, however, whether we actually develop a cosmopolitan outlook will be dependent upon a range of factors other than just having greater 'cosmopolitan opportunities' and the pressures generated by the problems associated with globalization. These include the type of globalizing process or processes being engaged with, the societies in which this interaction is taking place, and the individuals experiencing these encounters. For example, not all societies are undergoing the processes of reflexive modernization outlined earlier. Moreover, whether understanding and even empathy develop from increased contact and greater familiarity with different cultures will be largely dependent upon the individuals involved, each with their own life experiences, predispositions and social and educational backgrounds. This will influence whether or not people wish to experience different cultures, regard migrants as a threat, are willing to do business with foreign companies, and so on. It is for these reasons that the nature and influence of globalizing processes are both complex and uneven.

In sum, whether cosmopolitanism emerges from increasing global flows and forms of interconnectedness will be dependent upon the particular contexts in which these forces are experienced and the individuals and groups that are experiencing them. Of course, these contexts will be permeated and to a varying extent shaped by globalizing processes, which again indicates the significance of examining the intersection of the global and the local and of employing a range of disciplinary approaches as part of our analyses rather than just or mainly undertaking a sociological and cultural investigation. It also means that different forms and degrees of cosmopolitanism will emerge – varieties of cosmopolitanism, if you will – which returns us to the point made at the beginning of this chapter: the emerging tendency to view cosmopolitanism in plural terms.

Recommended reading

Cosmopolitanism is a concept that is receiving increasing academic and critical attention. One theorist in particular who has sought to explore the relationship between globalization and cosmopolitanism is Ulrich Beck, notably in works such as *What is Globalization?* (2000) and an essay entitled 'The Cosmopolitan Perspective: Sociology in the Second Age of Modernity' (2002). Ulf Hannerz's article 'Cosmopolitans and Locals in World Culture' (1990) has come to be regarded as something of a classic in this subject area. For an interesting insight into the relationship between cosmopolitanism and the nation-state and the issue of sovereignty, see Kymlicka and Straehle (1999) and Pogge (1992), respectively. And for books that deal with the cultural and sociological dimension of cosmopolitanism, see C.A. Breckenridge et al. (eds), *Cosmopolitanism* (2002), John Tomlinson, *Globalisation and Culture* (1999a), and John Urry, *Global Complexity* (2003).

Conclusion

Cultural Globalizations

So, what is cultural globalization? What is the nature of the relationship between culture and globalization? Moreover, what implications does globalization have for our understanding of culture? These questions will now be addressed by bringing together the key arguments and themes of this book.

Cultural globalization: analytical challenges

From the outset, however, we should recognize what has hopefully become evident during the course of this work, namely that cultural globalization presents us with a number of analytical challenges, notably the vast scale of the subject and the fact that global processes have not spread to all parts of the world, and even in those places where they have reached they have done so unevenly. In turn, this creates problems when it comes to considering how, for instance, forms of global connectivity are impacting upon national cultures or contributing to patterns of cultural conflict, all of which needs to be factored into our investigations. We must also bear in mind that the local can have a global resonance. For example, cultural artefacts, texts and other material forms can come to transcend particular cultures and places and have universal appeal and influence. Further adding to the complexity, cultural globalization has a long but uneven history. As we saw in chapter 1, the foundations for its current phase were laid in earlier epochs, though there are aspects of contemporary globalization that ensure its distinctiveness from other periods, including the unprecedented volume of cultural traffic and increased cultural mixing, developments that generate their own analytical challenges. But most importantly, defining cultural globalization is far from straightforward, as will now be shown.

Globalization

If we begin by breaking down the concept of cultural globalization into its constituent parts, starting with globalization, it soon becomes apparent that there is a lack of agreement over what it actually *is* or entails. This ranges from figures presenting globalization as the challenge of our age (e.g., Blair, 1996) through to those who consider it to be 'crushing cultural diversity and personal experiences' and turning the 'citizen into the consumer' (Touraine, 1997: 68). The contested nature of globalization is reflected in the particular approaches that different disciplines take towards it. As we have seen, while many sociologists associate globalization with modernity and the modern era, many historians take a longer view of its history. Another reason for this divergence is often the criteria that we employ as part of our respective definitions of globalization. For example, conceiving of globalization as simply multiple forms of global interconnectedness does not imply deep human relationships and encourages a conception of globalization as a long-term historical process, given that societies have been interacting and interconnecting in this way for some considerable time. However, if we view globalization as multiple forms of global interdependence, then this necessitates a qualitatively different type of human relationship, one which is harder to forge and maintain. Given the difficulties of travelling and communicating in earlier periods of human history, from this standpoint globalization could only be a modern phenomenon.

Culture

'Culture' is a similarly problematic concept resisting neat definitions, as is testified by the multiple perceptions of it. However, as was argued in chapter 2, given that cultures are not discrete entities and are invariably informed by their encounters with other cultural influences, it is appropriate to conceptualize culture as a process rather than something that is permanent and stable. Although, as that chapter also made clear, we should not overplay the idea of travel, fluidity and transculturality in relation to culture, because to do so risks neglecting processes of cultural formation and patterns of resistance and, in turn, underestimating cultural differences. An example of these dual tendencies can be seen in the case of the Brazilian carnival. Concern is now being expressed by some Brazilians that their carnivals are becoming dominated by foreign DJs and musicians, and especially by their electronic music, which is considered to be undermining the authentic Afro-

Brazilian carnival. Indeed, such has been the concern about the challenge this presents to Brazilian cultural identity that a number of samba schools in Río de Janeiro have banned foreigners from participating in their carnival parades. At the same time, Brazilian bloggers have been comparing the foreign musical performers with the Dutch invaders that came to their country in the seventeenth century (Phillips, 2007). Thus, there is a conception of Brazilian culture as something unique and worthy of preservation, yet it is inevitably evolving as part of an ongoing process, with this latest foreign intrusion simply the latest stage in its development.

Cultural globalization

If we combine these two concepts and address cultural globalization, what conclusions can we draw from this study about this subject? Our immediate problem is that we are confronted with so many things going on that it has led Ulf Hannerz (1989b) to express this as the 'global ecumene', a world culture of cultural interrelatedness. In spite of the fact that this may be an accurate description of the contemporary condition, it does not explain it, and for this we need to probe a little deeper and in particular recognize that we cannot fully understand globalization through the cultural prism. While, of all the forms of globalization, the cultural is the one that we experience daily and is the most visible, we must nevertheless take into account its other aspects and dimensions. In this sense, economic and political forms of globalization are often less easy to detect, though this does not mean that our experience of them is any less tangible. For instance, an investment decision made by a multinational corporation with its head office in, say, Tokyo can have a direct impact upon the employment prospects, and it follows lifestyles, of its workers in many parts of the world. More importantly, as we have seen, these dimensions of globalization are invariably intertwined, and consequently it necessitates an interdisciplinary approach to this subject even when the focus of our analysis is upon cultural globalization. For example, many of the cultural products that we come across, ranging from television programmes to consumer goods, are products of the economic, technological and political dimensions of globalization. To take just the case of the political dimension of globalization, it is the expansion of global governance, especially in the form of world trade agreements, that enables us to encounter these cultural products. In sum, the processes of cultural globalization do not exist in isolation, but are intermeshed with the other dimensions and processes of globalization.

As for the nature of the relationship between globalization and culture, we should recognize that globalizing processes do not define culture in the contemporary period, but they do profoundly shape it. In other words, cultures – be they national, religious, local or some other form – have histories and are forged from human endeavours, and therefore are not simply fluid and intangible, yet they are inevitably informed by our involvement in globalizing processes and cultural flows. However, if we are to determine the impact of such flows we need to acknowledge concerns that employing metaphors in this way can lead to our discussions remaining abstract and generalized. To rectify this problem we need to dissect such flows, establishing what they consist of (ideas, images, sounds, symbols, people, capital and products), whether they are global, regional or transnational in nature, and take into account their differing levels of intensity and velocity. Our investigations will almost certainly reveal not only the diverse and multiple origins of contemporary cultural flows, but also their multi-directional nature, and this in turn serves to undermine the notion of a unitary global culture (chapter 4). Even if we accept that there will always be dominant players and forces informing this aspect of cultural globalization, this does not preclude the possibility of there being countervailing flows as well as forms of resistance. In this regard, migration, travel and information and communications technologies are leading to cultural influences of the non-Western world permeating the West, and shaping culture accordingly, whether it be in the form of music, fashion, theatre or some other cultural practice. Moreover, numerous writers consider that the flows and processes of globalization are serving to blur existing cultural identities and generate more complex identities, reflected in increasing hybridity, polyethnicity and multiculturality (e.g., Nederveen Pieterse, 2004; García Canclini, 1995).

The global–local problem

Analysing cultural flows and seeking to determine any influence that they are having is even more complicated than has thus far been suggested. This is because we are immediately confronted with what Roland Robertson has termed the interpenetration of the global and the local. Thus, the global is informed by local influences, and vice versa. And there are interests and groups actively encouraging such a reciprocal relationship. As is well known, environmentalists have been urging us for many years to 'think globally, act locally'. Similarly, global companies are pursuing glocalization and adapting their products to local markets. But even without such encouragement and inducement, individuals and groups of their own accord are indigenizing the objects, sounds, symbols and images that go to make up cultural flows (chapter 4). Further complicating matters is that 'the local', which already assumes numerous forms (nation-state, neighbourhood, tradition, etc.), is likely to be much more internally diverse than ever before, as a result of the greater connectedness to the rest of world and the movement of new cultures into our localities – a point that even applies to nation-states, which have their own regimes and techniques for promoting national consolidation and coherence. Doreen Massey (2005) writes of the internal disjunctive multiplicities of place and suggests that we need to think of connection rather than place in relation to human interaction, although we should not overlook the fact that these connections under contemporary globalization are often flexible, dynamic and hard to pin down. And the cumulative effect of these developments leads Robert Holton (2005) to suggest that our unit of analysis should no longer be the national/local or the global but the glocal, which necessitates employing a *methodological glocalism*.

The idea of a binary relationship between the global and the local would therefore appear to be increasingly outdated under contemporary conditions. Indeed, as we saw in chapter 2, developments such as transnationalism further complicate matters by highlighting linkages that cut across this dualism. It is not just the global–local distinction that is under pressure from contemporary globalizing developments; the same applies to notions of home and abroad, internal and external, private and public. Furthermore, a combination of technological developments and shifts in the nature of capitalist production entails greater individuation when it comes to how we experience cultural flows. It means, for instance, that the music and programmes we download from the Internet, the increased array of television programmes we choose from, the satellite channels we subscribe to, and the digital newspapers and other sources of information we sign up to receive are all a product of our individual tastes. Hence, cultural differentiation is further ensured by the fact that individuals are themselves increasingly engaged in shaping many of their own cultural experiences. Such a transformation engenders reflexivity, with the individual becoming more aware of the processes of cultural production and consumption and their role within these processes, but in addition it means that the variety of responses at the local level will grow exponentially as more and more people pursue such lifestyles.

For many of the preceding reasons, it is now being argued that we should cease viewing the local as the stopping point of global circulations (Tsing, 2002) and move beyond the global–local dualism (Nustad, 2003). At the very least, the notion of the global consisting of a 'multiplicity of localities' (Morley and Robins, 1995), or that the local is a relational concept owing its existence to its relationship with the global, must be viewed as problematic. Given that it has been argued here that culture is more appropriately conceived of as a process founded upon webs of meaning, travel and plurality, it would indeed seem unnecessary to become overly preoccupied with identifying the global and the local. In other words, culture should not be considered solely in relation to particular places, especially as during the course of our everyday lives we move around, carrying our cultures with us, and engaging with global and transnational flows and processes in a variety of contexts (chapter 3). There is therefore much in our culturally connected lives that does not rely upon places, as listeners of world music, religious followers, and participants in social movements would testify. For this reason, to identify some of the connections and linkages that exist between globalization and culture, we need to examine both the circumstances and the ways in which individuals, groups and institutions, each with their own cultures and histories, are experiencing, interpreting and contributing to globalization's different flows and processes. Thus, people are not just at home passively waiting for global cultural flows; instead they are often actively contributing to them, something that is especially evident with transnational, migrant and diaspora communities. Even the immobile and the sedentary are globally connecting every time that they go online and send emails and use the World Wide Web, albeit in a limited sense. They are also becoming part of media and communication flows every time that they turn on their television and radios and make international telephone calls. At any single moment, therefore, alongside institutions (such as the UN), events (e.g., the Olympics) and powerful corporations (media MNCs), there will be a myriad of ways that ordinary people will be contributing to global connectivity. It also means that there is a dual sense to the notion of context in the contemporary period: the specific circumstances in which individuals and groups are operating, but also the overarching global context of more intensified forms of interconnectedness.

Human agency and cultural globalization

With human agents placed at the centre of our investigations, this necessitates taking into account our perceptions of globalization, something which will be informed by the ideologies and rhetoric surrounding it, that is, the discourse of globalization. It also demands factoring into our investigations any signs of an emerging global consciousness. Of course, many of us who are contributing to greater global connectedness will not always be aware that we are doing so, although it has been suggested here that one of the distinguishing features of our age is that people are engaged in a more critically reflexive relationship with dominant processes. Moreover, undertaking the type of investigations argued for here is likely to reveal both that people have different types of relationships, with globalizing flows and processes – passive, reflexive, indifferent, oppositional, and so forth – reflecting their own circumstances and cultural frameworks (which are informed by these encounters), and that in turn there are many more forms of engagement with and responses to globalizing processes than, say, the attempts to preserve national cultures or the generation of cosmopolitan attitudes and lifestyles addressed here. All of this is an indication of the intricate nature of the relationship between globalization and culture, and ensures that cultural globalization is complex, heterogeneous and plural, and as such should be conceived of as cultural globalizations, rather than in the singular. It follows that it is problematic both to seek to determine the cultural consequences of globalization, as Holton (2000), Barber (1996) and Huntington (1997) and others have done, and to discuss causality in relation to globalization, as if it is an autonomous agent with its own motivations and agenda. Indeed, in globalization literature there is a growing recognition of the complex nature of this subject, reflected in a shift towards empirical research and micro-level analyses of actors and agents engaged in global and transnational processes and the avoidance of general theorizing at a macro-level. For example, in academic journals such as *Global Networks* there are extensive studies of globe-spanning networks and transnational practices of extended families, migrants, business and professional organizations, INGOs and cyber communities. Such investigations are also being undertaken into institutions, examining the ways in which they are interacting and connecting with other bodies. In this regard, Martin Carnoy and Manuel Castells (2001) have applied such an approach to the nation-state and, based upon their findings, articulate the idea of the Network State. Similarly, global flows are being critically examined, with an emphasis upon how they intersect with institutions, the degrees of global–local interpenetration and, from a wider perspective, how forms of stability persist under conditions of fluidity (e.g., Street, 2003).

Cumulatively, the analysis of global networks, electronic communities and various transnational connections is providing more detailed and sophisticated insights into the ways in which the cultural processes of globalization are evolving, how they are informing our personal lives and societies, and how they our changing our conceptions of space and place. It is

also providing further evidence of the multiple sources and processes contributing to globalization, and notably how individuals and groups are, for a
variety of reasons – economic, familial, technological, personal, cultural, to
cite just a few – increasingly operating in a global and transnational manner.
In addition, it strongly suggests that, while there are clearly powerful
influences generating the processes of globalization, such as capitalism,
there is no unitary power or force defining them. Consequently, it would be
unwise to reduce such phenomena to a single influence, as this would struggle to account for the range of human motivations behind such activity.
Furthermore, the different contexts in which individuals and groups are
operating, such as their institutional settings, localities, workplaces, regions
and countries, will inform their actions. A further complication is that the
influence of these different layers of cultural and social life will often overlap
and be interdependent. Indeed, such tendencies apply not only for individuals and groups, but also to institutions and events, networks and flows,
making it difficult to identify truly global phenomena. For example, in the
case of the World Cup, while football or soccer is marketed at these events
as the world's game (global), the actual tournament contains only thirty-two
countries (international), the teams and the supporters involved inevitably
demonstrate their patriotism (national), and many of the policing, monitoring and other arrangements are dependent upon forms of regional and
transnational cooperation. Thus, a seemingly global phenomenon is actually constituted by the merging or interdependence of a number of non-
global elements. This breaking down of the global into constituent
complementary parts could also be applied to institutions, such as the UN,
and cultures, such as Islam, and even to movements such as al-Qaeda
(chapter 6). What this means, therefore, is that phenomena cited as evidence
of globalization or cultural globalization are not necessarily global in either
territorial extent or outcome, but taken together they are intensifying levels
and forms of interconnectedness across the globe (Holton, 2005: 13).

The above position is unlikely to gain universal acceptance, especially in
relation to cultural globalization. For many commentators the cultural
realm of globalization is more globalized than its political and economic or
material realms (e.g., Waters, 1995). This is because cultural globalization
is in part constituted by symbolic exchanges – the economy of signs and
symbols – ranging from advertisements to data accumulation and transfer,
which are lifted from terra firma and the restrictions of being tied to physical places and hence are more mobile. However, as we have seen, even in
the contemporary period institutions such as the nation-state and national
governments and, at the level of ideas, cultural fundamentalisms and ethnic

nationalisms have all served to limit the spread of cultural flows. And it is not just ideas, images and symbols that governments will seek to restrict, but also the movement of people, by legislating on immigration and citizenship. We therefore need to counterbalance the emphasis upon mobility that can be found in some accounts (e.g., Urry, 2000) with recognition of the practical constraints on everyday life. More broadly, there is a danger that we become too hung up on identifying what is global and what is not, and, given the claim here that much of what is taking place involves levels and forms of interpenetration and indigenization, along with the unevenness of cultural flows it means we will find little if anything that is truly global and homogenized, culturally speaking. Of course, there are still significant changes afoot that we need to acknowledge and account for. In this regard, if we lose our preoccupation with identifying globalization as an end-state, it soon becomes clear, as was stated above, that there are numerous developments and processes whose cumulative effect is to contribute to greater connectedness within the world but which are not necessarily global in their own right. Cultural globalization is therefore most appropriately viewed as a catch-all term or concept to describe international, transnational, regional, local and global developments that have a cultural dimension, as well as counter-developments such as forms of cultural consolidation. It follows that cultural globalization is not a unitary condition but a multilateral set of interrelated and interpenetrating processes and tendencies, and this again lends support to the idea of conceiving of this subject in plural terms (Holton, 2005).

Thus, increased cultural mixing, the plural nature of cultural flows, the complexities of global–local interconnections, and the forms and levels of interdependence identified above all reinforce the need to consider cultural globalization in relation to human agents and the particular circumstances in which they are operating, otherwise we are relying upon conjecture. In short, the starting point of our investigation into this subject should be a recognition that the cultural flows, networks, capitalist markets, and other developments that are generating multiple forms of global interconnectedness are both engaged with and contributed to by individuals, groups and institutions in a range of contexts, and the form that this interaction takes will be significantly shaped by their respective cultural dispositions. And as cultural beings and situated agents we are neither passive nor neutral, but are actively creating, shaping and negotiating our way through these processes over time. It should also be noted that this more anthropological or human-centred approach to this subject area is in line with third-wave globalization theory (see Hay and Marsh, 2001; Holton, 2005) and transnational approaches (see Ong, 1999). Furthermore, adopting this approach will enhance our understanding of cultural globalization and associated debates, enabling us to determine the accuracy of claims that engagement with global processes engenders, among other things, homogenization, hybridization, cultural retreatism and cosmopolitanism. Of course, when we undertake such micro-level analyses we may well discover that even within particular settings it will be possible to detect some or all of these patterns of behaviour, and more besides, but crucially this behaviour is not simply determined by any of the elements of globalization.

However, we should not become so focused upon micro-level analysis that we lose sight of how global structural inequalities, power relations, international regulatory frameworks and dominant corporations inform cultural developments and encounters, and this can be avoided by synthesizing the insights of disciplines such as sociology, politics and economics, and is a reminder of the necessity of pursuing an interdisciplinary approach to this subject. We naturally should apply such an approach when we are analysing networks, so that we take into account the vertical and horizontal relations between and within networks, as well as how unequal access to global telecommunications technology inhibits participation in them for some individuals and societies (chapter 3). Similarly, Zygmunt Bauman identifies 'a global hierarchy of mobility' (1998a) and makes a distinction between an affluent mobile elite and a localized poor, with the latter struggling to participate in globalizing processes. In this vein, our discussions of cultural flows should never lose sight of the fact that capitalism and economic and financial motives lie behind much cultural production, drive the expansion of the telecommunications industry, and encourage many people to migrate. Likewise, we need to acknowledge that some flows emanate more intensively from particular sources than others – such as those originating from powerful media and entertainment corporations (CNN, MTV, the BBC) – ensuring that some cultures are subject to repeated exposure to other cultures, which inevitably generates its own power differentials, as well as informing the nature of transculturality (chapter 2). People's experiences of and engagement with the global and the transnational are often profoundly shaped by the preceding factors, and must be considered an important part of our investigations. In short, in stressing the novelty and complexity of our age we must avoid neglecting established patterns of domination. All of this relates to a wider point touched upon at various points during the course of this work, namely that we should not overestimate contemporary developments and the degree of change that is taking place. Even in these more fluid times, characterized by travel, networks and transitoriness, there still remain structures and centres of power, and institutions that retain their vitality, such as the nation-state. Thus, as we move further into the twenty-first century, we will not simply be entering a new global or transnational era. Rather, our century, will be marked by the playing out of an ongoing tension between twentieth-century internationalism and contemporary transnational and globalizing tendencies, and the developments and debates surrounding cultural globalization will be an integral part of this contest.

Recommended reading

In my view, works that are taking globalization studies forward and contributing to our understanding of cultural globalization are part of the third-wave approach to globalization, such as Colin Hay and David Marsh's *Demystifying Globalization* (2001) and Robert Holton's *Making Globalisation* (2005). In addition, two journals that consistently recognize the complexities of this subject and provide useful case studies are *Globalizations* and *Global Networks*.

Notes

Introduction: Approaching Cultural Globalization

1 The emphasis upon multidimensionality and plurality in relation to globalization is in line with much of the recent literature in this area. In this regard, a new academic journal entitled *Globalizations* was launched in 2004.

2 For a good example of this type of analysis and approach, see Massimiliano Monaci et al. (2003), who undertook a three-year research project in Milan and the surrounding region between 1998 and 2000 into how local actors in a range of occupational fields (teachers, artists, journalists, financial operators and corporate top managers) were responding to and perceiving globalization.

3 It is a moot point whether such a neat distinction can be made between the humanities and social sciences. In practice, there is considerable overlap amongst the different disciplines that constitute these two categories.

4 The term 'globalists' is employed here to encapsulate a range of opinion within a particular but rather broad approach to globalization. They are variously termed by other writers, 'strong globalizers', 'globalizers', 'hyperglobalizers' or simply advocates or supporters of globalization. These terms will be used interchangeably here.

Chapter 1 The Histories of Cultural Globalization

1 The identification of different historical phases of globalization can be found in other works (see Held et al., 1999; Hopkins, 2002; Nederveen Pieterse, 2004). In particular, *Global Transformations* by David Held et al. (1999) has influenced my own approach to this subject.

2 When the premodern phase of globalization begins is a source of contestation, and will be dealt with in the next section of this chapter.

3 J.H. Bentley (1993) maintains that while these cross-cultural encounters generally did not generate cross-cultural conversions, they nevertheless were effective agents of change in the premodern world, playing 'a prominent role – perhaps even the major role – in the shaping of the world's cultural patterns' (ibid., 5). Furthermore, Bentley identifies a number of periods in the premodern era that 'witnessed sustained and systematic cross-cultural encounters of high intensity' (ibid., 28).

4 However, this contention is disputed by the pioneer of world-systems analysis, Immanuel Wallerstein (2004), who maintains that the world-system emerged during the sixteenth century. Other writers question whether capitalism can be equated with market exchange (e.g., Hopkins, 2002). Lack of space entails that this important and complex debate cannot be gone into here, but the different positions can be found in Frank and Gills (1996).

5 This episode is an indication of the ebbs and flows of globalization, but also strengthens the case of those writers who stress the contribution of the combined forces of

modernity to globalization. From this perspective, as will be shown in more detail in the next subsection, contemporary globalization is based upon the later globalization of the modern industrial period. It is from this point onwards, it is argued, that forces such as capitalist expansionism and industrial technology ensured that globalization reached its true global – as opposed to regional – extent, reflected in the establishment of genuine interconnectedness and interdependency.

6 However, John Elliott (1970) believes Europe's encounter with the New World had a negligible impact upon European culture, arguing that many writers and philosophers simply incorporated the new knowledge from America into established patterns of thinking mainly because Europeans had confidence in their own beliefs and practices, and generally felt superior to the peoples they encountered. Indeed, many European writers simply congratulated their own culture on the magnificent achievement of the discoveries.

7 As with the other phases of globalization, there is some debate about when the contemporary epoch begins (e.g., Held et al., 1999; Hopkins, 2002; Nederveen Pieterse, 2004; Scholte, 2005).

8 For the most sophisticated and comprehensive implementation of this type of approach, see Held et al. (1999).

Chapter 2 Travelling Cultures

1 However, some anthropologists believe alterity or otherness can be overplayed, noting how most people operating in different cultural contexts adapt relatively easily to their new surroundings (see Baumann, 1996a; Keesing, 1994). Quite simply, fewer people would migrate if the prospects of moving to another society were likely to be too traumatic, culturally speaking. Moreover, an excessive emphasis upon the 'other' can merely exacerbate difference and cultural conflict as well as disguise what we have in common, notably the fact that human beings have basic needs that cut across cultures (see Doyal and Gough, 1991).

2 In the mid-1990s, the head of the International Organization for Migration estimated that there were 120 million international migrants, which is less than 2 per cent of the world's population (Castles and Miller, 1998: 4). In 2000, approximately 130 million people lived outside of their nation of birth (Suarez-Orozco, 2000).

3 For an example of this type of analysis, see Claudia de Lima Costa's article 'Between North and South: Travelling Feminisms and Homeless Women' (1999), which examines the adaptations involved as feminist theory travels between the USA and Brazil.

4 There are writers who question whether the notion and rhetoric of flows is an appropriate way of conceptualizing globalization (e.g., see Tsing, 2002).

5 David Held and his co-writers concede that focusing on cultural flows does not tell us anything about 'the experience of participants at either end of the flows' (1999: 329). In this regard, some writers maintain that to understand globalization we need to pay greater attention to how its flows and processes are being variously experienced and perceived, which includes examining associated ideologies (Hay and Marsh, 2001; Hopper, 2006).

6 However, Michael Kearney argues in *Reconceptualising the Peasantry: Anthropology in Global Perspective* (1996) that in a world of global flows the idea of spatial and cultural distinctions and patterns of domination is difficult to sustain.

7 Urry's emphasis upon mobility, as well as more generally the emphasis within the globalization literature upon metaphors such as scapes, networks and flows, has been criticized for being light on empirical data and research (e.g., Favell, 2001).

8 Of course, migrant communities will continue to face pressures to assimilate in most countries. For this reason, some writers consider transnationalism to be a form of resistance on the part of migrants, and in particular a reaction against their invariably marginalized position within their host countries (see Basch et al., 1994).

9 Nevertheless, the notion of cultures travelling is applicable to our era in the sense that cultural flows are indicative of a broader shift away from group cultures and identities towards the self-constituting individual forging their own lifestyles (see chapter 7). In other words, we are constantly passing through and absorbing multiple global and transnational flows of ideas, sounds, symbols, media images and information that inform to varying degrees our outlooks and behaviour patterns.

10 In the Conclusion, it is stressed that employing this approach is made more difficult by the increasingly complex and porous nature of localities, which in turn indicates a need for the type of detailed and sophisticated investigations undertaken by many contemporary anthropologists who incorporate an awareness of global or external influences upon places.

Chapter 3 Global Communication, Media and Technology

1 However, Chris Barker detects certain differences between soaps and telenovelas, notably with regard to the number of episodes and the themes covered, see *Global Television* (1997).

2 There are claims that increased competition is leading national broadcasters to become more entertainment-driven, and in turn this reduction in their public-service role is eroding the public sphere (Herman and McChesney, 1997).

3 John Thompson describes this media-created experience as 'non-reciprocal intimacy at a distance' (1995: 219). For a comprehensive discussion of mediated communication and interaction, see Thompson (1995) and Tomlinson (1999a, ch. 5).

4 Although Kai Hafez (2007) notes that the main artery of data exchange continues to be the transatlantic exchange between the USA and Europe, and contends this is therefore not a genuinely global exchange.

5 However, determining the amount of Internet usage is difficult because, within many households, workplaces, institutions, libraries, and of course cybercafés, even a single connection is likely to be accessed by multiple users.

6 A useful start has been made in gathering such information in the research undertaken for many of the essays in the book edited by Barry Wellman and Caroline Haythornwaite entitled *The Internet in Everyday Life* (2002).

7 Pippa Norris identifies a third aspect of the digital divide, namely a democratic divide, but alas this debate lies beyond the scope of this work (see Norris, 2001).

8 Indeed, inadequate telephony is also a problem for other developing regions, restricting as it does access to the 'information superhighway' (Tehranian and Tehranian, 1997).

9 Given the continued difficulties many people in developing societies face in accessing the Internet, the points made here should generally not be viewed as applicable to them.

Chapter 4 Globalization and Global Culture

1 John Tomlinson contends that cultural homogenization is unlikely to be the primary concern of ordinary citizens, who will have more pressing everyday concerns, such as their personal relations and the state of their finances (1991: 87). However, a counter-argument to this point is that being able to choose one's own culture or cultures is an integral part of leading a flourishing life.

2 For a discussion of Toyotism and the impact of the transfer of Japanese management and working practices abroad, see Elger and Smith (1994).

3 However, it should be noted that China is making significant inroads into global communications. In January 2007, China had 137 million Internet users, making it the largest online community in the world after the USA, and it is estimated that by 2009 Chinese Internet users will outnumber American users (Ramesh, 2007). Some commentators

predict that the Chinese-language Internet will eventually be larger than its English-language counterpart.

4   One such claim is that global capitalism is encouraging cultural convergence by eroding national distinctiveness, but this will be considered in more detail in the next chapter.

5   For Wallerstein's response to this charge, see his essay 'Culture is the World-System: A Reply to Boyne' (1990b).

6   However, in comparison with Wallerstein, Sklair does at least allow for a greater role for human agency within the global system, noting that 'globalization is driven by actors working through institutions they own and/or control' (2001: 1–2).

7   Indeed, Robertson believes Giddens's conception of globalization is also historically inaccurate, arguing that 'globalisation of the contemporary type was set in motion long before whatever we might mean by modernity' (1992: 170).

8   In *Living with Globalisation* (2006), I examine the intersection of the global and the local in a more empirical and contextualized manner, examining a number of case studies where this confluence occurs.

9   Zygmunt Bauman is another writer who has detected a loss of Western self-confidence, evident as he sees it in the contemporary distinction between the universal and the global. The former is associated with the 'proud project' of modernity, while globality, 'in contrast, is a meek acquiescence to what is happening "out there"' (1995: 24).

10 Globalization is of course also an 'ization' and this issue of the conflation of process with end-state needs to be borne in mind when we consider the major critical perspectives on globalization, namely the globalist, sceptical and transformationalist accounts. To what extent, if at all, do they replicate this tendency?

11 Although John Beynon and David Dunkerley (2000) consider that 'the global' and 'the local' constitute a crude dichotomy, and have called for intermediate concepts in the analysis of cultural globalization.

Chapter 5   Globalization and National Culture

1   As will be shown in chapter 6, not all national cultures are associated with nation-states – for example, Montserrat Guibernau (1999) writes of nations without states such as the Welsh and the Basques – but here the focus will be upon the relationship between the nation-state and national culture.

2   Given that the primary concern of this chapter is to consider national culture in relation to globalization rather than undertaking an extensive examination of these terms, such conceptual slippage is likely to be in evidence here, with national culture considered in the broadest sense to encompass and to be constituted by all of these elements.

3   According to Huntington, the US 'Census Bureau estimates that by 2050 the American population will be 23 per cent Hispanic, 16 per cent black and 10 per cent Asian-American' (1996: 61).

4   Within cultural studies, other notable writers that have addressed the issue of hybridity are Arjun Appadurai, Homi Bhabha, Néstor García Canclini and Ulf Hannerz.

5   For a range of criticisms of hybridity theory, see Brah and Coombes (2000) and Friedman (1995, 1999). Unfortunately, given this chapter's focus upon national culture, the nature of the debate between hybridity theorists and their critics cannot be discussed in any detail here.

Chapter 6   Globalization and Cultural Conflict

1   Huntington denies that he seeks to portray civilizations as unified blocs. In an interview he gave shortly after 9/11, he pointed out that: 'The major section on Islam in my book is called "Consciousness Without Cohesion", in which I talk about all the divisions in

the Islamic world, about Muslim-on-Muslim fighting. Even in the current crisis, they are still divided. You have a billion people with all these subcultures, the tribes. Islam is less unified than any other civilisation' (Huntington, 2001).

2 However, this thesis should not be overstated. For instance, detraditionalization, if it exists, best describes a process or tendency; we have not simply moved beyond tradition and entered a post-traditional epoch. In other words, while we are generally more critical of traditional institutions and practices than compared to even the recent past, nevertheless they almost certainly still continue to exert some influence upon most of us (Heelas, 1996).

3 However, this view of the USA as being plagued by 'culture wars' has been challenged (see Fiorina et al., 2005). Alan Wolfe in *One Nation After All* (1998) contends that many Americans simply do not view their country in this way. Based upon attitudinal research of middle-class Americans, he discovered a strong degree of toleration and acceptance of other cultures. While Wolfe's research tells us nothing about the views of other sections of American society, it nevertheless serves to counter some of the gloomier assessments about cultural relations within the USA.

4 In relation to image, an extensive Kuwaiti government survey conducted in 2005 revealed that the depiction of Muslims in the US and European media was 'typically stereotypical and negative' largely because the West's image of Islam has been hijacked by extremists (see Feuilherade, 2005).

5 Wahhabism or Wahhabi Islam, a conservative movement that first emerged in the eighteenth century, seeking to purify Islam and rid it of the accretions gained since the death of the Prophet, was founded by Muhammad ibn 'Abd al-Wahhab (1703–92) and has profoundly shaped Osama bin Laden's religious outlook. With 'Wahhabi' becoming something of a blanket term, some prefer the term *Salafi* when applied to groups beyond the borders of Saudi Arabia (Oliveti, 2002). But as John Esposito has noted: 'both Wahhabi and Salafi can be misleading, as they are used as umbrella terms that incorporate diverse ideologies and movements' (2002: 106).

6 For an informed insight into the different forms of Islam and Islamism, see Burgat (2003).

7 The Middle East and parts of Central Asia are actually fairly disconnected from aspects of economic globalization, with the primary flows of capital trade taking place between other regions of the world. But, as is often the case, perception can be as important as reality when it comes to globalization.

8 Barber et al. would contend that at this juncture tribalist forces are more powerful than the cosmopolitan and the democratic ones identified here. For instance, INGO activity currently remains the preserve of only a limited number of people.

Chapter 7 Globalization and Cosmopolitanism

1 Reflecting these different ways of approaching cosmopolitanism, Samuel Scheffler (1999) makes an interesting distinction between 'cosmopolitanism about justice' and 'cosmopolitanism about culture'. Similarly, Jeremy Waldron (2000) distinguishes between cosmopolitanism in culture and the Kantian idea of a cosmopolitan right. However, it is debatable whether such distinctions can be made. Put simply, can we live in a cosmopolitan manner culturally without having a cosmopolitan sense of justice and ethics?

2 However, the issue of authenticity is raised by these cultural encounters. More specifically, to what extent have these foods, cuisines, religious faiths, music, etc. been modified to suit domestic tastes? For example, with regard to world music, doubts have been expressed as to whether leading artists and their music are truly representative of their respective societies and cultures. On a profounder level, there is the matter of what constitutes authentic culture within the context of cultural globalization. Alas, for such issues and questions to be tackled would require a book in themselves.

3 The terminology of this subject area is contested. Writers such as King (1990) and Sassen (2001) employ the term 'global city', which the latter believes is only applicable to London, New York and Tokyo. Other writers discuss 'world cities' (Knox, 2002) and even 'transnational urbanism' (Smith, 2001). Here the notion of globalizing cities will be employed to indicate that cities other than the three mentioned are becoming important global centres. The term also expresses the unevenness of globalization (Marcuse and van Kempen, 2000).

4 For a fuller explanation of how globalizing processes can foster individualism, see my book *Rebuilding Communities in an Age of Individualism* (2003), especially chapter 3.

5 However, the concept of global civil society has been challenged; see, for example, Shaw (1994).

6 However, the points made here need to be weighed against the contention of those writers who consider that nations and national identities retain their vitality even in our globalizing era (see Smith, 1995).

7 Of course, it is not necessarily the case that global communication technologies will lead to cosmopolitan outcomes or even that they will be used for cosmopolitan purposes. As we saw in the previous chapter, non- or anti-cosmopolitan forces, such as ethnic nationalist groups and the extreme right, are also utilizing these technologies.

8 Ulrich Beck draws similar conclusions in relation to his discussion of the 'Second Age of Modernity', which globalization has helped to ensure that we are entering. In particular, Beck regards cosmopolitanism as an ally of globalization in that it challenges the nation-state: 'globalization means that an increasing number of social processes are indifferent to national boundaries' (2002: 62). However, Beck warns this does not mean that we are all going to become cosmopolitans, as counter-movements will remain.

9 Of course, not all nations function in this way. Amy Gutmann contends that 'most nations do not teach, let alone practice, anything close to basic human rights' (Gutmann, 1996: 66). This is an important point. In this regard, Gerard Delanty (2000) believes cosmopolitanism has its roots in what he terms 'civic communities'.

10 For an interesting discussion of whether we are likely to have more commitment to our particular communities than the universal community of humankind, see Samuel Scheffler (1999).

11 This point was inspired by Hilary Putnam's article 'Must We Choose between Patriotism and Universal Reason?' (1996).

12 Although we should not forget that writers who are sceptical about globalization would undoubtedly challenge the nature and even the existence of these processes.

References and Bibliography

Abu-Lughod, J.L. (1989), *Before European Hegemony: The World-System, 1250–1350*, Oxford: Oxford University Press.

Abu-Lughod, L. (1991), 'Writing against Culture', in R.G. Fox (ed.), *Recapturing Anthropology*, Santa Fe, NM: School of America Research Press.

Adorno, T. (1991), *The Culture Industry*, London: Routledge.

Ajami, F. (1996), 'The Summoning', in *Samuel P. Huntington's The Clash of Civilizations? The Debate*, New York: Foreign Affairs, pp. 26–35.

Al-Ali, N. and Koser, K. (eds) (2001), *New Approaches to Migration?*, London: Routledge.

Albert, M. (1993), *Capitalism against Capitalism*, London: Whurr.

Albrow, M. (1996), *The Global Age*, Cambridge: Polity.

Albrow, M. (1997), 'Travelling Beyond Local Cultures', in J. Eade (ed.), *Living the Global City*, London: Routledge, pp. 37–55.

Alexander, J. (1996), 'Critical Reflections on "Reflexive Modernisation"', *Theory, Culture and Society*, 13, 4, pp. 133–8.

Alexander, J. and Seidman, S. (eds) (1991), *Culture and Society: Contemporary Debates*, New York: Cambridge University Press.

Alibhai-Brown, Y. (2001), 'Ramadan's True Spirit is Threatened', *The Independent*, 19 November.

Alibhai-Brown, Y. (2002), 'Reformist Muslims are Bringing New Hope to Islam', *The Independent*, 9 September.

Alsayyad, N. (ed.) (2001), *Hybrid Urbanism*, Westport, CT: Praeger.

Amin, A. (2001), 'Immigrants, Cosmopolitans and the Idea of Europe', in H. Wallace (ed.), *Interlocking Dimensions of European Integration*, Basingstoke: Palgrave, pp. 280–301.

Amin, S. (1996), 'The Challenge of Globalization', *Review of International Political Economy*, 2.

Amin, S. (1997), *Capitalism in the Age of Globalization*, London: Zed Books.

Anderson, B. (1983), *Imagined Communities: Reflections on the Origin and Spread of Nationalism*, London: Verso.

Anderson, B. (1994), 'Exodus', *Critical Enquiry*, 20, 2, pp. 314–27.

Anderson, B. (1995), 'Ice Empire and Ice Hockey: Two *Fin de Siècle* Dreams', *New Left Review*, 214, pp. 146–50.

Anderson, K. (1999), 'Clinton: End "Digital Divide"', *BBC News Online*, 9 December, www.bbcnews.co.uk (accessed 17/9/06).

Anderson-Gold, S. (2001), *Cosmopolitanism and Human Rights*, Cardiff: University of Wales Press.

Appadurai, A. (1990), 'Disjuncture and Difference in the Global Cultural Economy', in M. Featherstone (ed.), *Global Culture*, London: Sage, pp. 295–310.

Appadurai, A. (1996), *Modernity at Large: Cultural Dimensions of Globalization*, Minneapolis: University of Minnesota Press.

Appadurai, A. (ed.) (2001), *Globalization*, Durham, NC: Duke University Press.

Appiah, K.A. (1994), 'Identity, Authenticity, Survival', in C. Taylor (ed.), *Multiculturalism: Examining the Politics of Recognition*, Princeton, NJ: Princeton University Press.

Appiah, K.A. (1996), 'Cosmopolitan Patriots', in M.C. Nussbaum et al., *For Love of Country*, Boston: Beacon Press, pp. 21–9.

Archibugi, D. and Held, D. (eds) (1995), *Cosmopolitan Democracy*, Cambridge: Polity.

Arlidge, J. (2004), 'Forget Black, Forget White: The Future is Generation EA', *The Observer*, 4 January, p. 19.

Armstrong, K. (2001), 'The War We Should Fight', *The Guardian*, 13 October.

Armstrong, K. (2002), 'The Curse of the Infidel', *The Guardian*, 20 June.

Arthur, C. (2006), 'How Is the Blogosphere Doing?' *Guardian Unlimited*, 9 February, www.guardian.co.uk (accessed 24/11/06).

Ash, L. (2002), 'China's Fearful Muslim Minority', *BBC News Online*, 8 January, www.bbc.co.uk (accessed 12/5/06).

Axford, B. (1995), *The Global System*, Cambridge: Polity.

Axtmann, R. (1997), 'Collective Identity and the Democratic Nation-State in the Age of Globalization', in A. Cvetkovich and D. Kellner (eds), *Articulating the Global and the Local*, Boulder, CO: Westview Press, pp. 33–54.

Barber, B. (1996), *Jihad vs. McWorld*, New York: Ballantine.

Barber, B. (2000), 'Jihad vs. McWorld', in P. O'Meara, H.D. Mehlinger and M. Krain (eds), *Globalization and the Challenges of the New Century*, Bloomington: Indiana University Press, pp. 23–33.

Barker, C. (1997), *Global Television*, Oxford: Blackwell.

Barney, D. (2004), *The Network Society*, Cambridge: Polity.

Barraclough, G. (ed.) (1984), *The Times Atlas of World History*, London, Guild.

Barry Jones, R.J. (2000), *The World Turned Upside Down? Globalization and the Future of the State*, Manchester: Manchester University Press.

Bartley, R.L. (1996), 'The Case for Optimism: The West Should Believe in Itself', in *Samuel P. Huntington's The Clash of Civilizations? The Debate*, New York: Foreign Affairs, pp. 41–5.

Basch, L., Schiller, N.G. and Blanc, C.S. (eds) (1994), *Nations Unbound*, Langhorne, PA: Gordon & Breach.

Baudrillard, J. (1983), *Simulations*, New York: Semiotext(e).

Bauman, Z. (1993), *Postmodern Ethics*, Oxford: Blackwell.

Bauman, Z. (1995), *Life in Fragments*, Oxford: Blackwell.

Bauman, Z. (1996a), 'From Pilgrim to Tourist – or A Short History of Identity', in S. Hall and P. du Gay (eds), *Questions of Cultural Identity*, London: Sage, pp. 18–36.

Bauman, Z. (1996b), 'Morality in the Age of Contingency', in P. Heelas et al. (eds), *Detraditionalization*, Oxford: Blackwell, pp. 49–58.

Bauman, Z. (1998a), *Globalization: The Human Consequences*, Cambridge: Polity.

Bauman, Z. (1998b), 'On Glocalisation: Or Globalisation for Some, Localisation for Others', *Thesis Eleven*, 54, pp. 37–49.

Bauman, Z. (2001), *The Individualized Society*, Cambridge: Polity.

Baumann, G. (1996), *Contesting Culture*, Cambridge: Cambridge University Press.

Bayly, C.A. (2002), '"Archaic" and "Modern" Globalization in the Eurasian and African Arena, c.1750–1850', in A.G. Hopkins (ed.), *Globalization in World History*, London: Pimlico, pp. 47–73.

BBC (1998), 'It's a Man's Cyberworld', *BBC News Online*, 27 March, www.bbcnews.co.uk (accessed 17/6/06).

BBC (2000a), 'Is the Web Widening the Poverty Gap?', *BBC News Online*, 29 January, www.bbcnews.co.uk (accessed 12/1/06).

BBC (2000b), 'Indian Net Users Set to Soar', *BBC News Online*, 24 July, www.bbcnews.co.uk (accessed 18/9/06).

BBC (2003), 'Digital Divide Figures Are "Flawed"', *BBC News Online*, 29 January, www.bbcnews.co.uk (accessed 7/1/06).

BBC (2004), 'Global Broadband Keeps Climbing', *BBC News Online*, 6 January, www.bbcnews.co.uk (accessed 12/10/06).

BBC (2005a), 'UK Majority Back Multiculturalism', *BBC News Online*, 10 August, www.bbcnews.co.uk (accessed 2/11/06).

BBC (2005b), 'Blog Reading Explodes in America', *BBC News Online*, 4 January, www.bbcnews.co.uk (accessed 3/10/06).

BBC (2005c), 'Blogging v Dogging', *BBC News Online*, 28 September, www.bbcnews.co.uk (accessed 1/8/06).

BBC (2006), 'Global Fair Trade Sales Taking Off', *BBC News Online*, 28 June, www.bbcnews.co.uk (accessed 12/1/07).

Beaumont, P. (2001), 'The Roots of Islamic Anger', *The Observer*, 14 October.

Beck, U. (1992), *Risk Society: Towards a New Modernity*, London: Sage.

Beck, U. (1997), *The Reinvention of Politics: Rethinking Modernity in the Global Social Order*, Cambridge: Polity.

Beck, U. (1999), *World Risk Society*, Cambridge: Polity.

Beck, U. (2000), *What Is Globalization?*, Cambridge: Polity.

Beck, U. (2002), 'The Cosmopolitan Perspective: Sociology in the Second Age of Modernity', in S. Vertovec and R. Cohen (eds), *Conceiving Cosmopolitanism*, Oxford: Oxford University Press, pp. 61–85.

Beck, U. and Beck-Gernsheim, E. (1996), 'Individualisation and "Precarious Freedoms": Perspectives and Controversies of a Subject-Orientated Society', in P. Heelas et al. (eds), *Detraditionalization*, Oxford: Blackwell, pp. 23–48.

Beck, U., Giddens, A. and Lash, S. (1994), *Reflexive Modernization*, Cambridge: Polity.

Bennison, A.K. (2002), 'Muslim Universalism and Western Globalisation', in A.G. Hopkins (ed.), *Globalization in World History*, London: Pimlico, pp. 74–97.

Bentley, J.H. (1993), *Old World Encounters: Cross-Cultural Contacts and Exchanges in Pre-Modern Times*, Oxford: Oxford University Press.

Berger, P.L. and Huntington, S.P. (eds) (2002), *Many Globalizations*, Oxford: Oxford University Press.

Berger, S. and Dore, R. (eds) (1996), *National Diversity and Global Capitalism*, Ithaca, NY: Cornell University Press.

Berman, M. (1983), *All that is Solid Melts into Air*, London: Verso.

Beynon, J. and Dunkerley, D. (eds) (2000), *Globalization: The Reader*, London: Athlone Press.

Bhabha, H. (1990), *Nation and Narration*, London: Routledge.

Bhabha, H. (1995), *The Location of Culture*, London: Routledge.

Billig, M. (1995), *Banal Nationalism*, London: Sage.

Billington, R., Strawbridge, S., Greensides, L. and Fitzsimmons, A. (1991), *Culture and Society*, Basingstoke: Macmillan.

Blair, T. (1996), *New Britain: My Vision of a Young Country*, London: Fourth Estate.

Boas, F. (1911), *The Mind of Primitive Man*, New York: Macmillan.

Boas, F. (1886), 'The Limitations of the Comparative Method of Anthropology, *Science*, 4, 103.

Bourdieu, P. (1977), *Outline of a Theory of Practice*, Cambridge: Cambridge University Press.

Bourdieu, P. (1990a), *The Logic of Practice*, Cambridge: Polity.

Bourdieu, P. (1990b), *In Other Words: Essays Toward a Reflexive Sociology*, Cambridge: Polity.

Bourdieu, P. (1993), *The Field of Cultural Production*, Cambridge: Polity.

Boyd, C. (2005), 'Persian Blogging around the Globe', *BBC News Online*, 6 March, www.bbcnews.co.uk (accessed 19/1/07).

Boyne, R. (1990), 'Culture and the World-System', in M. Featherstone (ed.), *Global Culture*, London: Sage, pp. 57–62.

Brah, A. (1996), *Cartographies of Diaspora*, London: Routledge.

Brah, A. and Coombes, A. (eds) (2000), *Hybridity and its Discontents*, London: Routledge.

Breckenridge, C.A., Bhabha, H.K., Pollock, S. and Chakrabarty, D. (eds) (2002), *Cosmopolitanism*, Durham, NC: Duke University Press.

Bredin, M. (1996) 'Transforming Images: Communication Technologies and Cultural Identity in Nishnawbe-Aski', in D. Howes (ed.), *Cross-Cultural Consumption*, London: Routledge, pp. 161–77.

Brenner, N. (1998), 'Global Cities, Glocal States: Global City Formation and State Territorial Restructuring in Contemporary Europe', *Review of International Political Economy*, 5, 1, pp. 1–37.

Brimelow, P. (1995), *Alien Nation: Common Sense about America's Immigration Disaster*, New York: Random House.

Brogan, H. (2001), *The Penguin History of the USA*, 2nd edn, London: Penguin.

Brunn, S. and Leinbach, T. (eds) (1991), *Collapsing Time and Space: Geographic Aspects of Communication and Information*, London: HarperCollins.

Buckley Ebrey, P. (ed.) (1996), *Cambridge Illustrated History of China*, Cambridge, Cambridge UP.

Buncombe, A. (2007), 'US Military Tells Jack Bauer: Cut out the Torture Scenes … or Else!', *Independent Online*, 13 February, www.independent.co.uk (accessed 15/2/07).

Burbach, R., Nuñez, O. and Kagarlitsky, B. (1997), *Globalization and its Discontents*, London: Pluto Press.

Burgat, F. (2003), *Face to Face with Political Islam*, London: I.B. Tauris.

Burke, J. (2003), *Al-Qaeda: Casting a Shadow of Terror*, London: I.B. Tauris.

Calhoun, C. (2002), 'The Class Consciousness of Frequent Travellers: Towards a Critique of Actually Existing Cosmopolitanism', in S. Vertovec and R. Cohen (eds), *Conceiving Cosmopolitanism*, Oxford: Oxford University Press, pp. 86–109.

Callinicos, A. (2003), *An Anti-Capitalist Manifesto*, Cambridge: Polity.

Cameron, A. and Palan, R. (2004), *The Imagined Economies of Globalization*, London: Sage.

Carnoy, M. and Castells, M. (2001), 'Globalisation, the Knowledge Society, and the Network State: Poulantzas at the Millennium', *Global Networks*, 1, 1, pp. 1–18.

Castells, M. (1993), 'European Cities, the Information Society and the Global Economy', in A. Gray and J. McGuigan (eds), *Studying Culture*, London: Arnold.

Castells, M. (1996), *The Rise of the Network Society*, vol. 1 of *The Information Age*, Oxford: Blackwell.

Castells, M. (1997a), *The Power of Identity*, vol. 2 of *The Information Age*, Oxford: Blackwell.

Castells, M. (1997b), 'An Introduction to the Information Age', *City*, 7, pp. 1–16.

Castells, M. (1998), *The End of the Millennium*, vol. 3 of *The Information Age*, Oxford: Blackwell.

Castells, M. (2001), *The Internet Galaxy*, Oxford: Oxford University Press.

Castells, M. (2004), 'Informationalism, Networks, and the Network Society: A Theoretical Blueprint', in M. Castells (ed.), *The Network Society: A Cross-Cultural Perspective*, Cheltenham: Edward Elgar, pp. 3–45.

Castells, M. and Ince, M. (2003), *Conversations with Manuel Castells*, Cambridge: Polity.

Castles, S. (1998), 'Globalization and Migration: Some Pressing Contradictions', *International Social Science Journal*, 50, 2, pp. 179–86.

Castles, S. and Miller, M.J. (1998), *The Age of Migration*, 2nd edn, Basingstoke: Macmillan.

Chalaby, J.K. (ed.) (2005), *Transnational Television Worldwide*, London: I.B. Tauris.

Chatterjee, P. (1986), *Nationalist Thought and the Colonial World*, London: Zed Books.

Chavez, L. (1996), 'Multiculturalism is Driving Us Apart', *USA Today*, 124, 2612, pp. 39–41.

Cheah, P. and Robbins, B. (eds) (1998), *Cosmopolitics: Thinking and Feeling beyond the Nation*, Minneapolis: University of Minnesota Press.

Chen, W., Boase, J. and Wellman, B. (2002), 'The Global Villagers: Comparing Internet Users and Uses around the World', in B. Wellman and C. Haythornwaite (eds), *The Internet in Everyday Life*, Oxford: Blackwell, pp. 74–113.

Clark, R.P. (1997), *The Global Imperative: An Interpretative History of the Spread of Humankind*, Boulder, CO: Westview Press.

Clarke, J.J. (1997), *Oriental Enlightenment*, London: Routledge.

Clifford, J. (1988), *The Predicament of Culture*, Cambridge, MA: Harvard University Press.

Clifford, J. (1992), 'Travelling Cultures', in L. Grossberg, C. Nelson and P. Treichler (eds), *Cultural Studies*, London: Routledge, pp. 96–116.

Clifford, J. (1997), *Routes: Travel and Translation in the Late Twentieth Century*, Cambridge, MA: Harvard University Press.

Cohen, R. (1997), *Global Diasporas: An Introduction*, London: Routledge.

Connor, W. (1978), 'A Nation is a Nation, is a State, is an Ethnic Group, is a …', *Ethnic and Racial Studies*, 1, 4, pp. 379–88.

Cooper, F. (2001), 'What is the Concept of Globalization Good for? An African Historian's Perspective', *African Affairs*, 1000, pp. 189–213.

Cowen, N. (2001), *Global History: A Short Overview*, Cambridge: Polity.

Crane, D. (ed.) (1994), *The Sociology of Culture: Emerging Theoretical Perspectives*, Oxford: Blackwell.

Crick, M. (1989), 'Representations of International Tourism in the Social Sciences', *Annual Review of Anthropology*, 18.

Crystal, D. (1995), *The Cambridge Encyclopaedia of the English Language*, Cambridge: Cambridge University Press.

Crystal, D. (2003), *English as a Global Language*, 2nd edn, Cambridge: Cambridge University Press.

Curtin, P.D. (1984), *Cross-Cultural Trade in World History*, Cambridge: Cambridge University Press.

Cvetkovich, A. and Kellner, D. (eds) (1997), *Articulating the Global and the Local*, Boulder, CO: Westview Press.

Dalby, A. (2000), *Empire of Pleasures: Luxury and Indulgence in the Roman World*, London: Routledge.

Dalrymple, W. (2001), 'Jesus the Prophet', *The Guardian*, 22 December.

Dawood, N.J. (trans.) (1997), *The Koran*, London: Penguin.

Dawoud, K. (2002), 'Egypt Terror Leaders Renounce Violence', *The Guardian*, 2 August.

Deibert, R.J. (1997), *Parchment, Printing, and Hypermedia*, New York: Columbia University Press.

Delanty, G. (1996), 'Beyond the Nation-State: National Identity and Citizenship in a Multicultural Society – A Response to Rex', *Sociological Research Online*, 1, 3, www.socresonline.org.uk/socresonline/1/3/1 (accessed 3/9/05).

Delanty, G. (2000), *Citizenship in a Global Age*, Buckingham: Open University Press.

Delanty, G. and O'Mahony, P. (2002), *Nationalism and Social Theory*, London: Sage.

De Swaan, A. (1991), 'Notes on the Emerging Global Language System: Regional, National and Supranational', *Media, Culture and Society*, 13.

De Swaan, A. (2001), *Words of the World*, Cambridge: Polity.

Dodd, V. (2004), '90% of Whites Have Few or No Black Friends', *The Guardian*, 19 July, p. 1.

Douglass, M. (1994), 'Culture and the City in East Asia: A Perspective for the 21st Century', *International Conference on Cities in Transition: Towards a Creative and Cooperative Order*, Seoul Development Institute, November.

Dower, N. (1998), *World Ethics: The New Agenda*, Edinburgh: Edinburgh University Press.

Doyal, L. and Gough, I. (1991), *A Theory of Human Need*, Basingstoke: Macmillan.

Drahos, P. and Braithwaite, J. (2002), *Information Feudalism*, London: Earthscan.

Drahos, P. and Mayne, R. (eds) (2002), *Global Intellectual Property Rights*, Basingstoke: Palgrave.

Dunkerley, D. et al. (2002), *Changing Europe: Identities, Nations and Citizens*, London: Routledge.

Dunn, J. (ed.) (1995), *Contemporary Crisis of the Nation-State?*, Oxford: Blackwell.

Eade, J. (ed.) (1997), *Living the Global City: Globalization as Local Process*, London: Routledge.

Eagleton, T. (1991), *Ideology: An Introduction*, London: Verso.

Eagleton, T. (2000), *The Idea of Culture*, Oxford: Blackwell.

Eckes, A.E., Jr. and Zeiler, T.W. (2003), *Globalization and the American Century*, Cambridge: Cambridge University Press.

The Economist (2000), 'The New Americans', 11 March, pp. 1–18.

Eisenstadt, S.N. (ed.) (2002), *Multiple Modernities*, New Brunswick, NJ: Transaction Books.

Eisenstadt, S.N. (2003), *Comparative Civilizations and Multiple Modernities*, vols 1 and 2, Leiden: Brill.

Eisenstein, Z. (1998), *Global Obscenities: Patriarchy, Capitalism and the Lure of Cyberfantasy*, New York: New York University Press.

Elger, T. and Smith, C. (eds) (1994), *Global Japanization?*, London: Routledge.

Elliott, J.H. (1970), *The Old World and the New, 1492–1650*, Cambridge: Cambridge University Press.

Elliott, L. (2004), 'Blake's Big Brother', *The Guardian*, 10 July, p. 23.

Eriksen, T.H. (1995), *Small Places, Large Issues: An Introduction to Social and Cultural Anthropology*, London: Pluto Press.

Eriksen, T.H. (1997), 'Multiculturalism, Individualism and Human Rights: Romanticism, the Enlightenment and Lessons from Mauritius', in R.A. Wilson (ed.), *Human Rights, Culture and Context*, London: Pluto Press, pp. 49–69.

Eriksen, T.H. (ed.) (2003), *Globalisation: Studies in Anthropology*, London, Pluto Press.

Escobar, A. (1995), *Encountering Development*, Princeton, NJ: Princeton University Press.

Esposito, J.L. (2002), *Unholy War: Terror in the Name of Islam*, Oxford: Oxford University Press.

Etzioni, A. (1997), 'Other Americans Help Break Down Racial Barriers', *International Herald Tribune*, 10 May.

Fagan, B.M. (1990), *The Journey from Eden: The Peopling of our World*, London: Thames & Hudson.

Falk, R. (1995), 'The World Order between Inter-State Law and the Law of Humanity: The Role of Civil Society Institutions', in D. Archibugi and D. Held (eds), *Cosmopolitan Democracy*, Cambridge: Polity, pp. 163–79.

Falk, R. (1996), 'Revisioning Cosmopolitanism', in M.C. Nussbaum et al. (eds), *For Love of Country*, Boston: Beacon Press, pp. 53–60.

Falk, R. (1999), *Predatory Globalization*, Cambridge: Polity.

Favell, A. (2001), 'Migration, Mobility and Globaloney: Metaphors and Rhetoric in the Sociology of Globalisation', *Global Networks*, 1, 4, pp. 389–98.

Featherstone, M. (ed.) (1990), *Global Culture*, London: Sage.

Featherstone, M. (1995), *Undoing Culture*, London: Sage.

Featherstone, M. and Lash, S. (1995), 'Globalization, Modernity and the Spatialization of Social Theory: An Introduction', in M. Featherstone et al. (eds), *Global Modernities*, London: Sage, pp. 1–24.

Featherstone, M. and Lash, S. (eds) (1999), *Spaces of Culture: City, Nation, World*, London: Sage.

Featherstone, M., Lash, S. and Robertson, R. (eds) (1995), *Global Modernities*, London: Sage.

Ferguson, Y.H. (2006), 'The Crisis of the State in a Globalizing World', *Globalizations*, 3, 1, pp. 5–8.

Fernández-Armesto, F. (1996), *Millennium*, London: Black Swan.

Ferro, M. (1997), *Colonization: A Global History*, London: Routledge.

Feuilherade, P. (2005), 'Extremists "Hijack Islam's image"', *BBC Monitoring*, 15 November, www.bbcnews.co.uk (accessed 6/11/06).

Fieldhouse, D.K. (1961), '"Imperialism": An Historiographical Revision', *Economic History Review*, 14, pp. 187–209.

Fiorina, M.P. with Abrams, S.J. and Pope, J.C. (2005), *Culture War? The Myth of a Polarized America*, New York: Pearson Longman.

Frank, A.G. (1998), *Re-Orient: Global Economy in the Asian Age*, Berkeley: University of California Press.

Frank, A.G. and Gills, B.K. (eds) (1996), *The World System*, London: Routledge.

Freedland, J. (2002), 'What Really Changed', *The Guardian*, 4 September.

Friedman, E. (1999), 'Reinterpreting the Asianisation of the World and the Role of the State in the Rise of China', in D.A. Smith et al. (eds), *States and Sovereignty in the Global Economy*, London: Routledge, pp. 246–63.

Friedman, J. (1990), 'Being in the World: Globalization and Localization', in M. Featherstone (ed.), *Global Culture*, London: Sage, pp. 311–28.

Friedman, J. (1994), *Cultural Identity and Global Process*, London: Sage.

Friedman, J. (1995), 'Global System, Globalization and the Parameters of Modernity', in M. Featherstone, S. Lash and R. Robertson (eds), *Global Modernities*, London: Sage, pp. 69–90.

Friedman, J. (1999), 'The Hybridisation of Roots and the Abhorrence of the Bush', in M. Featherstone and S. Lash (eds), *Spaces of Culture*, London: Sage, pp. 230–56.

Fukuyama, F. (1992), *The End of History and the Last Man*, New York: Free Press.

Fuller, G. and Lesser, I. (1995), *A Sense of Siege: The Geopolitics of Islam and the West*, Boulder, CO: Westview Press.

García Canclini, N. (1995), *Hybrid Cultures*, Minneapolis: University of Minnesota Press.

Gearhart, S. (2005), 'Inclusions: Psychoanalysis, Transnationalism, and Minority Cultures', in F. Lionnet and S. Shih (eds), *Minor Transnationalism*, Durham, NC: Duke University Press, pp. 27–40.

Geertz, C. (ed.) (1963), *Old Societies and New States*, New York: Free Press.

Geertz, C. (1973), *The Interpretation of Cultures*, New York: Basic Books.

Geertz, C. (1980), *Negara*, Princeton, NJ: Princeton University Press.

Gellner, E. (1983), *Nations and Nationalism*, Oxford: Blackwell.

Gessner, V. and Schade, A. (1990), 'Conflicts of Culture in Cross-Border Legal Relations: The Conception of a Research Topic in the Sociology of Law', in M. Featherstone (ed.) (1990), *Global Culture*, London: Sage, pp. 253–79.

Giddens, A. (1990), *The Consequences of Modernity*, Cambridge: Polity.

Giddens, A. (1994), *Beyond Left and Right*, Cambridge: Polity.

Giddens, A. (1999), *Runaway World: How Globalisation is Reshaping our Lives*, London: Profile Books.

Gills, B.K. and Thompson, W.R. (eds) (2006), *Globalisation and Global History*, London: Routledge.

Gilpin, R. (1987), *The Political Economy of International Relations*, Princeton, NJ: Princeton University Press.

Gilroy, P. (1993), *The Black Atlantic*, London: Verso.

Glazer, N. (1997), *We Are All Multiculturalists Now*, Cambridge, MA: Harvard University Press.

Goodenough, W. (1989), 'Culture: Concept and Phenomenon', in M. Freilich (ed.), *The Relevance of Culture*, New York: Bergin & Garvey.

Gowan, P. (2001), 'Neoliberal Cosmopolitanism', *New Left Review*, 11, pp. 79–93.

Graham, S. and Marvin, S. (2001), *Splintering Urbanism*, London: Routledge.

Gray, J. (2003), *Al Qaeda and What it Means to be Modern*, London: Faber & Faber.

Green, D.M. (2000), 'The End of Identity? The Implications of Postmodernity for Political Identification', *Nationalism and Ethnic Politics*, 6, 3, pp. 68–90.

Greider, W. (1997), *One World, Ready or Not: The Manic Logic of Global Capitalism*, London: Penguin.

Griffiths, I.L. (1995), *The African Inheritance*, London: Routledge.

Guardian Unlimited (2003), 'Across the Great Divide', 10 December, www.guardian.co.uk (accessed 22/11/06).

Guéhenno, J.-M. (1995), *The End of the Nation-State*, Minneapolis: University of Minnesota Press.

Guerrina, R. (2002), *Europe: History, Ideas and Ideologies*, London: Arnold.

Guibernau, M. (1999), *Nations without States*, Cambridge: Polity.

Gupta, A. and Ferguson, J. (2002), 'Beyond "Culture": Space, Identity, and the Politics of Difference', in J. Xavier Inda and R. Rosaldo (eds), *The Anthropology of Globalization: A Reader*, Oxford: Blackwell, pp. 65–80.

Gutmann, A. (1996), 'Democratic Citizenship', in J. Cohen (ed.), *For Love of Country: Debating the Limits of Patriotism*, Boston: Beacon Press, pp. 66–71.

Habermas, J. (1984), *The Theory of Communicative Action*, vol. 1, Boston: Beacon Press.

Hafez, K. (2007), *The Myth of Media Globalization*, Cambridge: Polity.

Hall, S. (1992), 'The Question of Cultural Identity', in S. Hall, D. Held and T. McGrew (eds), *Modernity and its Futures*, Cambridge: Polity, pp. 273–316.

Hall, S. (1996), 'Who Needs Identity?', in S. Hall and P. du Gay (eds), *Questions of Cultural Identity*, London: Sage, pp. 1–17.

Halliday, F. (1996), *Islam and the Myth of Confrontation*, London: I.B. Tauris.

Hamelink, C.J. (1983), *Cultural Autonomy in Global Communications*, London: Longman.

Hannerz, U. (1987), 'The World in Creolisation', *Africa*, 57, 4, pp. 546–59.

Hannerz, U. (1989a), 'Culture between Centre and Periphery: Toward a Macroanthropology', *Ethnos*, 54, pp. 200–16.

Hannerz, U. (1989b), 'Notes on the Global Ecumene', *Public Culture*, 1, 2, pp. 66–75.

Hannerz, U. (1990), 'Cosmopolitans and Locals in World Culture', in M. Featherstone (ed.), *Global Culture*, London: Sage, pp. 237–51.

Hannerz, U. (1991), 'Scenarios for Peripheral Cultures', in A.D. King (ed.), *Culture, Globalisation and the World System*, London: Macmillan, pp. 107–28.

Hannerz, U. (1992a), *Cultural Complexity*, New York: Columbia University Press.

Hannerz, U. (1992b), 'The Global Ecumene as a Network of Networks', in A. Kuper (ed.), *Conceptualising Society*, London: Routledge, pp. 34–56.

Hannerz, U. (1996), *Transnational Connections*, London: Routledge.

Hannerz, U. (2003), 'Special Issue Devoted to the Work of Ulf Hannerz', *Global Networks*, 3, 3.

Harman, C. (1996), 'Globalisation: A Critique of a New Orthodoxy', *International Socialism*, 73, pp. 3–33.

Harries, O. (1994), 'Power and Civilization', *National Interest*, no. 35.

Harrison, L.E. and Huntington S.P. (eds) (2000), *Culture Matters*, New York: Basic Books.

Harvey, D. (1989), *The Condition of Postmodernity*, Oxford: Blackwell.

Hay, C. and Marsh, D. (eds) (2001), *Demystifying Globalization*, Basingstoke: Palgrave.

Headrick, D.R. (1988), *The Tentacles of Progress: Technology Transfer in the Age of Imperialism, 1850–1940*, Oxford: Oxford University Press.

Heater, D. (2003), *World Citizenship: Cosmopolitan Thinking and its Opponents*, London: Continuum.

Heelas, P. (1996), 'Introduction: Detraditionalization and its Rivals', in P. Heelas et al. (eds), *Detraditionalization*, Oxford: Blackwell, pp. 1–20.

Heelas, P., Lash, S. and Morris, P. (eds) (1996), *Detraditionalization*, Oxford: Blackwell.

Held, D. (1995), *Democracy and the Global Order*, Cambridge: Polity.

Held, D. (2004), *Global Covenant*, Cambridge: Polity.

Held, D. and Koenig-Archibugi, M. (2003), *Taming Globalization*, Cambridge: Polity.

Held, D. and McGrew, A. (eds) (2000), *The Global Transformations Reader*, Cambridge: Polity.

Held, D. and McGrew, A. (eds) (2002a), *Governing Globalization*, Cambridge: Polity.

Held, D. and McGrew, A. (2002b), *Globalization/Anti-Globalization*, Cambridge: Polity.

Held, D., McGrew, A., Goldblatt, D. and Perraton, J. (1999), *Global Transformations*, Cambridge: Polity.

Helleiner, E. (1997), 'Braudelian Reflections on Economic Globalization: The Historian as Pioneer', in S. Gill and J. Mittleman (eds), *Innovation and Transformation in International Studies*, Cambridge: Cambridge University Press, pp. 90–104.

Hendy, D. (2000), *Radio in the Global Age*, Cambridge: Polity.

Hepworth, M. (1989), *The Geography of the Information Economy*, London: Belhaven Press.

Herman, E. and McChesney, R. (1997), *The Global Media*, London: Cassell.

Hermida, A. (2006), 'Young Challenge Mainstream Media', *BBC News Online*, 3 May, www.bbcnews.co.uk (accessed 3/11/06).

Hewitt, D. (2000), 'China Clampdown on Muslim Region', *BBC News Online*, 29 May, www.bbcnews.co.uk (accessed 4/11/05).

Hiebert, D. (2002), 'Cosmopolitanism at the Local Level: The Development of Transnational Neighbourhoods', in S. Vertovec and R. Cohen (eds), *Conceiving Cosmopolitanism*, Oxford: Oxford University Press, pp. 209–23.

Hirst, P. and Thompson, G. (1996), *Globalization in Question*, Cambridge: Polity.

Hirst, P. and Thompson, G. (2000), 'Global Myths and National Policies', in B. Holden (ed.), *Global Democracy: Key Debates*, London: Routledge, pp. 47–59.

Hobsbawm, E. (1987), *The Age of Empire, 1875–1914*, London: Weidenfeld & Nicolson.

Hobsbawm, E. (1992), *Nations and Nationalism since 1780*, Cambridge: Cambridge University Press.

Hobsbawm, E. and Ranger, T.O. (eds) (1983), *The Invention of Tradition*, Cambridge: Cambridge University Press.

Holmes, D. (ed.) (1997), *Virtual Politics: Identity and Community in Cyberspace*, London: Sage.

Holton, R.J. (1998), *Globalisation and the Nation-State*, Basingstoke: Macmillan.

Holton, R.J. (2000), 'Globalisation's Cultural Consequences', *Annals of the American Academy of Political and Social Sciences*, 570, pp. 140–52.

Holton, R.J. (2005), *Making Globalisation*, Basingstoke: Palgrave.

Hopkins, A.G. (ed.) (2002), *Globalization in World History*, London: Pimlico.

Hopper, P. (2003), *Rebuilding Communities in an Age of Individualism*, Aldershot: Ashgate.

Hopper, P. (2004), 'Who Wants to Be a European? Community and Identity in the European Union', *Human Affairs*, 14, pp. 141–51.

Hopper, P. (2006), *Living with Globalisation*, Oxford: Berg.

Horrigan, J. and Raine, L. (2002), *The Broadband Difference: How Online Behavior Changes with High-Speed Internet Connections*, Washington, DC: Pew Internet and American Life Project.

Horsman, M. and Marshall, A. (1995), *After the Nation-State: Citizens, Tribalism and the New World Disorder*, London: HarperCollins.

Hsü, I.C.Y. (1995), *The Rise of Modern China*, 5th edn, Oxford: Oxford University Press.

Hunter, J.D. (1991), *Culture Wars: The Struggle to Define America*, New York: Basic Books.

Hunter, J.D. and Yates, J. (2002), 'In the Vanguard of Globalization: The World of American Globalizers', in P.L. Berger and S.P. Huntington (eds), *Many Globalizations*, Oxford: Oxford University Press, pp. 323–57.

Huntington, S.P. (1993), 'The Clash of Civilizations', *Foreign Affairs*, 72, 3, pp. 22–49.

Huntington, S.P. (1996), 'If Not Civilizations, What?', in *Samuel P. Huntington's The Clash of Civilizations? The Debate*, New York: Foreign Affairs, pp. 56–67.

Huntington, S.P. (1997), *The Clash of Civilizations and the Remaking of World Order*, London: Touchstone.

Huntington, S.P. (2001), 'So, Are Civilizations at War?', interview by Michael Steinberger, *The Observer*, 21 October.

Huntington, S.P. (2004), *Who Are We? America's Great Debate*, New York: Free Press.

Hutchinson, J. (2005), *Nations as Zones of Conflict*, London: Sage.

Inglis, F. (1993), *Cultural Studies*, Oxford: Blackwell.

Ingold, T. (1994), 'Introduction to Culture', in T. Ingold (ed.), *Companion Encyclopedia of Anthropology: Humanity, Culture and Social Life*, London: Routledge.

ITU (1994), *Direction of Traffic: International Telephone Traffic 1994*, Geneva: International Telecommunication Union.

ITU (2003), *ITU Internet Reports: Birth of Broadband*, Geneva: International Telecommunication Union.

ITU (2006), 'Key Global Telecom Indicators for the World Telecommunication Service Sector', International Telecommunication Union, www.itu.int (accessed 10/9/06).

Iwabuchi, K. (2002), *Recentering Globalization: Popular Culture and Japanese Transnationalism*, Durham, NC: Duke University Press.

Jackson, P., Crang, P. and Dwyer, C. et al. (eds) (2003), *Transnational Spaces*, London: Routledge.

Jacquin, D., Oros, A. and Verweij, M. (1993), 'Culture in International Relations', *Millennium*, 22, 3, pp. 375–77.

Jameson, F. and Miyoshi, M. (eds) (1998), *The Cultures of Globalization*, Durham, NC: Duke University Press.

Jenkins, B.M. (2001), 'The Organization Men: Anatomy of a Terrorist Attack', in J.F. Hoge and G. Rose (eds), *How Did This Happen?*, Oxford: Public Affairs, pp. 1–14.

Jones, S.G. (ed.) (1997), *Virtual Culture: Identity and Communication in Cybersociety*, London: Sage.

Jones, S.G. (ed.) (1998), *CyberSociety 2.0*, London: Sage.

Judah, T. (2002), 'Via TV and the Net, Iran's Youth Plot Social Revolution', *The Observer*, 25 August.

Julius, D. (1990), *Global Companies and Public Policy*, London: Pinter.

Kagan, R. (2003), *Paradise and Power: America and Europe in the New World Order*, London: Atlantic Books.

Kaldor, M. (2003), *Global Civil Society*, Cambridge: Polity.

Katz, J.E. and Aakhus, M. (eds) (2002), *Perpetual Contact*, Cambridge: Cambridge University Press.

Katz, J.E. and Rice, R. (2002), 'Synoptia: Access, Civic Involvement, and Social Interaction on the Net', in B. Wellman and C. Haythornwaite (eds), *The Internet in Everyday Life*, Oxford: Blackwell, pp. 114–38.

Kavolis, V. (1988), 'Contemporary Moral Cultures and the "Return of the Sacred"', *Sociological Analysis*, 49, 3.

Keane, J. (2003), *Global Civil Society?*, Cambridge: Cambridge University Press.

Kearney, M. (1995), 'The Local and the Global: The Anthropology of Globalisation and Transnationalism', *Annual Review of Anthropology*, 24, pp. 547–65.

Kearney, M. (1996), *Reconceptualizing the Peasantry: Anthropology in Global Perspective*, Boulder, CO: Westview Press.

Keck, M. and Sikkunk, K. (1998), *Activists beyond Borders*, Ithaca, NY: Cornell University Press.

Keesing, R.M. (1974), 'Theories of Culture', *Annual Review of Anthropology*, 3, pp. 73–97.

Keesing, R.M. (1994), 'Theories of Cultures Revisited', in R. Borofsky (ed.), *Assessing Cultural Anthropology*, New York: McGraw-Hill.

Kellas, J.G. (1991), *The Politics of Nationalism and Ethnicity*, Basingstoke: Macmillan.

Kelly, G. (ed.) (1999), *The New European Left*, London: Fabian Society.

Kennedy, P. and Roudometof, V. (eds) (2002), *Communities across Borders*, London: Routledge.

Keohane, R.O. (1995), 'Hobbes' Dilemma and Institutional Change in World Politics: Sovereignty in International Society', in H.-H. Holm and G. Sorensen (eds), *Whose World Order? Uneven Globalization and the End of the Cold War*, Boulder, CO: Westview Press, pp. 165–86.

Kepel, G. (2002), *Jihad: The Trail of Political Islam*, trans. A.F. Roberts, London: I.B. Tauris.

Khazanov, A.M. (1994), *Nomads and the Outside World*, Madison: University of Wisconsin Press.

Kiernan, V.G. (1988), *The Lords of Humankind*, London: Cresset Library.

King, A.D. (1990), *Global Cities*, London: Routledge.

King, A.D. (1995), 'The Times and Spaces of Modernity (or Who Needs Postmodernism?)', in M. Featherstone et al. (eds), *Global Modernities*, London: Sage, pp. 108–23.

Kivisto, P. (2002), *Multiculturalism in a Global Society*, Oxford: Blackwell.

Klein, N. (2000), *No Logo*, London: Flamingo.

Kline, D. and Burstein, D. (eds) (2005), *Blog!*, New York: CDS Books.

Knox, P.L. (2002), 'World Cities and the Organization of Global Space', in R.J. Johnson, P.J. Taylor and M.J. Watts (eds), *Geographies of Global Change*, 2nd edn, Oxford: Blackwell, pp. 328–39.

Kogut, B. (ed.) (2004), *The Global Internet Economy*, London: MIT Press.

Kotkin, J. (1992), *Tribes: How Race, Religion, and Identity Determine Success in the New Global Economy*, New York: Random House.

Kuper, A. (1999), *Culture: The Anthropologists' Account*, Cambridge, MA: Harvard University Press.

Kymlicka, W. and Straehle, C. (1999), 'Cosmopolitanism, Nation-States, and Minority Nationalism: A Critical Review of Recent Literature', *European Journal of Philosophy*, 7, 1, pp. 65–88.

Lak, D. (1999), 'Analysis: Chronic Instability of Indian Politics', *BBC News Online*, 18 April.

Lapham, L.H. (1992), 'Who and What is American?', *Harper's*, January, 43.

Lash, S. (2000), 'Risk Culture', in B. Adam, U. Beck and J. van Loon (eds), *The Risk Society and Beyond*, London: Sage, pp. 47–62.

Lash, S. and Lury, C. (2007), *Global Culture Industry: The Mediation of Things*, Cambridge: Polity.

Lash, S. and Urry, J. (1987), *The End of Organized Capitalism*, Cambridge: Polity.

Lash, S. and Urry, J. (1994), *Economies of Signs and Space*, London: Sage.

Latouche, S. (1996), *The Westernization of the World*, Cambridge: Polity.

Lelic, S. (2006), 'Brand Awareness', *Guardian Online*, 28 April.

Lesser, J. (ed.) (2003), *Searching for Home Abroad*, Durham, NC: Duke University Press.

Lévi-Strauss, C. (1969), *The Raw and the Cooked: Introduction to a Science of Mythology*, New York: Harper & Row.

Levitt, P. (2001), *The Transnational Villagers*, Berkeley: University of California Press.

Lima Costa, C. de (1999), 'Between North and South: Travelling Feminisms and Homeless Women', in D. Slater and P.J. Taylor (eds), *The American Century*, Oxford: Blackwell, pp. 298–316.

Linger, D.T. (2003), 'Do Japanese Brazilians Exist?', in J. Lesser (ed.), *Searching for Home Abroad*, Durham, NC: Duke University Press, pp. 201–14.

Lowe, L. and Lloyd, D. (eds) (1997), *The Politics of Culture in the Shadow of Capital*, Durham, NC: Duke University Press.

Luke, T.W. (1995), 'New World Order or Neo-World Orders: Power, Politics and Ideology in Informationalizing Glocalities', in M. Featherstone et al. (eds), *Global Modernities*, London: Sage, pp. 91–107.

Lull, J. (2000), *Media, Communication, Culture: A Global Approach*, 2nd edn, Cambridge: Polity.

Lury, C. (1996), *Consumer Culture*, Cambridge: Polity.

Lury, C. (1997), 'The Objects of Travel', in C. Rojek and J. Urry (eds), *Touring Cultures*, London: Routledge, pp. 75–95.

Lynch, M.D. (1997), 'Information Highways', in Y. Courrier and A. Large (eds), *World Information Report 1997/98*, Paris: UNESCO, pp. 258–303.

Lyon, D. (1988), *The Information Society*, Cambridge: Polity.

Maalouf, A. (2000), *On Identity*, London: Harvill.

McBride, S. (1980), *Many Voices, One World*, Paris: UNESCO.

McClintock, A. (1996), '"No Longer in a Future Heaven": Nationalism, Gender and Race', in G. Eley and R.G. Suny (eds), *Becoming National: A Reader*, Oxford: Oxford University Press, pp. 260–85.

Macfie, A.L. (2000), *Orientalism: A Reader*, Edinburgh: Edinburgh University Press.

Mackay, H. (2000), 'The Globalization of Culture?', in D. Held (ed.), *A Globalizing World?*, London: Routledge, pp. 47–84.

MacKenzie, J.M. (1983), *The Partition of Africa, 1880–1900*, London: Methuen.

MacKenzie, J.M. (1995), *Orientalism: History, Theory and the Arts*, Manchester: Manchester University Press.

McLuhan, M. and Fiore, Q. (1967), *The Medium is the Message*, Harmondsworth: Penguin.

McNeill, W.H. (1963), *The Rise of the West: A History of the Human Community*, Chicago: University of Chicago Press.

McNeill, W.H. (1979), *Plagues and Peoples*, London: Penguin.

McNeill, W.H. (1986), *Polyethnicity and National Unity in World History*, Toronto: Toronto University Press.

McPhail, T.L. (2006), *Global Communication: Theories, Stakeholders, and Trends*, 2nd edn, Oxford: Blackwell.

Makiya, K. (2001), 'Fighting Islam's Ku Klux Klan', *The Observer*, 7 October.

Mann, M. (1986), *The Sources of Social Power*, vol. 1: *A History of Power from the Beginning to AD 1760*, Cambridge: Cambridge University Press.

Mann, M. (1997), 'Has Globalization Ended the Rise and Rise of the Nation-State?' *Review of International Political Economy*, 4.

Mar, P. (1998), 'Just the Place is Different: Comparisons of Place and Settlement Practices of Some Hong Kong Migrants in Sydney', *Australian Journal of Anthropology*, 9, 1.

Martin-Barbero, J. (1993), *Communication, Culture and Hegemony*, London: Sage.

Marcuse, P. and van Kempen, R. (2000), *Globalizing Cities*, Oxford: Blackwell.

Massey, D. (1994), *Space, Place and Gender*, Cambridge: Polity.

Massey, D. (2005), *For Space*, London: Sage.

Mattelart, A. and Siegelaud, A. (eds) (1978), *Communication and Class Struggle*, New York: International General.

Mattelart, A., Delacourt, X. and Mattelart, M. (1984), *International Image Markets*, London: Comedia.

May, C. (2002), *The Information Society*, Cambridge: Polity.

Mayer-Schönberger, V. and Hurley, D. (2000), 'Globalization of Communication', in J.S. Nye and J.D. Donahue (eds), *Governance in a Globalizing World*, Washington, DC: Brookings Institution, pp. 135–51.

Maylam, P. (1986), *A History of the African People of South Africa*, London: Croom Helm.

Mazlish, B. and Buultjens, R. (eds) (1993), *Conceptualizing Global History*, Boulder, CO: Westview Press.

Mehendale, S. and Atabaki, T. (2005), *Central Asia and the Caucasus: Transnationalism and Diaspora*, London: Routledge.

Melucci, A. (1989), *Nomads of the Present: Social Movements and Individual Needs in Contemporary Society*, London: Hutchinson Radius.

Merelman, R. (1994), 'Racial Conflict and Cultural Politics in the United States', *Journal of Politics*, 5, 1, pp. 1–21.

Merry, S.E. (1997), 'Legal Pluralism and Transnational Culture: The *Ka Ho'okolokolonui Kananka Maoli* Tribunal, Hawai'i, 1993', in R.A. Wilson (ed.), *Human Rights, Culture and Context*, London: Pluto Press, pp. 28–48.

Meyer, B. and Geschiere, P. (eds) (1999), *Globalization and Identity*, Oxford: Blackwell.

Miles, R. (1994), 'Explaining Racism in Contemporary Europe', in A. Rattansi and S. Westwood (eds), *Racism, Modernity and Identity on the Western Front*, Cambridge: Polity, pp. 189–221.

Millar, F. et al. (1967), *The Roman Empire and its Neighbours*, London: Weidenfeld & Nicolson.

Miller, D. (ed.) (1995), *Acknowledging Consumption*, London: Routledge.

Minges, M. (2006), 'Tracking ICTs: World Summit on the Information Society Targets', *2006 Information and Communications for Development: Global Trends and Policies*, Washington, DC: World Bank, pp. 125–46.

Mohammad, M. (2001), *Islam and the Muslim Ummah*, Putrajaya, Malaysia: Prime Minister's Office.

Monaci, M., Magatti, M. and Caselli, M. (2003), 'Network, Exposure and Rhetoric: Italian Occupational Fields and Heterogeneity in Constructing the Globalised Self', *Global Networks*, 3, 4, pp. 457–80.

Morley, D. and Robins, K. (1995), *Spaces of Identity: Global Media, Electronic Landscapes and Cultural Boundaries*, London: Routledge.

Morris, N. and Waisbord, S. (eds) (2001), *Media and Globalization*, Lanham, MD: Rowman & Littlefield.

Mowlana, H. (1997), *Global Information and World Communication*, 2nd edn, London: Sage.

Mozfarri, M. (ed.) (2002), *Globalization and Civilizations*, London and New York: Routledge.

Munch, R. and Smelser, N.J. (eds) (1992), *Theory of Culture*, Berkeley: University of California Press.

Nas, P.J.M. and Houweling, A.J. (1998), 'The Network Metaphor: An Assessment of Castells' Network Society Paradigm', *Journal of Social Sciences*, 2, 4, pp. 221–32.

Nederveen Pieterse, J. (1994), 'Unpacking the West: How European is Europe', in A. Rattansi and S. Westwood (eds), *Racism, Modernity and Identity on the Western Front*, Cambridge: Polity, pp. 129–49.

Nederveen Pieterse, J. (1998), 'Hybrid Modernities: Mélange Modernities in Asia', *Sociological Analysis*, 1, 3, pp. 75–86.

Nederveen Pieterse, J. (ed.) (2000), *Global Futures*, London: Zed Books.

Nederveen Pieterse, J. (2004), *Globalization and Culture*, Lanham, MD: Rowman & Littlefield.

Newhouse, J. (1998) 'Europe's Rising Regionalism', *A New Europe? A Foreign Affairs Reader*, New York: Council on Foreign Relations, pp. 19–36.

Nie, N. and Erbring, L. (2000), *Internet and Society: A Preliminary Report*, Stanford, CA: Stanford Institute for the Quantitative Study of Society.

Norris, P. (2000), 'Global Governance and Cosmopolitan Citizens', in J. Nye and J. Donahue (eds), *Governance in a Globalizing World*, Washington, DC: Brookings Institution, pp. 155–77.

Norris, P. (2001), *Digital Divide*, Cambridge: Cambridge University Press.

Norton-Taylor, R. (2001), 'Bleak New World, as Seen by the MoD', *The Guardian*, 8 February.

Nussbaum, M.C. (1996), 'Patriotism and Cosmopolitanism', in M.C. Nussbaum et al., *For Love of Country*, Boston: Beacon Press, pp. 2–17.

Nustad, K.G. (2003), 'Considering Global/Local Relations: Beyond Dualism', in T.H. Eriksen (ed.), *Globalisation: Studies in Anthropology*, London: Pluto Press, pp. 122–37.

Nye, J.S., Jr. (2002), *The Paradox of American Power*, Oxford: Oxford University Press.

Ohmae, K. (1990), *The Borderless World*, London: Collins.

Ohmae, K. (2000), 'The Rise of the Region State', in P. O'Meara, H.D. Melinger and M. Krain (eds), *Globalization and the Challenges of a New Century*, Bloomington: Indiana University Press, pp. 93–100.

Ohmae, K. (2005), *The Next Global Stage*, Upper Saddle River, NJ: Wharton.

Oliveti, V. (2002), *Terror's Source: The Ideology of Wahhabi-Salafism and its Consequences*, Birmingham, Amadeus.

Ong, A. (1999), *Flexible Citizenship: The Cultural Logics of Transnationality*, Durham, NC: Duke University Press.

O'Sullivan, J. (1996), 'Mistaken Identities', *National Review*, 48, 22, pp. 50–5.

Osterhammel, J. and Petersson, N.P. (2005), *Globalization: A Short History*, Princeton, NJ: Princeton University Press.

Özkirimli, U. (2000), *Theories of Nationalism: A Critical Introduction*, Basingstoke: Macmillan.

Papastergiadis, N. (2000), *The Turbulence of Migration*, Cambridge: Polity.

Parekh, B. (2000), *Rethinking Multiculturalism*, Basingstoke: Palgrave.

Patterson, O. (2000), 'Taking Culture Seriously: A Framework and an Afro-American Illustration', in L.E. Harrison and S.P. Huntington (eds), *Culture Matters*, New York: Basic Books, pp. 202–18.

Perkin, H. (1996), *The Third Revolution: Professional Elites in the Modern World*, London: Routledge.

Perrone, J. (2005), 'Every Second a Blog – but Not for the Long Slog', *Guardian Online*, 3 August, www.guardian.co.uk (accessed 7/10/06).

Perry, N. (1998), *Hyper-Reality and Global Culture*, London: Routledge.

Phillips, T. (2007), 'Brazilian Carnival Loses its Rhythm to Foreign DJs', *The Guardian*, 12 February, p. 16.

Pogge, T.W. (1992), 'Cosmopolitanism and Sovereignty', *Ethics*, 103, pp. 48–75.

Porter, B. (1984), *The Lion's Share: A Short History of British Imperialism, 1850–1983*, 2nd edn, London: Longman.

Porter, B.D. (1993), 'Can American Democracy Survive?', *Commentary*, November, pp. 37–40.

Portes, A. (1996), 'Global Villagers: The Rise of Transnational Communities', *American Prospect*, 25, pp. 74–7.

Portes, A. (2001), 'Introduction: The Debates and Significance of Immigrant Transnationalism', *Global Networks*, 1, 3, pp. 181–93.

Price, S. (2001), 'Pakistan Tackles Sectarian Violence', *BBC News Online*, 15 March, www.bbcnews.co.uk (accessed 2/1/06).

Pries, L. (ed.) (2001), *New Transnational Social Spaces: International Migration and Transnational Companies in the Early Twenty-First Century*, London: Routledge.

Putnam, H. (1996), 'Must We Choose between Patriotism and Universal Reason?', in M.C. Nussbaum et al., *For Love of Country*, Boston: Beacon Press, pp. 91–7.

Ramesh, R. (2007), 'China, Soon to Be World's Biggest Internet User', *The Guardian*, 25 January, p. 17.

Rantanen, T. (2005), *The Media and Globalisation*, London: Sage.

Rapport, N. and Overing, J. (2000), *Social and Cultural Anthropology: The Key Concepts*, London: Routledge.

Rex, J. (1996), 'National Identity in the Democratic Multi-Cultural State', *Sociological Research Online*, 1, 2, www.socresonline.org.uk/socresonline/1/2/1 (accessed 3/9/05).

Rheingold, H. (2000), *The Virtual Community*, rev. edn, London: MIT Press.

Richmond, A.H. (1984), 'Ethnic Nationalism and Post-Industrialism', *Ethnic and Racial Studies*, 7, 1, pp. 4–18.

Rieff, D. (1995), *Slaughterhouse: Bosnia and the Failure of the West*, London: Vintage.

Ritzer, G. (1993), *The McDonaldization of Society*, London: Sage.

Ritzer, G. (1998), *The McDonaldization Thesis*, London: Sage.

Ritzer, G. (ed.) (2002), *McDonaldization: The Reader*, Thousand Oaks, CA: Pine Forge Press.

Ritzer, G. and Liska, A. (1997), '"McDisneyization" and "Post-Tourism"', in C. Rojek and J. Urry (eds), *Touring Cultures: Transformations of Travel and Theory*, London: Routledge, pp. 96–109.

Robertson, R. (1992), *Globalization: Social Theory and Global Culture*, London: Sage.

Robertson, R. (1995), 'Glocalization: Time–Space and Homogeneity–Heterogeneity', in M. Featherstone, S. Lash and R. Robertson (eds), *Global Modernities*, London: Sage, pp. 25–44.

Robertson, R. and Inglis, D. (2006), 'The Global *Animus*', in B.K. Gills and W.R. Thompson (eds), *Globalisation and Global History*, London: Routledge, pp. 33–47.

Robison, R. and Goodman, D.S.G. (eds) (1996), *The New Rich in Asia: Mobile Phones, McDonald's and Middle-Class Revolution*, London: Routledge.

Rojek, C. and Urry, J. (eds) (1997), *Touring Cultures*, London: Routledge.

Rosenau, J. (1997), *Along the Domestic–Foreign Frontier*, Cambridge: Cambridge University Press.

Rosendorf, N.M. (2000), 'Social and Cultural Globalization: Concepts, History, and America's Role', in J.S. Nye and J.D. Donahue, *Governance in a Globalizing World*, Washington, DC: Brookings Institution, pp. 109–34.

Rouse, R. (1991), 'Mexican Migration and the Social Space of Postmodernism', *Diaspora*, 1, 1, pp. 8–23.

Rushdie, S. (2001), 'A War that Presents Us All with a Crisis of Faith', *The Guardian*, 3 November.

Rushdie, S. (2002), 'Anti-Americanism Has Taken the World by Storm', *The Guardian*, 6 February.

Ruthven, M. (1995), 'The West's Secret Weapon against Islam', *Sunday Times*, 1 January, p. 6.

Sabloff, J. and Lamberg-Karlovsky, C. (eds) (1975), *Ancient Civilization and Trade*, Albuquerque: University of New Mexico Press.

Said, E. (1994), *Culture and Imperialism*, London: Vintage.

Said, E. (1995), *Orientalism*, Harmondsworth: Penguin.

Said, E. (2001), 'Islam and the West are Inadequate Banners', *The Observer*, 16 September.

Sanderson, S.K. (ed.) (1995), *Civilizations and World Systems*, Walnut Creek, CA: Altamira Press.

Sardar, Z. (1999), *Orientalism*, Buckingham: Open University Press.

Sardar, Z. (2001), 'Islam Has Become its own Enemy', *The Observer*, 21 October.

Sardar, Z. and Wyn Davies, M. (2002), *Why Do People Hate America?*, Cambridge: Icon Books.

Sassen, S. (2000), *Cities in a World Economy*, 2nd edn, Thousand Oaks, CA: Pine Forge Press.

Sassen, S. (2001), *The Global City*, 2nd edn, Princeton, NJ: Princeton University Press.

Sassen, S. (ed.) (2002), *Global Networks, Linked Cities*, London: Routledge.

Sassoon, D. (1998), 'Fin-de-Siècle Socialism: The United, Modest Left', *New Left Review*, 227, pp. 88–96.

Schech, S. and Haggis, J. (2000), *Culture and Development: A Critical Introduction*, Oxford: Blackwell.

Scheffler, S. (1999), 'Conceptions of Cosmopolitanism', *Utilitas*, 11, 3, pp. 255–76.

Schiller, H.I. (1979), 'Transnational Media and National Development', in K. Nordenstreng and H.I. Schiller (eds), *National Sovereignty and International Communication*, Norwood, NJ: Ablex.

Schiller, H.I. (1989), *Culture Inc.*, New York: Oxford University Press.

Schiller, H.I. (1991), 'Not Yet the Post-Imperialist Era', *Critical Studies in Mass Communication*, 8, pp. 13–28.

Schiller, H.I. (1995), 'The Global Information Highway', in J. Brook and I.A. Boal (eds), *Resisting the Virtual Life: The Culture and Politics of Information*, San Francisco: City Lights Press.

Schiller, H.I. (1996), *Information Inequality*, London: Routledge.

Schirm, S.A. (2002), *Globalization and the New Regionalism*, Cambridge: Polity.

Schlesinger, P. (1991), *Media, State and Nation*, London: Sage.

Scholte, J.A. (2000), *Globalization: A Critical Introduction*, Basingstoke: Macmillan.

Scholte, J.A. (2005), *Globalization: A Critical Introduction*, 2nd edn, Basingstoke: Palgrave.

Screen Digest (1997), 'World Cinema Market: Start of the European Fightback', August.

Segal, G. (2002), 'Does China Matter?' in *The Rise of China*, New York: Foreign Affairs, pp. 27–39.

Senghaas, D. (2002), *The Clash within Civilizations: Coming to Terms with Cultural Conflicts*, London: Routledge.

Sennett, R. (2002), 'Cosmopolitanism and the Social Experience of Cities', in S. Vertovec and R. Cohen (eds), *Conceiving Cosmopolitanism*, Oxford: Oxford University Press, pp. 42–7.

Servon, L.J. (2002), *Bridging the Digital Divide*, Oxford: Blackwell.

Shain, Y. (1995), 'Multicultural Foreign Policy', *Foreign Policy*, 100, pp. 69–88.

Shaw, M. (1994), 'Civil Society and Global Politics: Beyond a Social Movements Approach', *Millennium: Journal of International Studies*, 23, 3, pp. 647–67.

Shields, R. (ed.) (1992), *Lifestyle Shopping*, London: Routledge.

Shikaki, K. (2002), 'This is a War on Islam', *The Guardian*, 11 September.

Shohat, E. and Stam, R. (1995), *Unthinking Eurocentrism*, London: Routledge.

Shore, C. (2000), *Building Europe*, London: Routledge.

Shweder, R.A. (2000), 'Moral Maps, "First World" Conceits, and the New Evangelists', in L.E. Harrison and S.P. Huntington (eds), *Culture Matters*, New York: Basic Books, pp. 158–76.

Sinclair, J., Jacka, A. and Cunningham, S. (eds) (1996), *New Patterns in Global Television: Peripheral Vision*, Oxford: Oxford University Press.

Sklair, L. (2001), *The Transnational Capitalist Class*, Oxford: Blackwell.

Sklair, L. (2002), *Globalization: Capitalism and its Alternatives*, 3rd edn, Oxford: Oxford University Press.

Smart, B. (ed.) (1999), *Resisting McDonaldization*, London: Sage.

Smelser, N. and Alexander, N. (eds) (1999), *Diversity and its Discontents: Conflict and Common Ground in Contemporary American Society*, Princeton, NJ: Princeton University Press.

Smith, A.D. (1986), *The Ethnic Origins of Nations*, Oxford: Blackwell.

Smith, A.D. (1990), 'Towards a Global Culture?', in M. Featherstone (ed.), *Global Culture*, London: Sage, pp. 171–91.

Smith, A.D. (1991), *National Identity*, London: Penguin.

Smith, A.D. (1995), *Nations and Nationalism in a Global Era*, Cambridge: Polity.

Smith, M.A. and Kollock, P. (eds) (1999), *Communities in Cyberspace*, London: Routledge.

Smith, M.P. (2001), *Transnational Urbanism*, Oxford: Blackwell.

Soysal, Y.N. (1994), *Limits of Citizenship: Migrants and Postnational Membership in Europe*, Chicago: University of Chicago Press.

Sparks, C. (1998), 'Is There a Global Public Sphere?', in D.K. Thussu (ed.), *Electronic Empires: Global Media and Local Resistance*, London: Arnold, pp. 108–24.

Spear, P. (1990), *A History of India*, vol. 2, Harmondsworth: Penguin.

Spybey, T. (1996), *Globalization and World Society*, Cambridge: Polity.

Stadler, F. (2006), *Manuel Castells*, Cambridge: Polity.

Standage, T. (1998), *The Victorian Internet*, London: Weidenfeld & Nicolson.

Staple, G. (1991), *The Global Telecommunications Report, 1991*, London: International Institute of Communications.

Staple, G. (1996), *Teleography, 1996*, London: International Institute of Communications.

Starr, A. (2000), *Naming the Enemy: Anti-Corporate Social Movements Confront Globalization*, London: Zed Books.

Stone, D. (2002), 'Knowledge Networks and Policy Expertise in the Global Polity', in M. Ougaard and R. Higgott (eds), *Towards a Global Polity*, London: Routledge, pp. 125–44.

Strange, S. (1990), 'Finance, Information and Power', *Review of International Studies*, 16, 3, pp. 259–74.

Strange, S. (1995), 'The Limits of Politics', *Government and Opposition*, 30, 3, pp. 291–311.

Street, B. (1993), 'Culture as a Verb: Anthropological Aspects of Language and Cultural Process', in D. Graddol, L. Thompson and M. Byram (eds), *Language and Culture*, Clevedon: BAAL and Multilingual Matters.

Street, P. (2003), 'Stabilising Flows in the Global Field: Illusions of Permanence, Intellectual Property Rights and the Transnationalisation of Law', *Global Networks*, 3, 1, pp. 7–28.

Strinati, D. (1995), *An Introduction to Theories of Popular Culture*, London: Routledge.

Suarez-Orozco, M. (2000), 'Everything You Ever Wanted to Know about Assimilation but Were Afraid to Ask', *Daedalus*, 129, 4, pp. 1–30.

Swidler, A. (1986), 'Culture in Action: Symbols and Strategies', *American Sociological Review*, 51, pp. 273–88.

Tait, R. (2006), 'Iran Bans Fast Internet to Cut West's Influence', *The Guardian*, 18 October, www.guardian.co.uk (accessed 9/12/06).

Talbott, S. and Chanda, N. (eds) (2001), *The Age of Terror*, Oxford: Perseus Press.

Taylor, C. (1992), *Multiculturalism and the 'Politics of Recognition'*, Princeton, NJ: Princeton University Press.

Taylor, C. (ed.) (1994), *Multiculturalism: Examining the Politics of Recognition*, Princeton, NJ: Princeton University Press.

Taylor, P.J. (2001), 'Isations of the World: Americanisation, Modernisation and Globalisation', in C. Hay and D. Marsh (eds), *Demystifying Globalisation*, Basingstoke: Palgrave, pp. 49–70.

Tehranian, M. and Tehranian, K.K. (1997), 'Taming Modernity: Toward a New Paradigm', in A. Mohammadi (ed.), *International Communication and Globalization*, London: Sage, pp 119–67.

Thompson, J.B. (1990), *Ideology and Modern Culture*, Cambridge: Polity.

Thompson, J.B. (1995), *The Media and Modernity*, Cambridge: Polity.

Thussu, D.K. (ed.) (1998), *Electronic Empires: Global Media and Local Resistance*, London: Arnold.

Tomlinson, J. (1991), *Cultural Imperialism*, London: Pinter.

Tomlinson, J. (1997a), 'Internationalism, Globalization and Cultural Imperialism', in K. Thompson (ed.), *Media and Cultural Regulation*, London: Sage, 117–62.

Tomlinson, J. (1997b), '"And Besides, the Wench is Dead": Media Scandals and the Globalization of Communication', in J. Lull and S. Hinerman (eds), *Media Scandals*, Cambridge: Polity.

Tomlinson, J. (1999a), *Globalization and Culture*, Cambridge: Polity.

Tomlinson, J. (1999b), 'Globalised Culture: The Triumph of the West?' in T. Skelton and T. Allen (eds), *Culture and Global Change*, London: Routledge, pp. 22–9.

Toulmin, S. (1999), 'The Ambiguities of Globalisation', *Futures*, 31, 9/10, pp. 905–12.

Touraine, A. (1997), *What is Democracy?*, Boulder, CO: Westview Press.

Tracey, M. (1988), 'Popular Culture and the Economics of Global Television', *Intermedia*, 16, 2.

Tran, M. (2000), 'Africa is Loser in Global Digital Divide', *The Guardian*, 14 August, www.guardian.co.uk (accessed 2/11/06).

Tsing, A. (2002), 'The Global Situation', in J. Xavier Inda and R. Rosaldo (eds) *The Anthropology of Globalization: A Reader*, Oxford: Blackwell, pp. 453–85.

Turkle, S. (1995), *Life on the Screen*, New York: Simon & Schuster.

Turner, B.S. (2006), 'Classical Sociology and Cosmopolitanism: A Critical Defence of the Social', *British Journal of Sociology*, 57, 1, pp. 133–51.

Twist, J. (2004), 'China Leads Way on Broadband', *BBC News Online*, 5 October, www.bbcnews.co.uk (accessed 12/11/06).

UNESCO (1998), *Statistical Yearbook, 1998*, Paris: UNESCO.

Urban, G. (2001), *Metaculture: How Culture Moves through the World*, Minneapolis: University of Minnesota Press.

Urry, J. (1990), *The Tourist Gaze*, London: Sage.

Urry, J. (1995), *Consuming Places*, London: Routledge.

Urry, J. (2000), *Sociology beyond Societies: Mobilities for the Twenty-First Century*, London: Routledge.

Urry, J. (2003), *Global Complexity*, Cambridge: Polity.

van de Ven, H. (2002), 'The Onrush of Modern Globalization in China', in A.G. Hopkins (ed.), *Globalization in World History*, London: Pimlico, pp. 167–93.

van den Berghe, P. (1979), *The Ethnic Phenomenon*, New York: Elsevier.

van Dijk, J.A.G.M. (2005), *The Deepening Divide*, London: Sage.

Vasagar, J. (2005), 'Talk is Cheap, and Getting Cheaper', *The Guardian*, 14 September, p. 25.

Vertovec, S. and Cohen, R. (eds), *Conceiving Cosmopolitanism*, Oxford: Oxford University Press.

Wagner, R. (1986), *Symbols that Stand for Themselves*, Chicago: University of Chicago Press.

Wagner, R. (1991), 'Poetics and the Recentering of Anthropology', in I. Brady (ed.), *Anthropological Poetics*, Savage, MD: Rowman & Littlefield.

Waldron, J. (2000), 'What is Cosmopolitan?', *Journal of Political Philosophy*, 8, pp. 227–43.

Wallerstein, I. (1974), *The Modern World-System*, New York: Academic.

Wallerstein, I. (1980), *The Modern World-System II*, New York: Academic.

Wallerstein, I. (1990a), 'Culture as the Ideological Battleground of the Modern World-System', in M. Featherstone (ed.), *Global Culture*, London: Sage, pp. 31–56.

Wallerstein, I. (1990b), 'Culture is the World-System: A Reply to Boyne', in M. Featherstone (ed.), *Global Culture*, London: Sage, pp. 63–5.

Wallerstein, I. (2003), *The Decline of American Power*, New York: New Press.

Wallerstein, I. (2004), *World-Systems Analysis*, Durham, NC: Duke University Press.

Walzer, M. (ed.) (1995), *Toward a Global Civil Society*, New York: Berghahn Books.

Warschauer, M. (2004), *Technology and Social Inclusion*, London: MIT Press.

Waters, M. (1995), *Globalisation*, London: Routledge.

Watson, J.L. (1997), *Golden Arches East: McDonald's in East Asia*, Stanford, CA: Stanford University Press.

Watts, J. (2004), 'China Orders TV Stars to Stop "Queer" Western Behaviour', *The Guardian*, 5 May, p. 18.

Webb, J., Schirato, T. and Danaher, G. (2002), *Understanding Bourdieu*, London: Sage.

Webster, F. (2002), *Theories of the Information Society*, 2nd edn, London: Routledge.

Weeks, A.L. (1996), 'Do Civilizations Hold?', in *Samuel P.Huntington's The Clash of Civilizations? The Debate*, New York: Foreign Affairs, pp. 53–4.

Wei-Ming, T. (2000), 'Multiple Modernities: A Preliminary Inquiry into the Implications of East Asian Modernity', in L.E. Harrison and S.P. Huntington (eds) (2000), *Culture Matters*, New York: Basic Books, pp. 256–66.

Wellman, B. and Gulia, M. (1999), 'Virtual Communities as Communities: Net Surfers Don't Ride Alone', in M.A. Smith and P. Kollock (eds), *Communities in Cyberspace*, London: Routledge, pp. 167–94.

Wellman, B. and Haythornwaite, C. (eds) (2002), *The Internet in Everyday Life*, Oxford: Blackwell.

Welsch, W. (1999), 'Transculturality: The Puzzling Form of Cultures Today', in M. Featherstone and S. Lash (eds) (1999), *Spaces of Culture: City, Nation, World*, London: Sage, pp. 194–213.

Werbner, P. (1999), 'Global Pathways: Working Class Cosmopolitans and the Creation of Transnational Ethnic Worlds', *Social Anthropology*, 7, 1, pp. 17–35.

Werbner, P. and Modood, T. (eds) (1997), *Debating Cultural Hybridity*, London: Zed Books.

Whitehouse, D. (1999), 'Circle of Light is Africa's Net Gain', *BBC News Online*, 23 June, www.bbcnews.co.uk (accessed 12/1/05).

Wieviorka, M. (1994), 'Racism in Europe: Unity and Diversity', in A. Rattansi and S. Westwood (eds), *Racism, Modernity and Identity on the Western Front*, Cambridge: Polity, pp. 173–88.

Williams, M. (1996), 'A Campus Erupts over Multiculturalism', *New York Times*, 28 June, p. A13 (N).

Williams, R. (1963), *Culture and Society, 1780–1950*, Harmondsworth: Penguin.

Williams, R. (1976), *Keywords*, London: Fontana.

Wilson, R.A. (ed.) (1997), *Human Rights, Culture and Context: Anthropological Perspectives*, London: Pluto Press.

Wolfe, A. (1998), *One Nation After All*, London: Viking.

Wolff, J. (1991), 'The Global and the Specific: Reconciling Conflicting Theories of Culture', in A.D. King (ed.), *Culture, Globalization and the World-System*, London: Macmillan, pp. 161–73.

Wolpert, S. (1989), *A New History of India*, 3rd edn, Oxford: Oxford University Press.

Woolgar. S. (ed.) (2002), *Virtual Society? Technology, Cyberbole, Reality*, Oxford: Oxford University Press.

Wray, R. (2007), 'China Overtaking US for Fast Internet Access as Africa Gets Left Behind', *The Guardian*, 14 June, p. 29.

Wriston, W. (1992), *The Twilight of Sovereignty*, New York: Charles Scribner.

Wurm, S.A. (ed.) (1996), *Atlas of the World's Languages in Danger of Disappearing*, Paris: UNESCO.

Wuthnow, R. and Witten, M. (1988), 'New Directions in the Study of Culture', *Annual Review of Sociology*, 14, pp. 46–67.

Xavier Inda, J. and Rosaldo, R. (eds) (2002), 'Introduction: A World in Motion', *The Anthropology of Globalization: A Reader*, Oxford: Blackwell, pp. 1–34.

Yang, M.M. (2004), 'Mass Media and Transnational Subjectivity in Shanghai: Notes on (Re)Cosmopolitanism in a Chinese Metropolis', in J. Xavier Inda and R. Rosaldo (eds), *The Anthropology of Globalization: A Reader*, Oxford: Blackwell, pp. 325–49.

Young, I.M. (1990), *Justice and the Politics of Difference*, Princeton, NJ: Princeton University Press.

Young, R.C. (1995), *Colonial Desire: Hybridity in Theory, Culture and Race*, London: Routledge.

Younge, G. (2004), 'Black Americans Move Back to Southern States, *The Guardian*, 25 May, p. 13.

Zakiara, F. (1997), 'Culture is Destiny: A Conversation with Lee Kuan Yew', in *The New Shape of World Politics*, New York: Foreign Affairs, pp. 219–33.

Zickmund, S. (1997), 'Approaching the Radical Other: The Discursive Culture of Cyberhate', in S.G. Jones (ed.), *Virtual Culture*, London: Sage, pp.185–205.

Zubaida, S. (2002), 'Middle Eastern Experiences of Cosmopolitanism', in S. Vertovec and R. Cohen (eds), *Conceiving Cosmopolitanism*, Oxford: Oxford University Press, pp. 32–41.

Index